D1710027

A
Broken Heart
and a Contrite
Spirit

The First Principles
and Ordinances Series
(Volume 2)

Philip M. Hudson

ISBN 978-1-50647-09-5

Library of Congress Control Number 2019908231

Illustrations - Google Images.

This book may be ordered from online bookstores.

Publishing Services by BookCrafters
Parker, Colorado.
www.bookcrafters.net

"I will ransom them from the power of the grave. I will redeem them from death. O death, I will be thy plagues; O grave, I will be thy destruction."
(Hosea 13:14).

Table of Contents

Acknowledgements..1

Preface...7

Introduction...13

Chapter One: Repentance and the seven deadly sins................................19
Chapter Two: The reduction sauce of repentance....................................41
Chapter Three: The Last Judgment...49
Chapter Four: The Fall..55
Chapter Five: Father forgive them..61
Chapter Six: Applying the Atonement in our lives...................................67
Chapter Seven: Opposition in all things..73
Chapter Eight: A key element of The Plan...93
Chapter Nine: Shed the weight of sin..99
Chapter Ten: Cherubim and a flaming sword..109

Chapter Eleven: Choices and worth..121
Chapter Twelve: Perfect in our repentance...141
Chapter Thirteen: Wickedness never was happiness..............................153

Chapter Fourteen: Purposeful repentance...161
Chapter Fifteen: Have I been forgiven?...165
Chapter Sixteen: Infinite and eternal forgiveness...................................171
Chapter Seventeen: Before a wound can heal...179
Chapter Eighteen: Just get back on the bike...189
Chapter Nineteen: Removing the barnacles of life...................................193
Chapter Twenty: The door swings both ways...197
Chapter Twenty One: We are works in progress.......................................203
Chapter Twenty Two: The rapids of life...223
Chapter Twenty Three: The Holy Ghost is an eternal optimist...................231
Chapter Twenty Four: Making intelligent choices...................................237
Chapter Twenty Five: Giving vitality to life's playbook...........................249
Chapter Twenty Six: Repentance and The Plan of Happiness...................257
Chapter Twenty Seven: The success strategy of repentance...................275
Chapter Twenty Eight: The pumpkin patch of the Lord...........................287
Chapter Twenty Nine: Let him cast the first stone.................................297
Chapter Thirty: Huckleberries, chokeberries and repentance...................305
Chapter Thirty One: Is repentance too good to be true?........................313
Chapter Thirty Two: Jumping out of our skin...323
Chapter Thirty Three: Redeemed by the grace of God...........................343
Chapter Thirty Four: The road to repentance.......................................357
Chapter Thirty Five: His Plan to save our souls...................................371
Chapter Thirty Six: Five keys to successful repentance........................381

What More Can I Say?...391
About The Author...393
Also By The Author..397

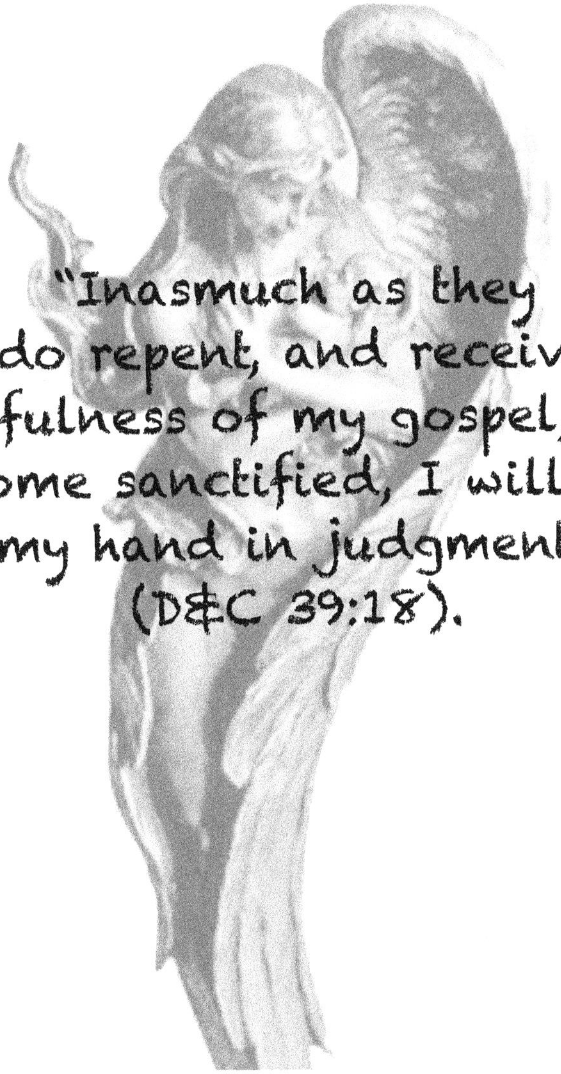

"Inasmuch as they
do repent, and receive
the fulness of my gospel, and
become sanctified, I will stay
my hand in judgment."
(D&C 39:18).

Acknowledgements

In this volume, I have attributed quotations to original authors whenever possible, as well as when I have editorialized their ideas. In many cases, however, my language will naturally reflect the teachings of leaders and members of The Church of Jesus Christ of Latter-day Saints.

The list of those who have contributed to this book is endless. As I have organized my own thoughts, I have realized how heavily I have borrowed from the towering examples of those who, over the years, have been my mystical mentors, my sensible chaperones, my spiritual guides, my surrogate saviors, my compassionate critics, and everything in between.

They are my avatars, manifestations of deity in bodily forms, my na'vi, the visionaries, who communicate with God on a level to which I can only aspire, and my tsaddik, whom I esteem as intuitive interpreters of biblical law and scripture. They are my divine teachers incarnate. They have offered listening ears,

extended open arms, lifted my spirits, shown me the way, emboldened me with words of encouragement, cheered me on with wise counsel, stretched my mind, reinforced my faith, strengthened my testimony, vitalized my conversion, helped me to discover my wings, given immaterial support, provided of their means, taught me humility, been there to steady me, soothed my troubled soul, stepped in to nurture me, led me to fountains of living water, wet my parched lips with inspired counsel, and bound up my wounds.

Every family member, teacher, student, classmate, business associate, mentor, friend, priesthood brother, relief society sister, ordinance worker, and temple patron with whom I have come in contact has influenced me. Every author, poet, journalist, essayist, thespian, satirist, and lyricist, has moved me in some positive way. They have taught me to find the silk purse in every sow's ear and the silver lining in every cloud. When I have been given a lemon, they have shown me where to find the recipe for lemonade.

With their positive influence, I have learned to keep tempests in teapots where they belong, and to put them in perspective. I have tried to retain the joyful anticipation of the optimistic little boy, who, when faced with the daunting task of shoveling up an enormous pile of manure in a horse stall near his home, enthusiastically set about his task with the exclamation: "There's got to be a pony in there, somewhere!" Well did the poet teach: "No man is an island, entire of itself. Every man is a piece of the continent, a part of the main. If a clod be washed away by the sea, Europe is the less, as well as if a promontory were, as well as if a manor of thy friends or of thine own were. Any man's death diminishes me, because I am involved in mankind, and therefore never send to know for whom the bell tolls. It tolls for thee." (John Donne).

When I think of the influence of a multitude of angels thinly disguised as my family, friends, and peers, I remember the words of Sir Isaac Newton, who, when pressed to reveal the great secret behind his accomplishments, simply replied: "I stood on the shoulders of giants." Of course, at the end of the day, I alone

am responsible for the contents of this volume. But I hope my interpretation of principles and doctrine will cultivate your interest to dig deeper into the themes woven into this tapestry, by turning to the scriptures and seeking inspiration from the Spirit. My only goal is to help you to expand your insights into the telestial mile markers, the terrestrial truths, and the celestial guidelines that accompany each of us during our quest for enlightenment.

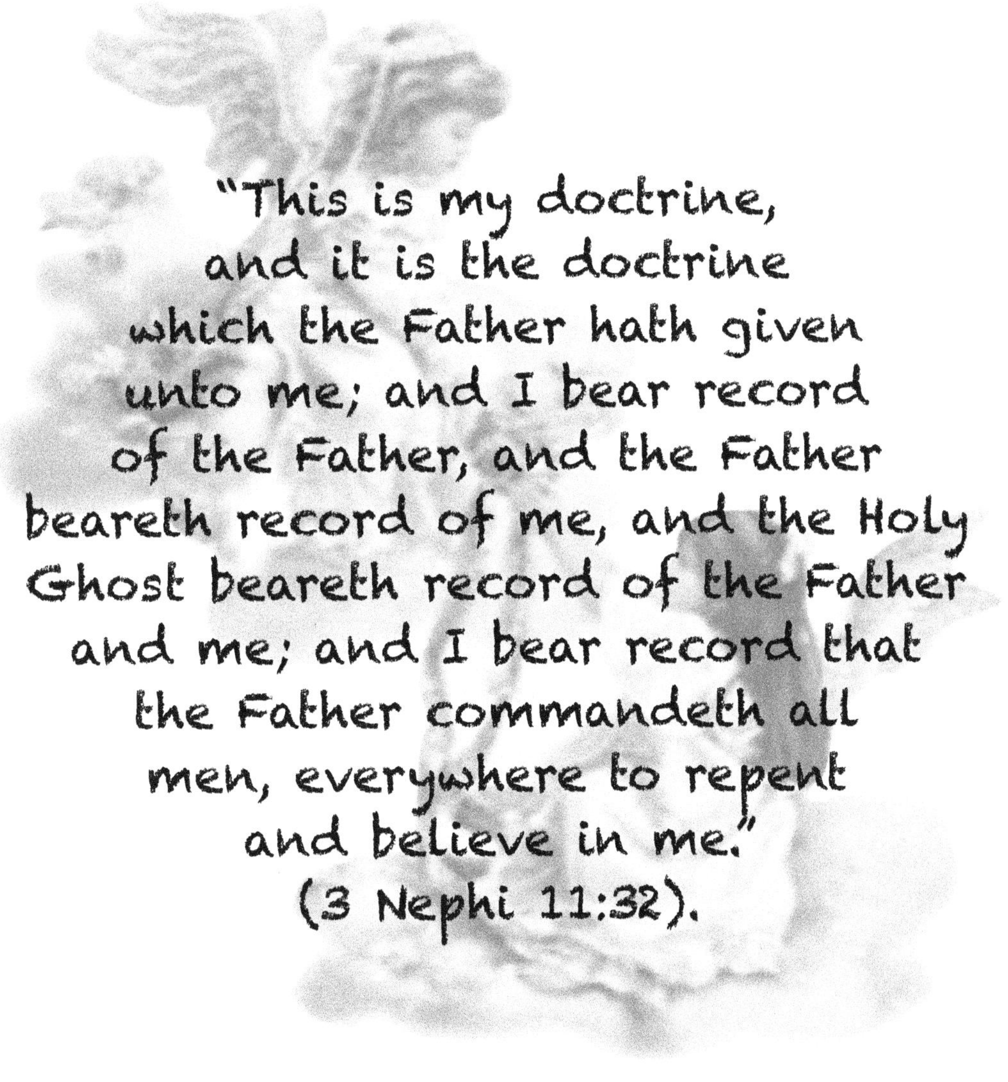

"This is my doctrine,
and it is the doctrine
which the Father hath given
unto me; and I bear record
of the Father, and the Father
beareth record of me, and the Holy
Ghost beareth record of the Father
and me; and I bear record that
the Father commandeth all
men, everywhere to repent
and believe in me."
(3 Nephi 11:32).

Preface

I love to learn by reading the Standard Works, and I often think of St. Hilary, who wrote in the third century: "Scripture consists not in what we read, but in what we understand." In each of the chapters in this volume, I have consistently tried to find a scriptural foundation and a spiritual confirmation as I put my pen to paper. For me, it has been exciting to find that the ideas swirling around inside my head can generally be anchored to, and find relevance in, the scriptures. Holy writ gives me a sense of coherence and stability. On a much smaller scale, I feel as Albert Einstein must have, when the mathematical equivalents to scriptural understanding crystallized, and he said of the experience: "A storm broke loose in my mind."

I believe the Spirit has the generative power to energize, vitalize, and quicken our axons and dendrites and craft a neural environment that stimulates creative thought. Those who have experienced the illumination of the Spirit know what Einstein meant when he said: "A splendid light dawned on me." So, the challenge for each of us is to enlist the aid of the Holy Ghost to assist in understanding, whenever, however,

and with whatever we utilize to process the world around us.

Every time I proofed a chapter (and I did this many times) I found myself scribbling additional notes in the margins, and thinking to myself, "Why didn't

I see that before." That is precisely what I hope will be the experience of those who read this volume, that in the process, they will be instructed by the Spirit to be led in directions that will later prove to be of personal value.

I hope that as you read these chapters, you will be uniquely impacted and that you will be touched differently each time you re-visit them. When I am long-gone, perhaps the considerable thought that went into their production will generate a palpable bond between us that will span the years separating us. It is my hope that the gulf that then divides us will be bridged by our shared energies to establish the foundation for an eventual joyous reunion.

One of the reasons why I am somewhat obsessed with writing is that I enjoy the rush when I find wisdom and great treasures of knowledge, and even hidden treasures. It has been my experience that a comprehension of doctrinal themes cannot often be discerned after only a cursory glance. I hope that within these pages you will find the pearls that generate within you a similar quest for greater understanding.

I had the opportunity to visit the Holy Land many years ago. We stopped, too briefly, at the ruins of Qumran. There, the Dead Sea Covenanters had lived, and in their scriptorium, I was able to pause and reflect upon their Eleventh Hymn that had been preserved on scrolls hidden in caves high above their community. It reads: "Behold, for mine own part I have reached the intervision, and through the spirit thou has placed within me, come to know Thee, my God." In a similar fashion, Moses wrote: "But now mine own eyes have beheld God; but not my natural, but my spiritual eyes, for … his glory was upon me; and I beheld his face." (Moses 1:11).

I am continually reminded of Nephi's counsel to press forward with complete

dedication and steadfastness, or confidence with a firm determination in Christ, having a perfect brightness of hope, or perfect faith, and charity, or a love of God and of all men. If we do this, feasting upon the word of Christ, or receiving strength and nourishment as we ponder the principles and doctrines of the Gospel, and as we endure to the end in righteousness, we shall have eternal life, which is the greatest of God's gifts. (See 2 Nephi 31:20).

It is with love, then, that I extend to you the invitation to enjoy this volume. Accept it at face value, and use its messages as a springboard to your own personal levels of discovery, as you are taught by the Spirit to move under the influence of the Holy Ghost in the direction of your dreams.

Ofa lahi atu!

"They that are whole have no need of the physician, but they that are sick. I came not to call the righteous, but sinners to repentance." (Mark 2:17).

Introduction

If they are fortunate, novice quilters quickly learn a bit of wisdom from the Amish, who make some of the finest quilts in the world. On purpose, the Amish build mistakes into their projects, because they believe that any attempt on their part to design and produce a flawless creation would be a mockery of God, Who alone is perfect. The humility of the Amish makes me think of my own weak attempts to put my thoughts to paper. In His infinite wisdom, God knows very well that I do not need to consciously plan on lacing my efforts with errors. That will come quite naturally, without the need for me to intentionally contribute to my short-comings.

Perhaps this volume will do little more than help to define quirks in my personality. Each of us is different, and many things, including our family and friends, the circumstances in which we find ourselves, the quality of our education, and our own personalities, inspire and mold our oral and written expressions. I would like to think that, in this text, all of these influences have been encouraging, affirmative, and constructive.

Most of the chapters within this volume weave and wobble their way to a conclusion, although finality has not been my goal. As a thinker, writer and teacher who values careful scholarship, I would rather leave the door ajar for the reader, to allow shafts of the light of understanding to creep in as the dawning of recognition awakens interest in particular subject areas. I would hope that within the pages of this volume there is enough latitude to allow for divergent opinions and independent ideas, not to mention constructive criticism. I hope each chapter poses more questions than it answers. If, as I laid down my thoughts utilizing just over one hundred thousand words, I mis-stated myself a few times, or flat-out got it wrong, I ask the patient indulgence and gentle correction of the reader.

I find that no matter how often I have re-read a chapter that has been under construction, I continue to come up with different ways of expressing myself. The ink on the page may barely have dried before I am busy at work on a significant revision. There is no way to complete the process, and I have given up trying to do so. So this printed volume is a work in progress. I think of it as a living and breathing entity because, even in its imperfection, it is my hope that it has the generative power to stimulate intellectual, philosophical, imaginative, and spiritual thought processes. If this volume has any real value, it would be to provoke inquiry in the minds of all who ponder its themes.

The chapters are somewhat random in their subject matter and sequentially they follow no particular pattern. If any seem indecipherable, I invite you to recall Albert Einstein's observation: "That which is impenetrable to us really exists. Behind the secrets remains something subtle, intangible, and inexplicable. Veneration for this force beyond anything that we can comprehend is my religion." My own trust in the Lord is less esoteric, and promises an understanding of some of the very things that one of the greatest minds of the Twentieth Century found "subtle, intangible, and inexplicable." Quite simply, because of my faith-based heritage, this volume does more than scratch the surface of spiritual inquiry; it reaches beyond the mathematical equations and plumbs the depth and measures the breadth of my understanding of the foundation principle of repentance. I hope it does the same for you, dear reader.

The subject matter of the chapters was conceived in the white-hot crucible of thought that is common to all of us, charged by 10 or 20 billion cerebral cortical neurons, each with 60 to 100 dendrites and axons making 60 to 240 trillion interconnections. Recent estimates suggest that our brains can store around one petabyte of information (four quadrillion bytes – more than the entire Internet). So, this volume could have been a lot worse. I've tried very hard to be mindful of the attention span of my target readership.

I've also tried to remember that the best way to arouse creative expression is to "read ourselves full, think ourselves straight, pray ourselves hot, and let ourselves go!" When we do this, we nurture nature and let it caper.

Just as a chef de cuisine might throw a number of ingredients into a "slow cooker" and let them simmer for hours on the stove, some of the chapters only found shape and substance over time as they were nurtured in the subconscious recesses of my mind. The reduction sauce that instilled flavor in other chapters was the product of the distillation of weeks, months, and even years of contemplation, and yet, now and then, a particular thought would quickly sizzle into existence as if the idea had been thrown into a cauldron of boiling oil.

At times a storm did break loose in my mind, but more often than not, my experiences were more like the whispers of a gentle breeze. I do not pretend to have provided much in the way of meaning to even my little corner of the cosmos, but I have enjoyed the mental and spiritual exercise during the journey.

When, in just 24 days, Handel created the 259 pages of musical score that comprise "The Messiah," the notes came to him so quickly that he could barely keep up, as he furiously scratched out the oratorio on whatever paper was handy. After he had written the "Hallelujah Chorus" in a fervor of divine inspiration, he exclaimed that he had "seen all heaven before him." At the end of the manuscript, in acknowledgement of his own puny efforts, he wrote the letters "SDG" that stood for "Soli Deo Gloria"

or "To God alone the glory."

On a much smaller scale, we have all had similar experiences with light and knowledge, and I have been permitted at times to catch a glimpse of the flurry of activity that takes place just beyond the parted veil. Revelatory experiences that have been both nurturing and stimulating have sometimes found their way into the grammar of this volume.

Too often, though, I realize that my thoughts and expressions can be "carefully disguised with hypocrisy and glittering words," as Einstein put it. Although I do fancy myself a wordsmith, I have tried to avoid pedestrian expressions, idle language, and lazy scholarship. I do not pretend to be an authority on the principle of repentance, inasmuch as I believe that we are all works in progress, but if the factual tone within the chapters is sometimes disengaging, the truth is that I typically experienced a deep personal involvement in the expression of the principles that illuminate their themes.

There are those among us who can write out pi (π) to tens of thousands of digits. In 2005, in China, Chao Lu memorized π to 67,890 digits, which was a world record. I cannot come close to that, 3.14 being the extent of my knowledge of this irrational number, but I have been blessed with an imperfect ability to grasp concepts and expand them to proportions that seem to me to be at once both timely and timeless. When you open this volume, I hope you read it with as much enjoyment as I have experienced while creating it.

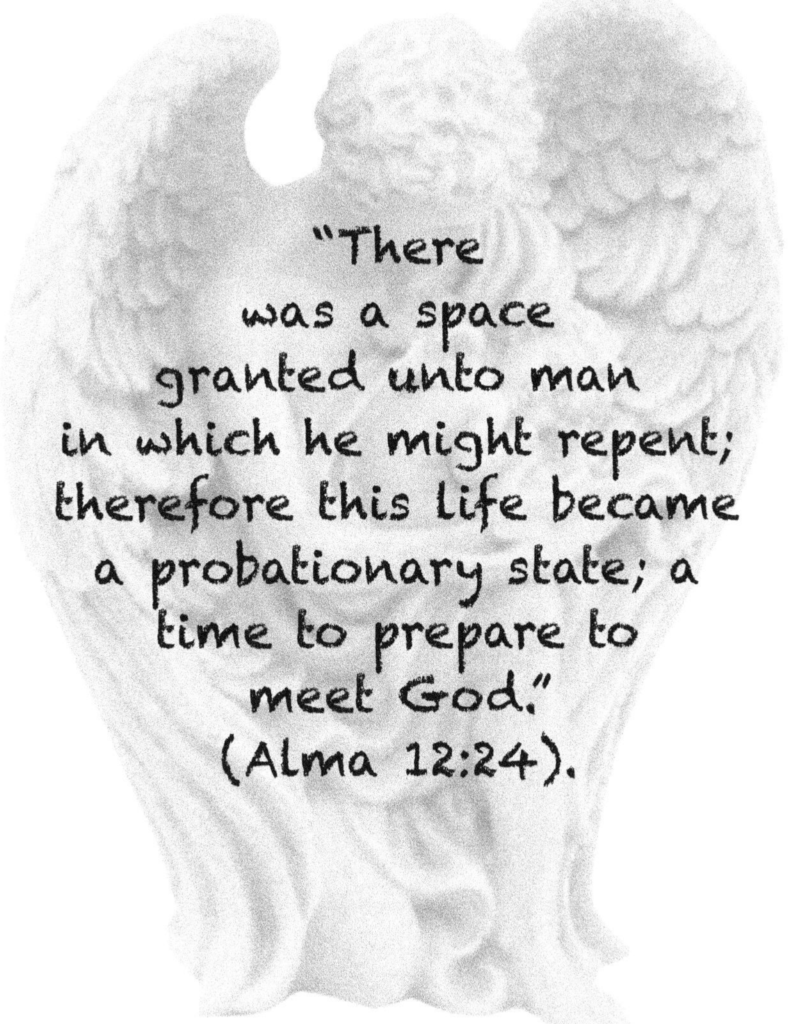

"There
was a space
granted unto man
in which he might repent;
therefore this life became
a probationary state; a
time to prepare to
meet God."
(Alma 12:24).

Chapter One

Repentance and the Seven deadly sins.

"These six things doth the Lord hate: yea, seven are an abomination unto him: A proud look, a lying tongue, and hands that shed innocent blood, an heart that deviseth wicked imaginations, feet that be swift in running to mischief, a false witness that speaketh lies, and he that soweth discord among brethren." (Proverbs 6:16-19).

We are assaulted on a daily basis by the Seven Deadly Sins, and to varying degrees, we are susceptible to their influences. In every instance, however, the Atonement of Christ stands ready to rescue us. Repentance puts a positive spin on our experiences and rekindles our joie de vivre, by recalibrating our celestial compass, rekindling our enthusiasm, and restoring our divine inspiration. It restores our faith in the mission statement of our Father in Heaven, that it is the purpose of lives to have joy. (See Moses 1:39 & 2 Nephi 2:25).

Repentance reaffirms the wisdom of Solomon, who wrote: "A merry heart maketh

a cheerful countenance: but by sorrow of the heart the spirit is broken." (Proverbs 15:13).

1). Solomon taught us that the Lord hates "a proud look."

Every character trait that has been tainted by pride has a counterpart in humility. For example, pride looks over to man and argues who is right, while humility looks up to God and cares only about what is right. Pride asks: "What do I want out of life?" while humility quietly inquires: "What would God have me do?" Pride is motivated by self-will, while humility is inspired by God's will. Pride is driven by the fear of man, while humility is nurtured by the love of God. The applause of the world rings in the ears of pride, while the accolades of heaven warm the hearts of the humble.

The arrogant, boastful, conceited, haughty, and self-centered nature of the proud is easily trumped by the altruistic, deferential, modest, and self-effacing behavior of the humble. Blind opposition, enmity, hatred, hostility, inflexibility, and intolerance are the raw manifestations of pride, but these are overwhelmed by the accommodation, approachability, charity, faith, hope, and sociability of the humble.

The proud feel more comfortable with their own perception of truth than they do with God's omniscience. They pit their own abilities against His priesthood power, their own paltry overtures against His mighty works, and their stubborn will against His gentle counsel. In truth, they have more won't power than will power. Those who refuse to accept His authority have hard-hearts, stiff-necks, and are overtly and covertly rebellious. They lack the malleability and pliability of the humble. The proud are unrepentant because they are smitten with themselves, while the humble experience remorse with the realization that they are less than the dust of the earth. The proud are easily offended and are sign seekers, and because they are past feeling, they require greater and greater intensities of stimulation to receive the same level of temporal or theological gratification. The humble are long-suffering and faithful, and when things seem that they could be no worse, they are at their best, because they are particularly sensitive to the whisperings of the comforting Spirit.

The proud stubbornly hold to their own opinions rather than aligning themselves with God's direction. They consume themselves in a senseless scramble for scarce resources. With self-serving interest, they fill their own lamps with oil, but are penurious when it comes to sharing their wealth with others. The humble, in contrast, foster an atmosphere of collaboration, conciliation, and cooperation, and they pool their resources with others in order to achieve mutually agreeable solutions to their problems.

The proud are argumentative; they fight, exercise unrighteous dominion, and abuse their position, while the humble speak softly, seek peaceful solutions, invite the Spirit to guide them in their interpersonal relationships, and acknowledge their love of God as the engine that drives their righteous behavior. The proud set the stage for secret combinations that are built up with one purpose in mind: "To get gain and the glory of the world." (Helaman 7:5). The humble, on the other hand, work openly, knowing that "nothing is secret that shall not be made manifest; neither any thing hid that shall not be known and come abroad." (Luke 8:17).

In their assessments and judgments, the humble are prone to blame softly and praise loudly. They understand that when straightening a bent nail, a pat on the back is better than a bump on the head. Before being critical of others, the humble remember that those whom they were about to reprove might not have had the same advantages as they. The humble have learned to seek out supportive and sustaining spiritual experiences in the peaceful countryside of clarity, and they encourage others to remove themselves from the madding crowd, to clear their heads, to listen more attentively and to see more plainly, to breathe more deeply as they inhale the fresh air of truth, and to be caressed by its gentle breeze, if they have not beforehand been reinvigorated by such influences and whisperings.

We can choose to humble ourselves, as we determine to repent, by receiving chastisement and counsel, by forgiving those who have offended us, by rendering selfless service, and by our good example that teaches others to do the same. We

can unconsciously choose to be humble by adopting a lifestyle that complements and honors God, and that acknowledges His "glory, honor, power, majesty, might, dominion, truth, justice, judgment, mercy, and an infinity of fulness, from everlasting to everlasting." (D&C 109:77).

The antidote to pride is actually quite simple. The quiet example of the Savior is illustration enough. Humility will conquer our pride even as repentance cleanses our inner vessel and we "yield to the enticings of the Holy Spirit, put off the natural man, and become (Saints) through the Atonement of Christ." (Mosiah 3:19).

2). Solomon taught us that the Lord hates "a lying tongue."

The process by which honesty is woven into and entrenched within our character is that of testing the mettle of our convictions. It is repentance that puts our money where our mouth is. We have no proof until we act on the basis of trust. Then comes the confirmation of the reality, as feelings of self-confidence grow and purposeful actions replace tentative overtures. Truly did Paul declare: "God hath not give us the spirit of fear, but of power, and of love, and of a sound mind." (2 Timothy 1:7). Honesty with ourselves and with God is clothed in the power stemming from the gratitude that only sound minds are capable of expressing. Honesty motivates us to do what is right, rather than what is expedient. Peter's admonition strikes a resonant chord with those whose actions are honest: "We ought to obey God rather than men." (Acts 5:29).

God has given us strong minds, great hearts, true faith, and ready hands, with the power to resist the lust of office, and the moral backbone to possess opinions and a will. We exercise our faith unto repentance to stand before demagogues and damn their treacherous flatteries without winking. We stand tall, and live above the fog in public duty and in private thinking. "For while the rabble, with their thumb worn creeds, their large professions and their little deeds, mingle in selfish strife, Lo! Freedom weeps, Wrong rules the land, and Justice sleeps." (Josiah Gilbert Holland).

All of us are repeatedly faced with occasions when withdrawals must be made from our spiritual bank accounts. When we rely upon the Atonement, and we put the principle of repentance to its ultimate test, we do not write checks that we cannot cash. We realize that only after regular deposits have been faithfully made over a period of time, can we rely upon the cornucopia of comfort created by the cushion of confidence that is a currency flowing from conduct that is consistent with the core curriculum of contrition.

When we repent, we never thirst, because we have sent taproots down through deep Gospel topsoil directly into a flowing fountain of living water. (See D&C 133:29 & Jeremiah 2:13). Repentance is the ultimate expression of honesty with ourselves, with Heavenly Father, with Jesus Christ, and with the Holy Ghost. It allows us to draw upon the power of all three members of the Godhead, so that we may experience the powerful manifestation of the glittering facets of the life of the Spirit. As the process is completed, we become increasingly receptive to flashes of insight as we are cast off into the stream of revelation and carried along in the quickening currents of direct experience with God. (See Mosiah 5:3).

Well did the poet observe that we should exercise our faculties to seek out that which is honest, true, chaste, benevolent, and virtuous. (See the 13th Article of Faith & Philippians 4:8). "The tree at the church next door to me turned up its roots and died. They had tried to brace its leaning, but it lowered and lowered, and then there it lay, leaves in grass and matted roots in air, like a loafer on a summer day. 'Look there,' said the gardener. "Short roots - all the growth went up. Big branches - short roots.' 'How come?' I asked. 'Too much water. This tree never had to hunt for drink.' Especially in thirsty times, my memory steps outside and looks at the tree at the church next door to me that turned up its roots and died." (Carol Lynn Pearson).

As we quietly repent, the righteousness of our cause will be revealed to us in marvelous simplicity and plainness. Walls of opposition to purposeful repentance will crumble and fall away. In our efforts, the Lord will comfort and succor us

with the bread of life. As we travel through the harsh environment of mortality, seeking the Lord while He may be found, oases will spring up in the desert and living waters will slake our thirst. Our roots will be deeply embedded in the bedrock of the Atonement.

We will engage in a partnership with God, and with His Spirit, as we become the architects of our own fate even as we draw upon powers and reserves that are greater than ourselves. Perhaps Victor Hugo heard that majestic clockwork when he wrote: "Be like a bird that pausing in her flight a while on boughs to light, feels them give way beneath her, and yet sings, knowing that she hath wings." As we repent, we will busily engage ourselves in fashioning defensive weapons in the armory of thought. With these tools, the Lord will show us how to build heavenly mansions of joy and strength and peace.

The Lord hates a lying tongue because it can overpower authenticity, decency, goodness, integrity, morality, rectitude, reliability, sincerity and trustworthiness. Repentance allows us to recapture these qualities, that we might become "the masters of thought, and the shapers of condition, environment, and destiny." (Spencer W. Kimball, "The Miracle of Forgiveness," p. 103).

Angels will attend us, as we repent: "For I will go before your face," promised the Lord. "I will be on your right hand, and on your left, and my Spirit shall be in your hearts, and mine angels round about you, to bear you up." (D&C 84:88). With such a promise, how could we then turn our backs on these reinforcements, and return to our wicked ways? Those who have received the holy anointing of forgiveness, will "never rest until the last enemy is conquered, death destroyed, and truth reigns triumphant." (Parley P. Pratt, "Deseret News," 4/30/1853).

3). Solomon taught us that the Lord hates "hands that shed innocent blood."

Aside from His obvious condemnation of murder, (see Exodus 20:13), the Lord hates those who obstruct the flow of living water from holy sources to parched lips, who prevent the innocent from embracing the truth, or who go about destroying

the faith and confidence of those who have already accepted Jesus Christ as their Savior. The scriptures record Alma's confession that, during the rebellious years of his youth, he "had murdered many of (Heavenly Father's spirit) children." Then, the

Book of Mormon record adds the clarification that his unrepentant example caused many to be led "away unto destruction." (Alma 36:14).

That he had contributed to their spiritual demise later caused him to be "racked, even with the pains of a damned soul." (Alma 24:15). "So great had been (his) iniquities, that the very thought of coming into the presence of (his) God did rack (his) soul with inexpressible horror." (Alma 36:14).

When Captain Moroni addressed what he supposed to be the neglect of the responsibilities of the government officials of his day, he asked: "Can you think to sit upon your thrones in a state of thoughtless stupor, while your enemies are spreading the work of death around you?" (Alma 60:6-7). One cannot but help to think of those today who are in a position to intervene when they see the unmistakable symptoms of societal collapse, but instead choose to sit on their hands, look the other way, or even encourage behavior worthy of the most sincere repentance.

Isaiah declared: "Behold, a king shall reign in righteousness, and princes shall rule in judgment." (Isaiah 32:1). But when bureaucrats lose their sense of divine purpose, and when the people are "past repentance," the temporal and spiritual equilibrium of entire societies hangs in the balance. Heaven sometimes holds its breath while waiting upon the initiative of those who are charged with the sacred responsibility to provide a good example, and to take the lead when it comes to repentance.

After his encounter with the leviathan, Jonah went to the wicked city of Nineveh, that is presumed by historians to have been the greatest city of the ancient world. Its people and their practices struck terror in the hearts of its neighbors. Given their reputation for shedding innocent blood, Jonah cried unto the king, who

was probably Shalmaneser III, "and said, yet forty days, and Nineveh shall be overthrown. So the people of Nineveh believed God, and proclaimed a fast, and put on sackcloth, from the greatest of them even to the least of them." They cried mightily unto God, and everyone turned from their evil ways, and from violence, saying "who can tell if God will ... turn away from His fierce anger, that we perish not? (Jonah 3:1-0).

When Jonah was then wroth with God for having spared the city, he was taught a great lesson. God asked him: "And should not I spare Nineveh, that great city, wherein are more than six score thousand persons that cannot discern between their right hand and their left hand?" (Jonah 4:11). In other words, God asked, should He not spare those who cannot discern between right and wrong, and yet are anxious to comply with His law when they are called to repentance?

The modern-day equivalent of Shalmaneser II is Abraham Lincoln, who issued a "Proclamation Appointing a National Fast Day" in response to the jolting reality of deteriorating conditions in the Union. It reads: "Whereas, the Senate of the United States, devoutly recognizing the supreme authority and just government of Almighty God, in all the affairs of men and of nations, has, by a resolution, requested the President to designate and set apart a day for national prayer and humiliation. And whereas it is the duty of nations as well as of men, to own their dependence upon the overruling power of God, to confess their sins and transgressions, in humble sorrow, yet with assured hope that genuine repentance will lead to mercy and pardon, and to recognize the sublime truth, announced in the holy scriptures and proven by all history, that those nations only are blessed whose God is the Lord. And, insomuch as we know that, by His divine law, nations like individuals are subjected to punishments and chastisements in this world, may we not justly fear that the awful calamity of civil war, which now desolates the land, may be but a punishment, inflicted upon us, for our presumptuous sins, to the needful end of our national reformation as a whole people?

We have been the recipients of the choicest bounties of heaven. We have been

preserved, these many years, in peace and prosperity. We have grown in numbers, wealth and power, as no other nation has ever grown. But we have forgotten God. We have forgotten the gracious hand which preserved us in peace, and multiplied and enriched and strengthened us, and we have vainly imagined, in the deceitfulness of our hearts, that all these blessings were produced by some superior wisdom and virtue of our own. Intoxicated with unbroken success, we have become too self-sufficient to feel the necessity of redeeming and preserving grace, too proud to pray to the God that made us! It behooves us then, to humble ourselves before the offended Power, to confess our national sins, and to pray for clemency and forgiveness.

Now, therefore, in compliance with the request, and fully concurring in the views of the Senate, I do, by this my proclamation, designate and set apart Thursday, the 30th day of April, 1863, as a day of national humiliation, fasting and prayer. And I do hereby request all the people to abstain, on that day, from their ordinary secular pursuits, and to unite, at their several places of public worship and their respective homes, in keeping the day holy to the Lord, and devoted to the humble discharge of the religious duties proper to that solemn occasion.

All this being done, in sincerity and truth, let us then rest humbly in the hope authorized by the divine teachings, that the united cry of the nation will be heard on high, and answered with blessings, no less than the pardon of our national sins, and the restoration of our now divided and suffering country, to its former happy condition of unity and peace."

In the Book of Mormon, we learn about Nephi, the son of Helaman, who found it necessary to withdraw from among the people, because "they did reject all his words, insomuch that he could not stay among them." Wicked leaders had "usurped the power and authority of the land, laying aside the commandments of God, and ... doing no justice unto the children of men; condemning the righteous because of their righteousness; letting the guilty and the wicked go unpunished because of their money; and moreover to be held in office at the head of government, to rule

and do according to their wills, that they might get gain and glory of the world, and, moreover, that they might the more easily commit adultery, and steal, and kill."(Helaman 7:2-5). "The past is prologue." (Shakespeare, "The Tempest," Act 2, Scene 1).

4). Solomon taught us that the Lord hates "a heart that deviseth wicked imaginations."

This is why He loves the innocence of little children, for they would never do such a thing. While they drew, a kindergarten teacher walked up and down the rows in her classroom, observing the work of her students. She stopped at the desk of one little girl and asked what her drawing was. The child replied: "I'm drawing a picture of God." The teacher paused, and then tentatively said: "But no one knows what God looks like." Without missing a beat or looking up from her paper, the five year old declared with certainty: "They will in a minute." Though tender in years, this child had what we might call untinctured imagination.

When repentant adults are equally pure in heart, they enjoy the intrinsic and self-reinforcing countermeasures to wicked imaginations. Their behavior is driven by altruism, self-denial, self-discipline, self-restraint, and self-sacrifice. The pure in heart are not easily offended, nor do they hold grudges. They never rationalize their weaknesses, frailties and failures. Rather, they seek the peace that comes with repentance and forgiveness of God. Their self-esteem hinges upon the approval of God, and not of the world.

What should we do when we are faced with wicked imaginations? Sometimes, the very "deceitfulness of riches choke(s) the word," and we are blinded to our characteristic good judgment, insomuch that we act irrationally. (Matthew 13:22). That is to say, the temptation of wicked imaginations clouds our vision and compromises our ability to make correct and prudent choices. Certainly, in these instances, we must speedily repent, in order to find our way back to the rod of iron. Repentance allows us to return to the secret garden of our childhood.

Every day, we are blitzed by any number of offers to spend obscene amounts of

money so we can save, and it is only natural to assume that some of the purveyors of promises "too good to be true" lie in wait to "falsify the balances by deceit." (Amos 8:5). They infiltrate the media, and like sharks prowling near the shoreline of our safety and security, they wait for the unwary to move into dangerously deep water. They disguise their evil purposes with tinsel, and invite the innocent to gamble away their fortunes and forfeit their birthright for a mess of pottage. They play upon our innate trust and the better angels of our nature, twisting the truth into caricatures of reality, reminiscent of the tangled Christmas lights of confusion. Wicked imaginations get our heads spinning so wildly that just about any outlandish offer makes it seem as if we have found Nirvana. If we think we have found the pot of gold at the end of the rainbow, we are more likely to discard the natural restraints that would have, under normal circumstances, tinctured our behavior with moderation.

Leprechauns who dance to the music of wicked imaginations stretch our comprehension of credibility, causing us to move to and fro unsteadily on our spiritual tip-toes. We roll the dice, and capitulate the determination of our destiny to the whims of lady luck. When wicked imaginations have so distorted our better judgment, it may be that the source of our improbable hope is the great deceiver himself, for Alma clearly taught: "Whatsoever is good cometh from God, and whatsoever is evil cometh from the Devil." (Alma 5:40). To narrow our search parameters, however, and to steer us back on course, Paul reminded us: "If there is anything virtuous, lovely, or of good report or praiseworthy, we seek after these things." (Philippians 4:8).

Paraphrasing the Apostle Paul, we should abhor wicked imaginations, and instead cleave unto that which a reasonable person would presume to be true. (See Romans 12:9). Paul was all too familiar with those who sowed false hope, writing: "For they that are such ... serve their own belly, and by good words and fair speeches deceive the hearts of the simple." (Romans 16:18). Such deceivers have sharpened their pencils, honed their skills, and loosed their tongues as consummate con men.

When confronting such swindlers, we cannot allow them to drag us down to the

lowest common denominator of their comfort level. Instead, we should yearn, as Paul did, for the light that will disperse the darkness. Repentance proffers the promise "that we henceforth be no more children, tossed to and fro," as flotsam and jetsam on the sea of life, "and carried about with every wind of doctrine, by the sleight of men, and cunning craftiness." (Ephesians 4:14).

Paul's simple counsel was: "Let no man deceive you with vain words." The trouble with vanity, a virulent form of wicked imaginations, is that it relies on false hope, and upon the strength of false premises. Vanity is the intangible expression of a pyramid scheme that cannot deliver on its promises. It writes checks it cannot cash because its spiritual reserves are running on empty and it is forever teetering on the brink of bankruptcy. In its worst form, vanity is an abomination because it thwarts God's Plan of Happiness. No wonder Paul counseled: "Beware lest any man spoil you through philosophy and vain deceit, after the tradition of men, after the rudiments of the world." (Colossians 2:8). Not only can our travel plans be spoiled by offers that seem too good to be true, but also the direction of our life's journey to the Celestial Kingdom ca be dangerously detoured when we succumb to wicked imaginations.

5). Solomon taught us that the Lord hates "feet that be swift in running to mischief."

We are slow to mischief when we possess the ability to look past telestial temptations and temporal trivia, and adjust our perspective so that the achievement of righteous goals that are worthy of our expenditure of energy becomes our obsession. As Ezra Taft Benson is reported to have stated: "When obedience ceases to be inconvenient, and becomes our quest, then God endows us with power."

Spiritual enlightenment endows us with an unsullied, uncorrupted focus. Input from the five natural senses is transformed by a spiritual sixth sense that orders our hierarchy of value and determines our priorities. When we have been conditioned through diligence, discipline, faith, patience, and repentance, the

activities, interests, and people that deserve our immediate attention are assigned the highest value. We draw upon all our physical and spiritual resources to address those concerns of greatest importance, while those whose feet are swift to run to mischief squander the enlightenment that is so freely given and yet is so casually and carelessly received. The Lord warned: "Wo unto him ... that wasteth the days of his probation, for awful is his state!" (2 Nephi 9:27). Particularly when unrepentant individuals groan "under darkness and under the bondage of sin," they grope about in a frantic and yet fruitless quest as they run to and fro desperately searching for focus, meaning, and stability in their lives. (D&C 84:49).

If we ignore the influences of the Light of Christ and the Holy Ghost that nurture our innate urge to abhor mischief, but instead allow ourselves to be habitually distracted by trifling concerns, we sin by omission and risk settling for life in a marshland of mediocrity. There is, after all, "a tide in the affairs of men, which, taken at the flood, leads on to fortune. Omitted, all the voyage of their life is bound in shallows and in miseries." (Shakespeare, "Julius Caesar," Act 4, Scene 2). "How carefully most men creep into nameless graves, while now and again one or two forget themselves into immortality." (Wendell Phillips, "Speech on Lovejoy").

There is always a price to be paid when we are swift to run to mischief. For example, when societal spiritual equilibrium is surrendered, its values are often adjusted in a vain attempt to re-establish a state of balance. When gods of wood and stone are nearly universally worshipped, it is justified as multiculturalism. If perversion is widely embraced, it is legitimized as an alternative lifestyle. When the poor are exploited, it is often disguised in the name of government-sponsored programs and policies. When unborn children are institutionally murdered, the collective conscience is soothed by coining terms like "pro-choice," and "women's rights" that deflect the issue away from the stark reality and brutality of the term "abortion." When public figures are caught in webs of lies, the sins are mollified and excused as "hyper-exaggeration." When power is abused, it is disguised as progressivism. When the media is polluted with obscenities, it is described as freedom of expression.

In the new millennium, underachievers have gotten so many participation trophies that they think that they are entitled to recognition and reward regardless of their lack of accomplishment. When asked about their goals in life, over 80% of them responded that they wanted to be rich and famous. The target has been moved so many times that they think they are scoring repetitive bulls-eyes, when in reality their arrows have strayed far from the mark.

When individuals are swift in running to mischief, they lose their desire to repent. They lose their focus, just as eyesight may be lost over time. First they squint, and then they hold the page a little closer or a little further away. They compensate for their inability to see clearly, and whether it is the printed page or their character that they cannot read, it is being unconsciously compromised, nevertheless. The faithful don't consciously intend to lose their testimony of the Savior, or their desire to repent. Conviction just fades away like a slow leak from an automobile tire, and not as a sudden blowout, and it can all be traced back to a capitulation to the tendency toward mischief that began at a specific point in time. As Benjamin warned: "This much I can tell you, that if ye do not watch yourselves, and your thoughts, and your words, and your deeds, and observe the commandments of God, and continue in the faith," and avoid running to mischief, "even unto the end of your lives, ye must perish." (Mosiah 4:30).

6). Solomon taught us that the Lord hates "a false witness that speaketh lies."

Those who bear false witness and speak lies often have only a weak foundation of doctrinal understanding of the Gospel. They fall into transgression in consequence of their shallow comprehension of principles. They ignorantly pick apart the scriptures and the words of those who preach the Gospel, distorting the doctrines into meaningless fragments without any coherent connection. They say: "Eat, drink, and be merry; nevertheless, fear God. He will justify in committing a little sin; yea, lie a little, take the advantage of one because of his words, dig a pit for thy neighbor; there is no harm in this; and do all these things, for tomorrow we die; and if it so be that we are guilty, God will beat us with a few stripes, and at last

we shall be saved in the kingdom of God." (2 Nephi 28:8). But as Alma declared to the inhabitants of Ammonihah: "Behold, the scriptures are before you; if ye will wrest them it shall be to your own destruction." (Alma 13:20).

The composite principles of the Gospel are the consummate compilation of affirmative actions. Together, they are as much the sum of "Thou shalt" commandments, as they are "Thou shalt not" commandments. Honesty, for example, is the mortar that holds together the building blocks of character, which is why the Lord hares a false witness that speaketh lies.

Those who are honest with themselves, their fellowmen, and the Lord have an unshakable moral and ethical standard upon which their belief system is securely anchored. Others, who make value judgments based on endocrine secretions, rather than on the unchanging and eternally validated laws of the Gospel, have no such foundation, but instead build their houses on the shifting sands of expediency and the fabrications of circumstance. Those who seek to be lights unto themselves fail to improve the quality of their disposition because their intellect can never bridge the gap between rational behavior and faith, nor can their deceptions provide the mortar that is necessary in the building of character.

The Lord hates those who speak lies, or seek to deceive through misrepresentation. A prospective employer asked a young man who had applied for a job, "If I hire you, can I count on you to be honest?" The young man replied, "You can count on me to be honest, whether you hire me or not." He delighted in being honest, and not because he was obligated to be so. Coercion counters agency, and those who are repetitively acted upon may ultimately forsake principles of conduct that are consistent with trustworthiness. Thus, the Lord instructed the Saints: "He that is compelled in all things, the same is a slothful and not a wise servant." Therefore, the Saints are admonished to be "anxiously engaged in a good cause, and do many things of their own free will, and bring to pass much righteousness. For the power is in them, wherein they are agents unto themselves." (D&C 58:26-28).

Free will implies the power and opportunity to choose, but not as the man who "walked the straight and narrow path, who never lied, and who kept the commandments until he died; who never went to the theatres, and never learned to dance; who never once on shapely legs bestowed a wicked glance; who never smoked or kissed another's wife, and never took a bit of liquor in his life; who never let his temper rise, never called his neighbor a fool, and kept strictly to the Golden Rule. Now you can be assured that he really lived on earth. But he was deaf, and dumb, and blind, and paralyzed from birth." (Anonymous).

Every day, we make the choice to repent or not to repent, and that is a decision that is illuminated and reinforced by our values. During the course of our lives, we may have examinations in math, or history, or economics. But another test will be in our determination to repent. If we must fail one, we need to make sure it is in math, history, or economics. There are faithful, repentant individuals who know nothing about these other subjects, but do just fine, thank you very much. They remain unmoved by the mendacities of Master Mahan.

Long ago, Alexis de Tocqueville wrote: "I sought for the greatness and genius of America in her commodious harbors and her ample rivers, and it was not there; in her fertile fields and boundless prairies, and it was not there; in her rich mines and her vast world commerce, and it was not there. Not until I went to the churches of America and heard her pulpits aflame with righteousness did I understand the secret of her genius and her power. America is great because she is good, and if America ever ceases to be good, America will cease to be great." ("Reflections of Alexis de Tocqueville," p. 71). In the words of the Apostle Paul: "Thanks be made for all men ... that we may lead a quiet and peaceful life in all godliness and honesty." (1 Timothy 2:1-2).

7). Solomon taught us that the Lord hates those who "soweth discord among brethren."

Those who sow discord are often jealous of the accomplishments of others. Their pride is a seductively successful satanic device designed to negatively influence

our spiritual well-being. "When pride has a hold on our hearts, we lose our independence of the world and deliver our freedoms to the bondage of men's judgment." (Ezra Taft Benson, C.R., 4/1989). In a shouting contest, the world will always prevail over the Spirit.

Murmuring is another way that Satan sows discord among brethren. It is the subdued and continually repeated expression of indistinct or inarticulate complaints or grumbling. Like an earthquake, the murmuring of the disgruntled and malcontented can build into harmonic waves with the power to undermine the foundations of both relationships and institutions. It is often conducted anonymously or behind the cloak of secrecy, but its effect is felt publicly. The pride of those who murmur compels them to expect a return without having made a legitimate investment. Especially in the case of those who murmur against the universality of God's command to repent, no tangible expenditure of faith has been made. Theirs is a cowardly act, and yet, they somehow expect results without responsibility.

Those who murmur are fault-finders, who throw dirt but lose ground in the process. They are like flies that pass over healthy parts of the body to feed only at open sores. At the dedication of the Kirtland Temple, Joseph Smith referred to those predatory individuals who had sought to tear down the Latter-day work through fault finding. "We ask thee," he prayed, "to confound, and astonish, and to bring to shame and confusion, all those who have spread lying reports abroad, over the world, against thy servants, if they will not repent." (D&C 109:29).

What can we do when we are assaulted by the Seven Deadly Sins?

When we are confronted by compromise, we should remember the counsel of Alma, who used the example of the Liahona, to teach: "For behold, it is as easy to give heed to the word of Christ, which will point to you a straight course to eternal bliss, as it was for our fathers to give heed to this compass, which would point unto them a straight course to the promised land." (Alma 37:44). As it was for Alma and his people, so it is for us. With our Liahona, we will find that no wind can blow except it fills our sails and carries us ever closer to our intended destination, without delay

or interruption, and without unnecessary cost, loss, or sacrifice. All that is required is the sacrifice of a broken heart and a contrite spirit. (See D&C 59:8).

The following are adapted from the Twelve Steps of Addiction Recovery (L.D.S.

Social Services). 1). We must acknowledge to ourselves that we are at risk of the constant and unrelenting assault of the seven deadly sins. 2). We must come to believe that only the power of God can restore us to complete spiritual health. 3). We must turn our lives over to His care and keeping. 4). We must constantly re-evaluate the stability and integrity of our moral shields. 5). We must acknowledge the power of the priesthood as a key ally in our fight against, and resistance to, Satan's onslaughts. 6). We must be ready to allow the power of God, and not our own puny efforts, to defeat Satan. 7). We must ask Jesus Christ to come to our defense, and in particular to help us through forgiveness following purposeful repentance, to heal the damage done in consequence of the weaknesses in our armor. 8). We must be true to our friends, family, and acquaintances; to be true to our word, and to honor our commitments and covenants, in order to draw upon the power of God through ordinances and covenants. 9). We must be absolutely honest in our dealings with our ourselves and our fellow warriors, and to enlist the aid of Heavenly Father, Jesus Christ, and the Holy Ghost, as we struggle to right the wrongs for which we are responsible. 10). We must constantly monitor the defensive network of systems within The Plan of Salvation to resist Satan, recognize when we have allowed them to fail, accept responsibility for the outcomes that are a natural consequence of the failure, and take steps to restore the integrity of the network. We must do everything within our ability to maintain the open lines of communication with the powers of heaven that have been established by The Plan. We must plan our work and work His Plan. 11). We must not only believe in Christ, but also believe Him when He says that He can heal us through the power of His Atonement. 12). We must then use the Atonement as our secret weapon in our defense against the seven deadly sins.

Whether we are combating the influences of the Seven Deadly Sins or the garden-variety sins that we commit every day, the Atonement stipulates that we go through

a process of repentance when we fall short of obedience to all of God's laws. Repentance requires that we Recognize our transgression, experience Remorse, Renounce the self-defeating behavior, Resolve to do better, make Restitution where possible, and then do our part through Repentance to establish a Reconciliation with the Spirit, in order to Receive a Remission of sin through the grace of God Who is our Redeemer.

"I beseech of you
that ye do not procrastinate
the day of your repentance until
the end; for after this day of life, which
is given us to prepare for eternity, behold,
if we do not improve upon our time while
in this life, then cometh the night of
darkness wherein there can be
no labor performed."
(Alma 34:33).

Chapter Two

The reduction sauce of repentance.

In The Book of Mormon, Alma Chapter 42 is the continuation of the counsel given by Alma to his son Corianton, that began in Alma Chapter 39. Mormon evidently chose to record this abridgment in the first person tense, in order to preserve the intensely personal quality of the counsel Alma gave to his sons Helaman, Shiblon, and Corianton. (See Alma Chapters 36 – 42). Alma taught Corianton the doctrine of Justice and Mercy as they relate to the principle of repentance, because the young man had wrested the scriptures in order to excuse his sinful behavior.

Alma refreshed Corianton's memory, reminding him that at the time of Adam and Eve's transgression, God "placed at the east end of the garden of Eden, cherubim, and a flaming sword which turned every way, to keep the Tree of Life." (Alma 42:2). He had very effectively used the same illustration 10 years earlier when teaching the people of Ammonihah, explaining to them that eternal life is gained by redemption through the reality of the Atonement of Jesus Christ, and not by physical cherubim who had metaphorically been set in place to guard the way to the Tree of Life.

He explained the purpose of the cherubim; that Heavenly Father had employed their service only to prevent Adam and his posterity from inappropriately partaking of its fruit before first being taught about The Plan of Salvation and the power of the Atonement through repentance.

In Ammonihah, Antionah had cited Genesis 3:24: God "placed at the east of the garden of Eden cherubims, and a flaming sword which turned every way, to keep the way of the Tree of Life." He had erroneously concluded that the only way to live forever was to "partake of the fruit of the Tree of Life." (See Alma 5:34). If this were so, Antionah had reasoned, the people would have had a justification for sinning. For if the key to immortality were simply partaking of the fruit, then with cherubim guarding the way, there would be "no possible chance that they (could) live forever." (Alma 12:21). But just as Alma had answered the question posed by Antionah, so did he for his son Corianton.

One of the foundation teachings of the Gospel is that we come into this world to die. "If it had been possible for Adam to have partaken of the fruit of the Tree of Life" in the Garden after the Fall, "there would have been no death, and the word would have been void, making God a liar, for he said: If thou eat, thou shalt surely die." (Alma 12:23). It was clearly understood before we came here that our experience would end in the death of our mortal body. It is part of the Merciful Plan of our Father. When Adam was sent into the Garden of Eden, it was with the understanding that he would violate, or in other words simply transgress, a law in order to trigger mortality.

The Fall has given each of us the privilege to come to the earth in order to prepare for a resurrection, through repentance because of the Atonement. "And we see that death comes upon mankind, yea, the death which has been spoken of by Amulek, which is the temporal death; nevertheless there was a space granted unto man in which he might repent; therefore this life became a probationary state; a time to prepare to meet God; a time to prepare for that endless state which has been spoken of by us, which is after the resurrection of the dead." (Alma 12:24). Through the Atonement, we will be raised in the resurrection, appropriately clothed in exactly

the kinds of bodies we will need in order to dwell in the degree of glory to which we are best suited by temperament.

Alma also taught that in the absence of repentance for their sins, and without the benefit of the ordinances and covenants of the Gospel Plan of Salvation, Adam and Eve must have ultimately been miserable, living forever in their sins. "And now behold, if it were possible that our first parents could have gone forth and partaken of the Tree of Life they would have been forever miserable, having no preparatory state; and thus The Plan of Redemption would have been frustrated, and the word of God would have been void, taking none effect." (Alma 12:26, see Alma 5:34).

Without redemption from sin, if they were to have partaken of the fruit of the Tree of Life, which is eternal life, or the highest expression of the love of God, it would not have been possible for them to sustain a celestial existence, inasmuch as in their current condition they would have been incapable of obedience to the principles that govern those who merit celestial glory. Thus, the Plan of Salvation would have been frustrated.

"The Fall had brought upon all mankind a spiritual death as well as a temporal (death), that is, we would be cut off from the presence of the Lord." (Alma 42:9). The violation of God's commandments inevitably results in alienation from His presence. The scriptures call this a spiritual death. This is illustrated by Adam and Eve's expulsion from the Garden, which resulted in their mortality, making their eventual temporal death inevitable. (See Moses 5:4). When we, the posterity of our first parents, come to earth, we experience our own "expulsion from the Garden," as we opengage our mission in the lone and dreary world. (See 1 Nephi 8:4).

But, in such a scenario, even as our hearts ache for the safety and security of our hearth and home in heaven, all is not lost. As Alma explained, it is expedient that we should be reclaimed from spiritual death by returning to the secret garden of our spiritual childhood. (See Alma 42:9).

It is for our benefit that we become acquainted with evil as well as with good, with pain as well as with pleasure, with darkness as well as with light, with error as well as with truth, and with punishment for the infraction of eternal laws, as well as with the blessings that follow obedience. Mortality is really our only opportunity to have these experiences. As Ralph Waldo Emerson once asked: "What is the use of immortality to one who cannot wisely use half an hour?" Every minute of mortality is precious. This is why Alma and so many other fathers have invested so much time and energy teaching their children correct principles, and training them in their proper execution. As Nephi explained: "We talk of Christ, we rejoice in Christ, we preach of Christ, we prophesy of Christ, and we write according to our prophecies, that our children may know to what source they may look for a remission of their sins." (2 Nephi 25:26).

In Alma Chapter 40, Alma had laid the groundwork for the counsel he now gave to his son, by explaining conditions in the Spirit World. He reminded Corianton: "If it were not for The Plan of Redemption, as soon as they were dead their souls were miserable, being cut off from the presence of the Lord." (Alma 42:11). Justice, or the law of compensation, would demand that they suffer eternally the consequences of their own actions. (See Alma 42:12). They would be in the grasp of "the justice of God, which (would have) consigned them forever to be cut off from his presence." (Alma 42:14).

The Plan of Redemption required that "an Atonement should be made. Therefore, God Himself atoneth for the sins of the world, to bring about The Plan of Mercy, to appease the demands of justice, that God might be a perfect, just God, and a merciful God also." (Alma 42:15). The Atonement allows God to satisfy Justice and still mercifully reclaim us from physical and spiritual death. The Savior thus becomes the Master of the situation. In His sacrifice, the debt is paid, redemption is made, the covenant of our Father is fulfilled, and Justice is satisfied, with all power, including the keys of resurrection, given to our Redeemer, all according to the will of our Heavenly Father.

"Mercy claimeth the penitent, and mercy cometh because of the Atonement; and the Atonement bringeth to pass the resurrection of the dead; and the resurrection of the dead bringeth back men into the presence of God. For behold, justice exerciseth all his demands, and also mercy claimeth all which is her own; and thus, none but the truly penitent are saved." (Alma 42:23-24, underlining mine).

Alma reminded Corianton that the only payment required for the gift of salvation is "the heart and a willing mind." (D&C 64:34). The only things that we must give up are our sins. (See Alma 22:18). Therefore, Alma counseled his son: "Only let your sins trouble you, with that trouble which shall bring you down unto repentance." (Alma 42:29).

The first step in the process that Alma outlined for Corianton was to consciously recognize his sin. (See Jeremiah 6:15). Secondly, Alma urged his son to cease excusing himself in sin. He warned: "O my son, I desire that ye should deny the justice of God no more. Do not endeavor to excuse yourself in the least point because of your sins, by denying the justice of God; but do let the justice of God, and his mercy, and his long-suffering have full sway in your heart; and let it bring you down to the dust in humility." (Alma 42:30).

Alma counseled Corianton that the Atonement of Jesus Christ is the only compelling alternative to overwhelmingly negative influences competing for dominance in our lives. The only stipulation of the Atonement is that we go through a process wherein we Recognize our transgression, experience Remorse, Renounce the self-defeating behavior, make Restitution where possible, Resolve to do better, and then establish a Reconciliation with the Spirit through Repentance, that we might ultimately Receive a Remission of sin through the grace of God our Redeemer.

Finally, Alma instructed his son to return to the missionary labor to which he had been previously called. "And now, O my son, ye are called of God to preach the word unto this people. And now, my son, go thy way, declare the word with truth

and soberness, that thou mayest bring souls unto repentance, that The Great Plan of Mercy may have claim upon them" also. (Alma 42:31).

That Corianton was faithful to his father's exhortation is evident from a reference to him in the abridged record of Shiblon. Mormon recorded that seventeen years after Alma's counsel was given, Shiblon "was a just man, and he did walk uprightly before God, and he did observe to do good continually, to keep the commandments of the Lord his God, and also did his brother" Corianton. (Alma 63:2).

"Speak with
the trump of God,
with a voice to shake
the earth, and cry
repentance unto
every people!"
(Alma 29:1).

Chapter Three

The Last Judgment

How will we be judged? John the Revelator "saw the dead, small and great, stand before God; and the books were opened; and another book was opened, which is the book of life. And the dead were judged out of those things which were written in the books, according to their works." (Revelation 20:12).

The "Final Judgment" is only the last in a long series of judgments. We were all judged in the pre-mortal existence, and we are judged throughout our lives. Finally, at the Last Judgment, if we have not repented, "our words will condemn us, yea, all our works will condemn us ... and our thoughts will also condemn us." (Alma 12:14). For "every idle word that men shall speak, they shall give account thereof in the day of judgment. For by thy words thou shalt be justified, and by thy words thou shalt be condemned." (Matthew 12:36-37).

Many years ago, the popular comedian Groucho Marx sued for 15 million dollars for breach of contract over obscene remarks he made 'off the record' and that were subsequently published. The plaintiff stated that he became ill when he read the final manuscript and needed medical attention because he was so shocked by its

contents. Ultimately, Marx had to face the music and stand by his comments.

One day Jan received a telephone call from a ward member. After their conversation was completed, Jan replaced the receiver in its cradle, but it didn't go all the way down, and the line was still open. Later, when the other person picked up the phone to use it again, she had instant access to the uninhibited conversations in our home. Fortunately, our family did not thereafter have to be like "the kings of the earth, and the great men, and the rich men, and the chief captains, and the mighty men, and every bondman, and every free man, (who) hid themselves in the dens and in the rocks of the mountains; and said to the mountains and rocks, Fall on us, and hide us from the face of him that sitteth on the throne and from the wrath of God." (Revelation 6:15-16).

"We are going to be judged out of the things written in books, out of the revelations of God, out of the temple records, out of those things which the Lord has commanded us to keep." (Joseph Fielding Smith, "Doctrines of Salvation," 2:200) Our own bodies will be the most accurate record of all, for "the work of the law (is) written in (our) hearts." (Romans 2:15). That record is "written not with ink, but with the Spirit of the living God; not in tables of stone, but in fleshy tables of the heart." (2 Corinthians 3:3). We tell the story ourselves, for it is written in the tablets of our own minds. "That record cannot lie and will be unfolded before God and angels, and those who sit as judges." (John Taylor).

The book of life is the record of our own acts that has been written in our own bodies. "It is the record engraven in the very bones, sinews, and flesh of the mortal body. That is, every thought, words, and deed has an effect on the human body; all these leave their marks, which can be read by Him who is Eternal as easily as the words in a book can be read." (Bruce R. McConkie, "Mormon Doctrine," p. 97).

By divine investiture of authority, Christ is the ultimate Judge, for "the Father judgeth no man, but hath committed all judgment unto the Son." (John 5:22). His Judgment Seat lies in a straight course. The gatekeeper will not be Saint Peter, but

Christ Himself, for "He employeth no servant there." (2 Nephi 9:41).

Today is the Day of Judgment. Continually, we speak, think, and act according to celestial, terrestrial, or telestial law. A barometer can be used to measure the direction in which the weather is headed. Our faith in Christ and our capacity for repentance keeps us pointed in the direction of our heavenly home.

Each day of our lives, we are 24 hours closer to the Pleasing Bar of Christ, if we pattern our behavior after the 13th Article of Faith. (See Alma 3:7 & Moroni 10:34). "We believe in being honest, true, chaste, benevolent, virtuous, and in doing good to all men. Indeed, we may say that we follow the admonition of Paul: We believe all things, we hope all things, we have endured many things, and hope to be able to endure all things. If there is anything that is virtuous, lovely, or of good report or praiseworthy, we seek after these things." (See Philippians 4:8).

"Happiness," after all, "is the object and design of our existence, and will be the end thereof, (at the Last Judgment), if we follow the path that leads to it, and this path is virtue, uprightness, faithfulness, holiness, and keeping all the commandments of God," including the injunction to repent. (Joseph Smith, "Teachings," p. 255)

At that banquet of consequences, "there will not be much that is satisfying at the table, unless we are able to bow our heads (in reverence), not hang them (in shame), in the presence of God, who will be there. " (Marion D. Hanks)

Blessed are those who walk "not in the counsel of the ungodly, nor standeth in the way of sinners, nor sitteth in the seat of the scornful. But (their) delight is in the law of the Lord, and in his law doth (they) meditate day and night. And (they) shall be like a tree planted by the rivers of water, that bringeth forth his fruit in his season; (their) leaf also shall not wither; and whatsoever (they) doeth shall prosper. The ungodly are not so: but are like the chaff which the wind driveth away. Therefore the ungodly shall not stand in the judgment, nor sinners in the congregation of the righteous. For the Lord knoweth the way of the righteous: but

the way of the ungodly shall perish." (Psalms 1:1-2).

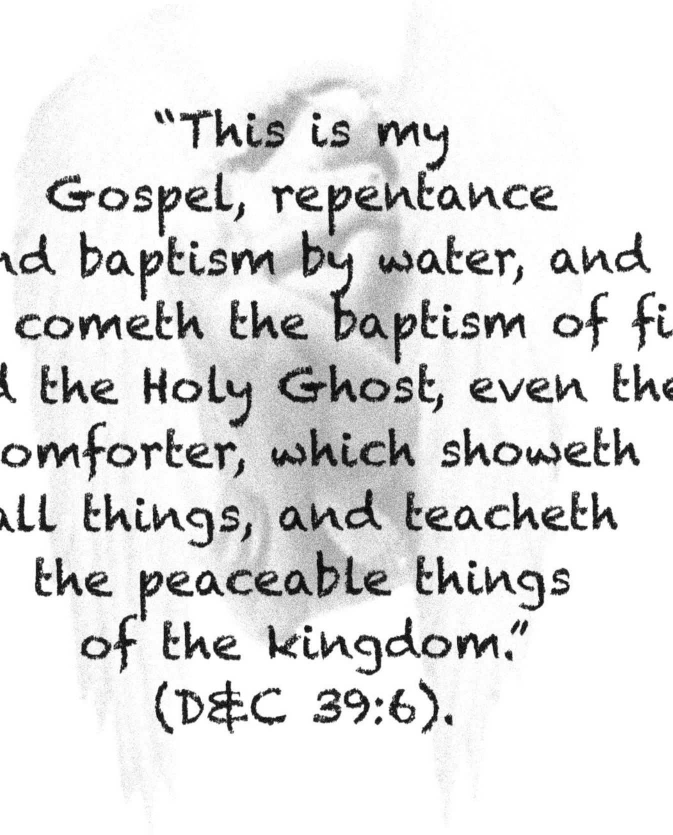

"This is my
Gospel, repentance
and baptism by water, and
then cometh the baptism of fire
and the Holy Ghost, even the
Comforter, which showeth
all things, and teacheth
the peaceable things
of the kingdom."
(D&C 39:6).

Chapter Four

The Fall

The world misinterprets the significance of the Fall of Adam because there have been "taken away from the Gospel of the Lamb many parts which are plain and most precious; and also many covenants of the Lord have they taken away. And all this have they done that they might pervert the right ways of the Lord, that they might blind the eyes and harden the hearts of the children of men." (1 Nephi 13:26-27). The account in Genesis treats the Fall as an event, without delving into the ramifications of its related doctrine. Fortunately, the accounts in The Pearl of Great Price and in the temple endowment, as well as within the inspired commentaries of Book of Mormon prophets, help to fill in the gaps.

We know that Satan "sought to beguile Eve, for he knew not the mind of God, wherefore he sought to destroy the world." (Moses 4:6). Eve was pure and without guile and was easily deceived. When Lucifer took advantage of her, the sin lay at his feet. ("What is this thou hast done?") Satan told Eve a truth and a lie. He said that she and Adam would have knowledge, but he also said that they should not die. (Genesis 3:4-5). Satan came to Eve with the intent to deceive. He was full of treachery, and he sought to mislead her. His offer was a forgery. He was, after all, a

liar from the beginning. (D&C 93:15).

After God created Adam and Eve, they were given the commandment to dress and keep the Garden and to abstain from partaking of the fruit of the Tree of

Knowledge of Good and Evil. (Moses 3:15 & 17). But they were also commanded to be fruitful, and multiply, and replenish the earth. (See Genesis 1:28). It is also possible that Eve, having been created at a later time, did not receive the same instructions that had earlier been given to Adam, although this hypothesis is not supported by the narrative in the temple endowment.

After the Fall, God put enmity between Satan and the family of Adam and Eve, for He recognized the dangers that would lie in their familiarity with sin. (Genesis 3:15). As Alexander Pope observed: "Vice is a monster of such frightful mien, as to be hated needs but to be seen. Yet seen too oft, familiar with her face, we first pity, then endure, then embrace."

Genesis tells us that after the Fall, Eve would have "sorrow" in her conception. But as Spencer W. Kimball observed: "I wonder if those who translated the Bible might have used the term distress instead of sorrow. It would mean much the same, except I think there is great gladness in most Latter-day Saint homes when there is to be a child there." ("Ensign," 3/1976).

When Adam and Eve were driven from the Garden, they were "punished" with the very things that would later prove to bring them the greatest happiness. As the Sufi poet Rumi observed: "Our wounds become portals that allow light to enter us." A Savior would be provided for them, but in the meantime, cherubim and a flaming sword were placed to keep the way of the Tree of Life, to preserve the principle of repentance that had just been explained to Adam and Eve. (See Genesis 3:24). Both Justice and Mercy would allow them and their posterity to experience all of the wonders of mortality, without harming their eternal identity or hampering The Plan. "For behold, if Adam had put forth his hand immediately, and partaken of the Tree of Life, he would have lived forever, according to the word of God, having no

space for repentance; yea, and also the word of God would have been void, and the great plan of salvation would have been frustrated." (Alma 42:5).

After the Fall, the door to Eden may have swung shut, but as it did so, another door opened that introduced Adam and Eve to a secret garden accessible only to those who would utilize the power of the Atonement. By obedience to the principles of The Plan, they would experience both good and evil, pleasure and pain, and light and darkness, in the wonderful learning laboratory of life.

Repent: for
the kingdom of
heaven is at hand."
(Matthew 4:17).

Chapter Five

Father forgive them.

On the Cross at Calvary, the Savior looked down upon the Roman soldiers who had crucified Him, and uttered these remarkable words: "Father, forgive them, for they know not what they do." (Luke 23:34). Incredibly, it was with the same spirit of forgiveness that He regarded His brethren the Jews, who had so recently condemned Him.

Their voices must have stung His ears, however, when He had heard them cry out: "His blood be on us, and on our children. (Matthew 27:5). These were the descendants of those of whom the Lord had spoken through the mouth of His prophet Isaiah: "Fear not, for ... with everlasting kindness will I have mercy on thee, saith the Lord thy Redeemer." (Isaiah 54:8). Through Isaiah, the Lord of all the earth promised His covenant children: "No weapon that is formed against thee shall prosper; and every tongue that shall revile against thee in judgment thou shalt condemn. This is the heritage of the servants of the Lord, and their righteousness is of me, saith the Lord." (Isaiah 54:17).

These promises notwithstanding, in the courtyard of Pilate, the Jews had betrayed

the Bridegroom to whom they had been betrothed. If there were ever justification for the Savior to harbor bitter feelings toward those who had wronged Him, it would be as He staggered under the weight of His cross, on the Via Dolorosa, or the "Way of Grief, Sorrow, and Suffering." As He struggled along "Painful Way," He knew that every step would bring Him closer to Calvary as the result of His betrayal by His brethren.

Long before the Savior's comforting words had illuminated the mind of His prophet Isaiah, and even before the foundation of the world, He had begun to consistently accumulate reserves in His spiritual bank account to be used against the day when He would need them most. He knew from the beginning, even before The Greet and Eternal Plan of Deliverance from Death (2 Nephi 11:5) had been explained to the Father's children, that His was to be an infinite and eternal Atonement for every sin that would ever be committed by His brothers and sisters. Thus, when the critical hour came in the Garden of Gethsemane, followed by the mockery of his trial before Pilate and His crucifixion on Calvary, He was able to plumb the limitless depths of His reserves of mercy and extend His magnificent forgiveness to those who had so grievously offended him. "He was wounded for our transgressions, he was bruised for our iniquities. The chastisement of our peace was upon him; and (yet) with his stripes we are healed." (Isaiah 53:5). Thus, did His prophet Isaiah describe the Atonement of the Savior, over 700 years before His mortal ministry. Truly, the reach of His sacrifice was infinite in both its temporal and eternal scope.

As Benjamin declared about 125 years before Christ's agony in Gethsemane: "The Atonement (was) prepared from the foundation of the world, that thereby salvation might come to him that should put his trust in the Lord, and should be diligent in keeping his commandments, and continue in the faith even unto the end of his life." (Mosiah 4:6). The Atonement to which Benjamin referred took into account every sin that would be individually or collectively committed by the family of man, beginning at the foundation of the world and only ending when the Lord comes a second time to usher in His millennial reign on earth.

The Atonement anticipated the sins of omission and of commission that would be frustratingly, repetitively, and painfully committed by every generation of the children of men, from the beginning to the end of time. It is all the more remarkable to realize that the Atonement anticipated sins that had not yet been committed. When the Savior stood before the Council and said to His Father: "Here am I, send me," (Abraham 3:27), He knew full well the price that would be required to satisfy Justice in order to obtain mercy for His brothers and sisters. He had the spiritual firepower to make such a statement, but even his maturity as a God in Heaven could not take away the pain He must have felt, even then, for the scriptures describe Him as the "lamb slain from the foundation of the world." (Revelation 13:8).

Could His brothers and sisters who were also in attendance at the Council, who so enthusiastically raised their arms to the square to support the Father's proposal, have truly felt the import of the moment? (See Job 38:7). He not only was making history, but He was also creating a binding foundation and precedent to re-write history itself? They were eyewitnesses to the vitalization of "the merciful plan of the great Creator." (2 Nephi 9:6). They must have palpably sensed in His condescension the enveloping reach of His love for them. They must have understood His supernal example of humility, His supreme act of selflessness, and His superlative expression of altruism. He had just become their personal Redeemer, and the power of the Atonement had just been initialized in their behalf. Could they have comprehended the significance of the events that were unfolding before them? The exercise of their free will had just been guaranteed, the principles of The Plan certified, the price of their future offenses successfully negotiated, the promise of payment confirmed in advance, and the demands of Justice satisfied and equally balanced against Mercy. Even cherubim and a flaming sword had been prepared to guard the way, that the eternal progression of Adam and Eve and their posterity might be assured. The legitimacy of God's work and glory had been warranted: To bring to pass our immortality and eternal life. (See Moses 1:39).

As Aaron taught King Lamoni's father, around a hundred years before the mortal ministry of the Savior: "Since man had fallen he could not merit anything of

himself; but the sufferings and death of Christ atone for their sins, through faith and repentance, (and) he breaketh the bands of death, that the grave shall have no victory ... that the sting of death should be swallowed up in the hopes of glory." (Alma 22:14).

"Whosoever repenteth and cometh unto me, the same is my Church." (D&C 10:67).

Chapter Six

Applying the Atonement in our lives.

On the Cross at Calvary, the Savior looked down upon the Roman soldiers who had crucified Him, and uttered these remarkable words: "Father, forgive them, for they know not what they do." (Luke 23:34). Incredibly, it was with the same spirit of forgiveness that He regarded His brethren the Jews, who had so recently condemned Him.

Their voices must have stung His ears, however, when He had heard them cry out: "His blood be on us, and on our children. (Matthew 27:5). These were the descendants of those of whom the Lord had spoken through the mouth of His prophet Isaiah: "Fear not, for ... with everlasting kindness will I have mercy on thee, saith the Lord thy Redeemer." (Isaiah 54:8). Through Isaiah, the Lord of all the earth promised His covenant children: "No weapon that is formed against thee shall prosper; and every tongue that shall revile against thee in judgment thou shalt condemn. This is the heritage of the servants of the Lord, and their righteousness is of me, saith the Lord." (Isaiah 54:17).

These promises notwithstanding, in the courtyard of Pilate, the Jews had betrayed the Bridegroom to whom they had been betrothed. If there were ever justification for the Savior to harbor bitter feelings toward those who had wronged Him, it would be as He staggered under the weight of His cross, on the Via Dolorosa, or the "Way of Grief, Sorrow, and Suffering." As He struggled along "Painful Way," He knew that every step would bring Him closer to Calvary as the result of His betrayal by His brethren.

Long before the Savior's comforting words had illuminated the mind of His prophet Isaiah, and even before the foundation of the world, He had begun to consistently accumulate reserves in His spiritual bank account to be used against the day when He would need them most. He knew from the beginning, even before The Greet and Eternal Plan of Deliverance from Death (2 Nephi 11:5) had been explained to the Father's children, that His was to be an infinite and eternal Atonement for every sin that would ever be committed by His brothers and sisters. Thus, when the critical hour came in the Garden of Gethsemane, followed by the mockery of his trial before Pilate and His crucifixion on Calvary, He was able to plumb the limitless depths of His reserves of mercy and extend His magnificent forgiveness to those who had so grievously offended him. "He was wounded for our transgressions, he was bruised for our iniquities. The chastisement of our peace was upon him; and (yet) with his stripes we are healed." (Isaiah 53:5). Thus, did His prophet Isaiah describe the Atonement of the Savior, over 700 years before His mortal ministry. Truly, the reach of His sacrifice was infinite in both its temporal and eternal scope.

As Benjamin declared about 125 years before Christ's agony in Gethsemane: "The Atonement (was) prepared from the foundation of the world, that thereby salvation might come to him that should put his trust in the Lord, and should be diligent in keeping his commandments, and continue in the faith even unto the end of his life." (Mosiah 4:6). The Atonement to which Benjamin referred took into account every sin that would be individually or collectively committed by the family of man, beginning at the foundation of the world and only ending when the Lord comes a second time to usher in His millennial reign on earth.

The Atonement anticipated the sins of omission and of commission that would be frustratingly, repetitively, and painfully committed by every generation of the children of men, from the beginning to the end of time. It is all the more remarkable to realize that the Atonement anticipated sins that had not yet been committed. When the Savior stood before the Council and said to His Father: "Here am I, send me," (Abraham 3:27), He knew full well the price that would be required to satisfy Justice in order to obtain mercy for His brothers and sisters. He had the spiritual firepower to make such a statement, but even his maturity as a God in Heaven could not take away the pain He must have felt, even then, for the scriptures describe Him as the "lamb slain from the foundation of the world." (Revelation 13:8).

Could His brothers and sisters who were also in attendance at the Council, who so enthusiastically raised their arms to the square to support the Father's proposal, have truly felt the import of the moment? (See Job 38:7). He not only was making history, but He was also creating a binding foundation and precedent to re-write history itself? They were eyewitnesses to the vitalization of "the merciful plan of the great Creator." (2 Nephi 9:6). They must have palpably sensed in His condescension the enveloping reach of His love for them. They must have understood His supernal example of humility, His supreme act of selflessness, and His superlative expression of altruism. He had just become their personal Redeemer, and the power of the Atonement had just been initialized in their behalf. Could they have comprehended the significance of the events that were unfolding before them? The exercise of their free will had just been guaranteed, the principles of The Plan certified, the price of their future offenses successfully negotiated, the promise of payment confirmed in advance, and the demands of Justice satisfied and equally balanced against Mercy. Even cherubim and a flaming sword had been prepared to guard the way, that the eternal progression of Adam and Eve and their posterity might be assured. The legitimacy of God's work and glory had been warranted: To bring to pass our immortality and eternal life. (See Moses 1:39).

As Aaron taught King Lamoni's father, around a hundred years before the mortal

ministry of the Savior: "Since man had fallen he could not merit anything of himself; but the sufferings and death of Christ atone for their sins, through faith and repentance, (and) he breaketh the bands of death, that the grave shall have no

victory ... that the sting of death should be swallowed up in the hopes of glory."
(Alma 22:14).

"These words are not
of men nor of man, but of me;
wherefore, you shall testify they are of
me and not of man; For it is my voice which
speaketh them unto you; for they are given by
my Spirit unto you, and by my power you can
read them one to another; and save it were by
my power you could not have them.
Wherefore, you can testify that
you have heard my voice,
and know my words."
(D&C 18:34-36).

Chapter Seven

Opposition in all things.

In a grand summary to Lehi's discourse on opposition and the Fall of Adam, begun in 2 Nephi 2:11, he provided eloquent closure to the principle, in verse 25, with an aphorism that is one of the basic messages of the Restoration: "Adam fell that men might be, and men are that they might have joy." When the Fall of Adam is considered in conjunction with the Atonement of Christ, it is clear that both are part of God's Plan of Progression, for we can only attain eternal happiness in a personal, tangible, reunification of our body and spirit. For we are "spirit, the elements are eternal, and spirit and element, inseparably connected, receive a fullness of joy." (D&C 93:33).

Beginning with 2 Nephi 2:26, Lehi continued to impress upon Jacob that it is Christ's way for us to act for ourselves by using our agency with responsibility, while it is Satan's way for us to be acted upon, by forfeiting our agency in exchange for the fleeting pleasures of the world. Whether we do the latter consciously or unwittingly, the consequences are the same. The "perfect law of liberty" allows us to do as we wish and to be free according to the flesh. (James 1:25). The exercise of agency in an atmosphere of diametrically opposed alternatives comes down to a choice

between liberty and eternal life, or captivity and spiritual death. (See 2 Nephi 2:27). But for agency to facilitate positive outcomes, our actions must be carried out within the context of the Gospel and its laws. Otherwise, unbridled freedom will lead to tyranny, which is its opposite. In every situation, we are free to choose from among alternatives that are in opposition to each other, but we cannot choose to escape the unfortunate consequences of our poor choices.

Of all God's creations, Satan is most miserable, and our adoption of his tactics and plan would have made us equally unhappy by denying agency, requiring obedience, relying upon compulsion, and preventing progression. Although the plan he proposed in heaven was counterfeit, fraudulent, inoperable, and ultimately rejected by the Council, basic elements have been transferred to the temporal battlefield, where they have been re-packaged and re-branded in a last ditch effort to gain acceptance among the children of men. Elements of its twisted ideology can be seen in social, political, cultural and economic programs that pander to the natural man's innate insecurity, lack of initiative, and desire for undeserved entitlements. Those of weak will who voluntarily or involuntarily give up their agency in exchange for whatever provocative pleasures their poor choices may provide, are snared by Satan and bound by his strong chains. (See 2 Nephi 1:13). Ultimately, when they feel the heavy cords of oppression around their necks, they realize too late that their loyalties have limited their options, restricted their actions, and fettered their self-expression. (See 2 Nephi 26:22).

Habitual sin is a quicksand that mires the unwary in a monotonously repetitive and underwhelming convention, and in a mind-numbing conformity. These are the opposites of imaginative spontaneity and refreshingly distinctive artistic individuality. The cloudy cataracts that are created by their concessions to sin hamper their vision. Their narrow perspective forces them into a comfortless compromise that leaves them as empty shells. Without the therapy of repentance, the prognosis for eyes that can no longer see clearly, and that cannot discern between good and evil, is pessimistic, at best.

Sometimes all too quickly, and sometimes agonizingly slowly, those who have sold their souls to the Devil for a mess of pottage are dragged down to a hell on earth that is of their own construction. Their bad habits are the result of repetitively impulsive behaviors that, in a rising tide of wickedness, continually erode away at the foundations of agency. Oddly enough, as Dallin Oaks observed, those who settle for the moral mediocrity of character crippling personality traits can never get enough of what they don't need, because what they don't need won't satisfy them. ("Ensign," 11/1991).

Heavenly Father does not operate this way. He honors free will, but with the codicil that repentance will be waiting in the wings, to be applied as a balm to repair bruised egos, bitter feelings, and battered birthrights. Unto those who fear his name shall the Sun of righteousness arise, with healing in his wings; and they shall go forth, and grow up as calves of the stall. (See Malachi 4:2).

Before the foundation of the world, God counseled Adam: "Thou mayest choose for thyself, for it is given unto thee." (Moses 3:17). That course entails risk, but it is the only option if we desire to progress eternally. "Behold," He declared with satisfaction in the Garden after the Fall, "the man is become as one of us, to know good and evil." (Moses 4:28). The exhilarating journey upon which Adam and Eve were about to embark was a good thing in the sight of God. He knew that their exercise of free will in an atmosphere of opposition would propel them toward immortality and eternal life, as long as they relied upon ordinances, covenants, and the Atonement of His Only Begotten Son.

Heavenly Father had prepared every needful thing before the commencement of their journey to Christ. Passage was booked on that telestial tour when His children raised their right arms to the square in support of His Plan at the Council in heaven before the world was. (See Abraham 3:25-26). It was there that He had determined to repeatedly give them the opportunity to voluntarily recommit themselves to covenants of obedience to true and eternal principles, rather than enslaving them in good habits.

"The Spirit is pure," declared Brigham Young, "and is under the special control and influence of the Lord, but the body is of the earth, and is subject to the power of the Devil, and is under the mighty influence of that fallen nature that is of the earth. If the Spirit yields to the body, the Devil then has power to overcome the body and spirit of that man, and he loses both." ("Discourses of Brigham Young," p. 69-70).

Beginning with the end in mind, Heavenly Father knew that at the end of their journey, all of His children would "reap their rewards according to their works, whether they were good or whether they were bad, to reap eternal happiness or eternal misery, according to the spirit which they listed to obey, whether it be a good spirit or a bad one. For every man receiveth wages of him whom he listeth to obey." (Alma 3:26-27).

Father Lehi closed his inspired blessing to Jacob by declaring that he had "chosen the good part," meaning that he had wisely elected to use his freedom of choice to yield himself to the redeeming power of the Atonement. (2 Nephi 2:30). "All things which pertain to our religion are only appendages" to the Atonement, declared the Prophet Joseph Smith. ("Teachings," p. 127). The principles that are fundamental to our understanding of the purpose and potential of life have to do with the Fall of Adam and the role of the Lord Jesus Christ as the Redeemer of mankind, because repentance was made possible according to The Plan of our Father. How appropriate that Lehi would choose to address these concepts in such a personal way, via a patriarchal blessing given to his son.

Jacob must have carefully studied and pondered his blessing numerous times, because a number of years later he expounded upon it in an address to his brethren. (See 2 Nephi 9). He reiterated many of its principles by structuring each element within the framework of God's goodness and greatness, and by relating covenants to all the house of Israel; thereby, by extension to members of The Church of Jesus Christ of Latter-day Saints. He began by affirming that it is a great gift to have a

body. With our knowledge of the casualty count from the ideological War in Heaven, we know that some of Heavenly Father's children have forfeited their privilege to obtain a body. For those who remained faithful in the pre-earth existence, however, came humbling liabilities, and so The Plan required the Creator to "become subject unto man in the flesh, and die for all men." (2 Nephi 9:5).

2 Nephi 9:6-15 contains one of the most important discussions to be found in all scripture of the power of the Atonement as it relates to the Resurrection and to the principles of agency and opposition. Death, taught Jacob, is a natural part of the "merciful plan of the great Creator." (2 Nephi 9:6). Life is sometimes short, and yet all that is required may be accomplished. Death, which from a mortal perspective is the opposite of life, is essential to The Plan of Salvation. It is our Golden Ticket that refamiliarizes us with the secret garden of our primeval childhood, and introduces us to the wonders of eternity.

Jacob would later write: "Our lives passed away like as it were unto us a dream, we being a lonesome and a solemn people, wanderers, cast out from Jerusalem, born in tribulation, in a wilderness, and hated of our brethren ... wherefore we did mourn out our days." (Jacob 7:26). Nevertheless, because of the Atonement, the elements of The Plan that, at first blush. seem to stand in opposition to life become the pathway and portal to a joyful reunion in the eternities, where we will meet our families "before the pleasing bar of God." (Jacob 6:13, see Alma 3:7).

The transgression of Adam, Jacob knew, was a necessary and integral part of The Plan. Jacob correctly understood that Adam did not sin in the Garden of Eden, in the classical sense, for he did not have true moral agency. The scriptures refer only to his "transgression," and the 2nd Article of Faith makes a specific distinction between it and our "sins." Mortality, the mirror of immortality, was the consequence of his transgression, but it was certainly not a punishment for sin. As Lehi firmly asserted: "Adam fell that men might be, and men are that they might have joy." (2 Nephi 2:25).

In any event, an Atonement was required to initialize The Plan and to forthrightly address the issue of reconciliation between Mercy and Justice. The Atonement removes the permanent effects of physical death and gives us the opportunity to have the effects of spiritual death removed through repentance. The Atonement can save us from our natural state of carnality, sensuality, and Devilish inclinations. It does this by activating the Law of Mercy, which mitigates for those who conform to its requirements the effects of the first Law, that demands Justice. It lifts us to a state of holiness, spirituality, angelic innocence, and happiness. Having explained this to his brethren, Jacob was enraptured by his vision of God's mercy, as was the Apostle Paul, who later confirmed: "By grace (we) are saved, thru faith, and that not of ourselves; it is the gift of God." (Ephesians 2:8).

Standing in opposition to grace is a darkness that is so great that it has the potential to cover the earth, "and gross darkness the people." (Isaiah 60:2). Without repentance and the Atonement, we would be subject to the evil source of that darkness, "to rise no more." (2 Nephi 9:8). Satan is "the prince of darkness." (J.S.T. John 14:30). When he was cast out of heaven, he set about to deceive the whole world into thinking that he is the god of this earth. (Revelation 12:9). He is a usurper, an embezzler, a thief, and an illegitimate claimant to the throne of God. He is Perdition, meaning "loss," "destruction," or "utter ruin," who becomes the master only of those who refuse to repent. How great, then, is our gratitude to the Holy One of Israel, Who broke the death-grip of that "awful monster" who personifies physical and spiritual death? (2 Nephi 9:10, see John 11:25).

The Savior has the power to exercise the priesthood keys of authority relating to our resurrection. With the Atonement, He Who lived a perfect life is able to influence Justice with Mercy. As a key part of that process, repentance becomes one of the most powerful expressions of the righteous exercise of agency, and when we activate that bargaining chip, the Redeemer of Israel is able to negotiate with Justice from a position of power the purchase of our sins, with the legally recognized currency of the Atonement. His voluntary act of sacrifice is perfectly

balanced and attuned to accomplish the task at hand, to overcome death and hell, which are the eternal opposites of life and glory in the Kingdom of God.

It is contrary to the law of God for the heavens to be opened and messengers to come and do anything for us that we can do for ourselves. But since we cannot redeem ourselves, a Savior had to be provided. In the supernal example of a vicarious act, the Lamb of God was slain from before the foundation of the world, in the sense that it was in the Council in Heaven that it was determined that He would become our Redeemer. Mention has been made that Lucifer was also present in that Council. He, too, was free to exercise his agency to promote his counterfeit alternative plan that was the exact opposite of Heavenly Father's Plan of Salvation.

In 2 Nephi 9:13, Jacob explained that "the paradise of God" in the Spirit World is the abode of the righteous. Its opposite is the Spirit Prison of the Unjust where the unrighteous go to await their day of redemption. (See 1 Peter 3:18, & D&C 76:73). That day will come only when Justice has been satisfied that they have paid the penalty for their own sins. This currency is characterized in the scriptures as "the uttermost farthing." (Matthew 5:26). Justice will be equally satisfied if those who are living in the Spirit World accept the Gospel and Jesus Christ as their Redeemer, and necessary priesthood ordinances have been performed for them, in vicarious acts that stand only next to the Atonement itself in their power to save.

This is one reason why the dead, who have been taught and who have accepted the Gospel in the Spirit World, who did not have the opportunity to join the Church of Jesus Christ while in mortality, are so anxious for members of His Church to engage in family history research. By performing vicarious ordinances in their behalf, patrons in the House of The Lord can literally become "saviors on Mount Zion," in the sense that their kindred dead will be able to experience the opposite of spiritual death. (See Obadiah 1:21).

Those in the Spirit Prison of the Unjust, who reject the Gospel and thus deny the power of the Atonement, will have to pay for their sins themselves, since they

are not at-one, or in harmony with the Savior and the doctrines of His kingdom. (See 1 Peter 3:19, Moses 7:57, J.S.T. 1 Peter 3:20, & J.S.T. 1 Peter 4:6). They will not be redeemed from the Fall until they have personally satisfied the requirements established by the unalterable demands of Justice.

Jacob then explained that because of the resurrection of Christ, all will pass from physical death to immortality, which is the condition of the body when it has been eternally reunited with the spirit. The Savior of mankind will exercise in their behalf the priesthood keys of resurrection. This will be a free gift to all who have ever been clothed in mortal clay. For the moment, all will be redeemed from spiritual death, as well, and will have the opportunity to meet God, perhaps for one last time, at the Judgment Bar. Thus, the Resurrection will totally overcome, at least briefly, the effects of the Fall, which are physical and spiritual death.

The principle of agency puts accountability squarely on our shoulders. (See Acts 10:34). The family of man will come "before the pleasing bar of the great Jehovah, the Eternal Judge of both quick and dead." Moroni 10:34). Because they are be at-one with the Savior, the nature of those who have refused to repent will be unmistakable. Their flawed character will consign them to the dark fringes of eternity, for in their filthy state they could not hope to endure His glory. There will be shadowy sanctuaries to which they may flee, and within which they will feel comfortable.

Those who have not been cleansed in the blood of the Lamb, who have not taken the opportunity to rely upon the merits of Christ and the power of His Atonement through the first principles and ordinances of the Gospel, are described as being "filthy." (1 Nephi 15:33). For them, the Atonement does not have the power to pay the penalty for their sins. Therefore, the Law of Mercy can be of no benefit to them. These individuals must live with the consequences of their poor choices. They must submit themselves to the demands of Justice, as if there had been no Atonement made, and their torment that follows has been symbolically described "as a lake of fire and brimstone, whose flame ascendeth up forever and ever" that "has no end." (2 Nephi 9:16). But for the righteous, the Last Judgment will be a model for

reconciliation through the Atonement between two opposites: damnation on the one hand and eternal life on the other.

In spite of the horror that is the fate of the unrepentant, God must be given credit for remaining resolutely even-handed. His justice is affirmed, "for he executeth all his words, and they have gone forth out of his mouth, and his law must be fulfilled." (2 Nephi 9:17). At the same time, His mercy is benevolently validated, for "he delivereth his saints from that awful monster the Devil, and death, and hell, and that lake of fire and brimstone, which is endless torment." (2 Nephi 9:19).

Psalms 149:1 characterized ancient Israel as a congregation of "Saints," and Jacob used the same term to describe the righteous who believe in the Holy One of Israel. (See 2 Nephi 9:18). Implied is its opposite, characterized by those unrighteous and unbelieving sinners who go about with hammers and nails, busily constructing the crosses of the world. The Saints are those who have endured these crosses. The Savior explained what this means: "For a man to take up his cross is to deny himself all ungodliness, and every worldly lust, and keep my commandments." (J.S.T. Matthew 16:25-26). The opposite of the path to Calvary is the road to indulgence, the opposite of submission to the will of God is self-gratification, and the opposite of reverential worship is idolatry.

God understands opposition. After all, He had one particularly rebellious son. He understands how the powerful forces of temptation influence the exercise of agency. But He also knows everything. He sees the end from the beginning, for He is not only Alpha, but also Omega. He is both the Beginning and the End. If He were not omniscient, He would cease to be God, and we could not have faith in Him. God progresses as His creations multiply, and as He brings to pass the immortality and eternal lives of those who inhabit these creations. His unimpaired innocence, proven virtue, unparalleled focus, and unimpeachable honesty harmonize His work with eternal law. The resistance of Satan is no match for God's power. The opposition of the deceiver disintegrates before the authority of God, Who needs only to say: "Depart," and it is done.

Because He knows what is best for us, and has confidence in our divine potential to develop His nature, God commands us to repent, to be baptized, and to develop perfect faith. Because these realistic goals are easily within the reach of all of

His children, they become the basic requirements for readmittance to His Kingdom. Perfect faith impels us to action as though we had God's perfect knowledge. The principles of the Gospel draw us to divine characteristics so that we may be repelled by sin. The Gospel is the only weapon we need to vanquish Satan. Our knowledge of Gospel principles re-enthrones the Savior in our hearts, as the God of this earth. (See Moses 3:3).

Jacob explained that the Law of Mercy satisfies the demands of Justice through the Atonement for those who do not have knowledge of God's laws. "Wherefore, he has given a law; and where there is no law given there is no punishment; and where there is no punishment there is no condemnation; and where there is no condemnation the mercies of the Holy One of Israel have claim upon them because of the Atonement; for they are delivered by the power of him. For the Atonement satisfieth the demands of his Justice upon all those who have not the law given to them." (2 Nephi 9:25-26). Nevertheless, all those who have reached the age of accountability may enjoy the Light of Christ, which allows them to have a foundation of understanding of what is good and what is evil. Because of the Atonement, all have equal opportunity before the Lord. All "have the privilege, living or dead, of accepting the conditions of the great plan of redemption provided by the Father, thru the Son, before the world was." (John Taylor, "Mediation and Atonement," p. 181).

Jacob then warned his brethren that an appeal to vanity is the Devil's way of turning our minds against The Plan of Salvation. "O that cunning plan of the evil one!" he lamented. "O the vainness, and the frailties, and the foolishness of men! When they are learned they think they are wise, and they hearken not unto the counsel of God, for they set it aside, supposing they know of themselves, wherefore, their wisdom is foolishness and it profiteth them not. And they shall perish." (2 Nephi

9:28). Jacob's counsel is a warning against the pitfalls of intellectual apostasy. It posts a conspicuous notice that education alone offers no protection against the forces of opposition that are always operating in the theater of life, and especially upon academic stages. Too much self-assurance is a dark contrast to the illumination of our minds that can come through learning when it is accompanied by the Spirit. Jacob's aphorism drives home the point: "But to be learned is good, if (we) hearken unto the counsels of God." (2 Nephi 9:29).

From 2 Nephi 9:29 to the end of the chapter, we find a parallel to Isaiah 50:11 and 2 Nephi 7:11. These verses concern the Final Judgment, and were written as much for Latter-day Saints as for Jacob's Nephite brethren. Satan uses telestial trash and temporal trivia in all their mutated forms as counterfeits for the living God. The baubles of Babylon are a bribery; they are the brazen opposites of celestial sureties and the incorruptible riches of eternity. Jeremiah asked the question: "Shall a man make gods unto himself, and they are no gods?" (Jeremiah 16:20). In His Preface to the Doctrine and Covenants, the Lord declared of those who lived at the time of Joseph Smith: "They seek not the Lord to establish his righteousness, but every man walketh in his own way, and after the image of his own god, whose image is in the likeness of the world, and whose substance is like that of an idol, which waxeth old and shall perish in Babylon, even Babylon the great, which shall fall." (D&C 1:16).

"Wo unto the rich, who are rich as to the things of the world," wrote Jacob. (2 Nephi 9:30). Satan's Golden Question is and always has been: "Do you have any money?" He would have us believe that we can have anything in this world for money. In opposition to that damnable doctrine that is embraced by the spiritually immature, Jacob declared: "Wo unto the deaf that will not hear." (2 Nephi 9:31). Tinkling cymbals and sounding brass mesmerize those who will not see or hear. Those who are uncircumcised of heart focus their attention on selfish pleasures, the things of the world, and the honors of men, but these are nothing more than low value terrestrial and telestial targets. (See 1 Corinthians 13:1). They cannot see the celestial sureties that are beyond the horizon of their limited vision, because they

are fettered by their self-inflicted blindness. Without the perspective of the Gospel, they "tend to fill space, as if what they have, what they are, is not enough. Being affluent, they strangle themselves with what they can buy, things whose opacity obstructs their ability to see what is really there." (Greta Erlich, "Under Wyoming Skies," "The Atlantic Monthly," 5/1985).

Verse 34 parallels Proverbs 19:9: "Wo unto the liar, for he shall be thrust down to hell." Those who bear false witness qualify only for the Telestial Kingdom. If we view the forces operating in the vortex of life as naturally occurring opposites, false witness is particularly damaging, since it poisons the atmosphere in which correct choices might otherwise have been made. Its fiction is a façade that may compellingly distort the facts in a way that makes the righteous application of agency very difficult.

"Wo unto the murderer who deliberately killeth, for he shall die." (2 Nephi 9:35). The sin of deliberately killing another robs the victim of agency and self-determination with abrupt and irreversible finality. Such a brutal act of selfishness places the perpetrator beyond the power of the Atonement. Hence, the doctrine of Blood Atonement, (which is not an accepted doctrine of The Church of Jesus Christ of Latter-day Saints) wherein those in transgression must atone with their own blood for their sins.

"Wo unto them who commit whoredoms, for they shall be thrust down to hell." (2 Nephi 9:36). A "whore" can be "a corrupt or idolatrous community" or individual. (O.E.D.). Thus, the worship of idols of any kind is a whoredom, and, in a figurative sense, is adulterous. Our worship of idols, wherein we turn our backs on the sacred covenants of the Priesthood, is akin to infidelity. It is the diametrical opposite of those who come to the marriage supper of the Lamb with their lamps of oil filled to overflowing.

"Wo unto those that worship idols, for the Devil of all Devils delighteth in them." (2

Nephi 9:37). In the final analysis, the Devil can only rule on the earth when he is able to seductively manipulate those who worship idols. His followers have traded their birthright for a mess of pottage. They have given up their agency for the rush that accompanies carnality and sensuality. The opposite of counterfeit sensory

stimulation is priesthood power, which "is the legitimate rule of God and is the only legitimate power that has a right to rule upon the earth. And when the will of God is done on the earth, as it is done in heaven, no other power will bear rule." (John Taylor, J.D., 5:187).

"O my beloved brethren," Jacob implored, "remember the awfulness in transgressing against that Holy God, and also the awfulness of yielding to the enticings of that cunning one." (2 Nephi 9:39). The Devil's bribery stands in sharp contrast and in opposition to the blessings that follow obedience to God's will. Satan costumes his wares in gaudy paraphernalia that attract the curious, and yet demand no commitment. Those jaded souls are as moths that are drawn to fire, who if they venture too closely, will wither and die in the radiant heat of brimstone. Although the Devil's powerful lures might even glitter in the sunlight of truth, they remain a deception and a snare.

They may seem attractive because they offer pleasure and advantage, but they are insidious and adroit, for he is, after all, a tempter. In the end, however, his impoverished and malnourished disciples will be left destitute and helpless, with rescue a near impossibility. The insolvency of Satan's seduction cannot be mitigated by a third-party bailout. The only solution to his nepotism is to 'throw the bum out,' wipe the slate clean, and begin anew with an Elector who truly represents our best interests.

The Plan that was provided for us takes into account the reality that we would exercise our agency to yield in varying degrees to temptation even as we learn to deal with opposition and experience consequences. Repentance was introduced into The Plan to serve as a fuel rod to energize the Atonement in our behalf. It allows us to make mistakes, to learn from them, and to then grasp the horns of sanctuary

so that at the end of the day we may be justified by the grace of God.

Only when these protocols of The Plan are promulgated does mortality become the wonderful center for the talented and gifted it was envisioned to be. Indeed, as Henri Bergson so intuitively observed: "The universe becomes a machine for the making of Gods." ("The Two Sources of Morality and Religion"). The Gospel is its mainspring, and when it is tightly wound by our faith, it becomes a majestic clockwork. Without it, with danger lurking around every corner and at every curve in the road, there are forces in our world that can become improvised explosive devices, evil traps, and snares of Satan. Agency and opposition are always before us, and repentance stands as a sentinel, beckoning us to enter in at heaven's gate.

"Remember," cautioned Jacob, "to be carnally-minded is death, and to be spiritually-minded is life eternal." (2 Nephi 9:39). His message was intended to pierce the hearts of unconfronted individuals who had not yet made a commitment to Christ. These, he urged to "come unto the Lord," while acknowledging that the way is narrow, meaning that there are no viable alternatives. (2 Nephi 9:41). He taught that agency must be exercised with great sensitivity and selectivity. Once we have pledged our allegiance to the Almighty, however, Jacob promised that the way before us will lie in an easily identifiable "straight course," in contrast and in opposition to Satan's alternative program that is twisted, deceptive, unreliable, and is indifferent to our needs. He beckons us to follow a detour from the strait and narrow way that leads only to telestial traffic jams, conceptual cul-de-sacs, religious roundabout, and doctrinal dead-ends.

Opportunities for recommitment and rededication, thanks to the principle of repentance, are critical to our spiritual well being, because, as disciples of Christ, we are painfully aware that two choices lie constantly before us. "Two forces are operating, two voices are calling, one coming out from the swamps of selfishness and force, where success means death, and the other from the hilltops of justice and progress, where even failure brings glory. Two lights are seen on our horizon, one, the last fading marsh light of power, and the other the slowly rising sun of

human brotherhood. Two ways lie open before us, one leading to an ever lower and lower plane, where are heard the cries of despair and the curses of the poor, where manhood shrivels and possessions rot down the possessor, and the other leading to the highlands of the morning, where are heard the glad shouts of humanity, and where honest effort is rewarded with immortality." (John P. Altgeld). Boyd Packer simply stated: "The choice in life is not between wealth and poverty, or between fame and obscurity. It is between good and evil." ("Ensign," 11/1980).

Jacob summarized his teachings with the exhortation: "And whoso knocketh, to him will he open; and the wise, and the learned, and they that are rich, who are puffed up, because of their learning, and their wisdom, and their riches - yea, they are they whom he despiseth; and save they shall cast these things away, and consider themselves fools before God, and come down in the depths of humility, he will not open unto them." (2 Nephi 9:42).

Blessings are predicated upon obedience to law, and when we are quick to repent, we will surely experience the "happiness which is prepared for the saints." (2 Nephi 9:43). Jacob had fulfilled the commandments of God from his childhood and now had taken to heart the patriarchal blessing he had received so many years earlier. As a responsible adult and priesthood leader, and perhaps as a patriarch himself, he now taught his brethren boldly and with plainness, and so, even though he had solemn responsibilities as an ecclesiastical leader, he was free from their sins.

Nevertheless, he was concerned that the "chains" of the Devil might yet shackle the Nephites and darken their minds. Hundreds of years later, the prophet Alma explained what these chains are. "And they that will harden their heart, to them is given the lesser portion of the word until they know nothing concerning his mysteries; and then they are taken captive by the Devil, and led by his will down to destruction. Now this is what is meant by the chains of hell." (Alma 12:11).

This warning applies equally to members of The Church of Jesus Christ of Latter-day Saints. When our hearts are hardened against the message of salvation,

and particularly against the injunction to repent, it is as though our portion is diminished further and further, until our defenses against the aggressive tactics of the Devil evaporate. Left to ourselves, we are more easily influenced by the lies of the deceiver, rather than by the illuminating truths of the Spirit, and we will be dragged down to hell. In the harsh light of day, the misuse of the exercise of agency in the midst of difficult choices and opposition can lead to devastating consequences.

The Day of Judgment will be glorious for the righteous, however, because the Holy Ghost will justify them. Repentance, made possible by the Atonement, will have removed our soul-scars and the stain of sin from the tapestry that is the tableau of our lives. As John Taylor wrote: "That record is written by ourselves in the tablets of own minds. It cannot lie, and will in that day be unfolded before God and angels." (J.D., 11:79).

Contemporary prose illustrates the principle: "My father focuses heart-gripping flashes across the wall screen. Family slides. I am small, my brother is smaller, and my sister is smallest. Days now dead re-open like old storybooks from memory's heaped box. Pulling out pictures of cooking in Grandfather's Dutch oven; playing cheetah in our backyard monkey-jungle; being beautifully Easter-bested with my coat buttoned wrong; hugging a mommy minus grey hair. Soberly, I think of another Father, Who someday shall open my mind, and flash reeling remembering of every day's minute across my soul, across the heavens, and kindly ask me to narrate." (Lora Lyn Stucker, "New Era," 8/1973).

The conclusion of Jacob's address begins in 2 Nephi 9:47. "Ye look upon me as a teacher," he said, and so "it must needs be expedient that I teach you the consequences of sin. Behold, my soul abhorreth sin, and my heart delighteth in righteousness." (2 Nephi 9:48-49). Only a fully committed individual, speaking with power and authority, could make such a bold statement. In the Church, the greatest qualities of teachers are that they have testimonies of the principles of the Gospel, believe revealed truth, and exercise their privileges in the spirit of prayer and of faith.

After explaining the great Plan of Redemption to his people, that solved the dilemma created by God's demand for perfection coupled with our inability to lead sinless lives, Jacob simply stated: "O be wise; what can I say more?" (Jacob

6:12). 2 Nephi Chapters 2 & 9 illustrate why Joseph Smith said: "The Book of Mormon (is) the most correct of any book on earth, and the keystone of our religion, and (we will) get nearer to God by abiding by its precepts than by any other book." ("Introduction to The Book of Mormon").

"I will go
before your face. I
will be on your right hand,
and on your left, and my Spirit
shall be in your hearts, and
mine angels round about
you, to bear you up."
(D&C 84:88).

Chapter Eight

A key element of The Plan

To appreciate just how thoughtfully the principle of repentance was conceived, we need to take ourselves back to the inventive periods when matter was organized, the elements were brought out of chaos into harmony, and a Garden was created eastward in Eden. When God had finished His work, He saw that it was "very good." (Genesis 1:31). As the Architect of The Plan, everything was as He had imagined and pre-determined it would be. Every detail had been pre-played in eternity before it was re-played in the vast expanse of the temporal universe. The storyboard had first been created spiritually and then physically.

As God explained: "By the power of my Spirit created I ... all things both spiritual and temporal. First spiritual, secondly temporal." (D&C 29:31-32). He did this that creation might fulfill its destiny, that the universe might become "a machine for the making of Gods." (Henri Bergson, "Two Sources of Religion & Morality").

At the Council, He had introduced the blueprints that were the operating instructions of His magnum opus. There, He had unfolded before the eyes of all of His children His vision for their progression from spiritual embryos to fully

mature adults. His Plan would shepherd them through the growing pains and mental, emotional, physical, and spiritual instability related to early childhood development. In that pre-mortal setting, as the eyes of their understanding were opened, they could even then begin to appreciate their potential as their Father did.

With awakening comprehension, they realized that He had provided a way for them to blossom to the full stature of their spirits.

From the beginning, it had been clear that Adam, who prominently stood out among his pre-mortal brothers and sisters, would become a catalyst to drive forward the process leading to their exaltation, for he was "among the great and mighty ones who were assembled in (that) vast congregation of the righteous." (D&C 138:38). At the conclusion of the Council, he was valiant in defending the Father's Plan. (See Revelation 12:7).

When he later transgressed God's law in the Garden, it was not because he was weak, but because he was strong, and believed "that men might be." He intuitively knew that "men are, that they might have joy." (2 Nephi 2:25). It is because of him that "the world (has become) a stage, and all the men and women players with their exits and their entrances." (Shakespeare, "As You Like It," Act 2, Scene 7).

At best, mortality is a brief interlude in the grand scheme of things, and yet all that is required of us may be accomplished before the book is closed on this chapter in our lives. Death is as much a part of life as is birth, and Adam's transgression was integral to the execution of The Plan, inasmuch as it provided the opportunity for us to be born into this world, to live, and to die. Living in eternity before our turn on earth, we were able to preview the big picture, and so we shouted for joy. (See Job 38:7). When it was finally our time to come to earth, others smiled at our birth, while we cried. When it is our time to leave, our loved ones will cry at our death, while we will smile. Only then, will we see death for what it really is, "a mere comma, and not an exclamation point." (Neal A. Maxwell, "Ensign," 5/1983). It is "not extinguishing the light, but rather putting out the lamp because the dawn has come." (Ramindraneth Tagore).

Because of the sacrifice of the "lamb slain from the foundation of the world," (Revelation 13:8), and our regularly recurring repentance, we "shall not taste of death, for it shall be sweet" unto us. (D&C 42:46). The Atonement made life eternal, love immortal, and death only a horizon, "and a horizon is nothing, save the limit of our sight." (Raymond W. Rossiter).

"I would that I could persuade all ye ends of the earth to repent and prepare to stand before the judgment-seat of Christ." (Moroni 3:22).

Chapter Nine

Shed the weight of sin.

Just like the food consumed by those on Weight Watchers, every action in life has "points" related to it. When we live our lives in moderation and in harmony with Gospel principles, the sum of our behaviors doesn't exceed the acceptable number of "points" associated with those activities. We stay fit and trim, and we are able to fulfil the measure of our creation.

Just like Weight Watchers, provident living requires our attendance at regular gatherings of like-minded individuals. We call these "Sacrament Meeting," "Relief Society Meeting," and "Priesthood Meeting," to name a few. The peer pressure generated is a powerful positive reinforcement to encourage us to conform to the prescribed program and helps us to develop the discipline to deter deviation, expand our energies in constructive directions, cultivate fortitude, and build mental toughness.

Weight-Watchers helps us to be aware of our lean body mass index, the sum of everything in our bodies except fat. Likewise, in life we need to be able to recognize the immaterial negative elements that influences our spiritual nature, namely the

sins that weigh us down. Then, we can develop programs to shed those offensive pounds and get back to our optimal weight, to fit into the spiritual clothes in which we were baptized. For at that time, when we were "born again," we were at our ideal form, because we weren't yet burdened by sin.

Alma, whom you might recall was an early Weight-Watcher motivational speaker, encouraged all who would listen to adhere to the program: "The spirit and the body shall be reunited again in its perfect form," he promised, "both limb and joint shall be restored to its proper frame." (Alma 11:43). Much later, Joseph Fielding Smith, Jr., himself a vocal proponent of Weight-Watchers, taught: "All deformities and imperfections will be removed, and the body will conform to the likeness of the Spirit." ("Doctrines of Salvation," 2:289). Moreover, he asserted "in the restoration of all things, there shall come perfection." ("Answers to Gospel Questions," 4:185-189). In neither case was there significant objection from the scientific community of nutritionists and sports physiologists. It seems the claims of both Alma and Joseph have withstood the tests of time.

No matter how heavy we have allowed ourselves to become, no matter how many pounds of sin have begun to pile on, no matter how ponderous a burden we have created from our own inattention to our spiritual health, Christ, the mediator of the Weight-Watcher Program, will still lift us up. No matter how weak we have become, no matter that our spiritual muscles have turned to flab, no matter that we are for all intents and purposes "dead weight," He has the strength to carry us until, revitalized, we can once again walk and not be weary and run and not faint.

"Heaven lies about us in our infancy," wrote William Wordsworth. "Shades of the prison house begin to close upon the growing boy, but he beholds the light and whence it flow. He sees it in his joy. The youth, who daily farther from the east must travel, still is nature's priest, and by the vision splendid, is on his way attended. At length the man perceives it die away, and fade into the light of common day." ("Ode: Intimations of Immortality"). And then, perhaps only when he has hit rock-bottom, does the natural man hear an awful noise ringing in his ears as "the whole earth groans under the weight of its iniquity." (D&C 123:7). This motivates him to

drag his battered and beaten body to the local chapter of Weight Watchers, known as The Church of Jesus Christ of Latter-day Saints.

The Weight-Watcher Program can give us the resolve to avoid food that is not nutritious. Our covenant-consciousness helps us to avoid the highly caloric snacks of sin, the empty calories of commotion that cannot satisfy our hunger for spiritual centricity, the enticements of excess that blind us to the stability of temperance, the hydrogenated oils of overindulgence that clog our avenues of intuition, the bribery of bewilderment that clouds our vision and makes acceptable choices difficult, the cupcakes of confusion that are little more than the spiritual equivalents of refined sugar, and the unwholesome processed factory food that is mechanically dispensed by the Devil's dieticians at the automats of life. As Dallin Oaks remarked: "You can never get enough of what you don't need, because what you don't need won't satisfy you."

In a scenario similar to that of Weight-Watchers, inattention allows the weight of sin to slowly creep up on us. We compensate for its added pounds by unconsciously working just a little harder to move around. Because we are exhausted by ordinary efforts to stabilize our behavior, we become passive participants rather than active combatants in the arena of life, where sin, Satan's tag-team partner, is always our eager enemy. We would rather be a couch potato than a determined disciple. We never even notice our poor spiritual fitness, because our neglect fogs the mirror on our soul when we step out of the shower. Our conscience, the calorie-counter provided by our Father, is pushed aside. Thus, we avoid the only certifiably reliable scale that would alert us to our condition.

The burden of unresolved sin makes it seem as if we are carrying the weight of the world on our shoulders, and our hearts are heavy as they pump ever harder just to keep our circulation going. We become familiar with after-hours emergency centers, and our loved ones become alarmed that the need for life-support could become a real possibility. Our congestive heart failure is a sign that our worldliness has worsened.

The only solution offered by the Lord's Weight-Watcher Program is to change our own heart. Technology can provide no alternatives because there are no donor hearts available even if transplants were possible. How wonderful it would be in these circumstances to say of us: "This day he hath spiritually begotten you, for ... your hearts are changed through faith on his name." (Mosiah 5:7).

We don't notice the increase in our resting heart rate or its inability to absorb compassion. As our respiration rate increases, we are short of spiritual breath after mechanically performing even routine tasks. The exercise and lifestyle changes that would have remedied our condition seem too difficult, and we're too busy to even think about these alterations to our routines, anyway.

If only we could participate in the spiritual equivalent of Weight-Watchers, we would have less trouble sleeping, less difficulty focusing, and less of a problem concentrating on the tasks at hand. We wouldn't have that nagging angina in our chest that is aggravated every time we neglect our responsibilities.

At Weight-Watchers, we learn that we burn protein at a rate of 4 calories per gram, and fat at 9 calories per gram. Unfortunately, sin is purged in the same way. It takes over twice as much energy to eliminate it as it does to retain righteousness. It's far better to resist the urge to sin, because we have to pay for it later, and in spades. It's harder to lose a pound of sin than it is to retain with righteousness our classic form. It's far less expensive to be clothed in righteousness than it is to be burdened down with iniquity. Sin might look fashionable at the moment, and to some, but the style that is popular today can change quickly.

Righteousness is always modest in its appearance, and its value is enduring. It has a certain "timelessness" about it, perhaps because it is always "on sale," while we pay a premium for sin. Righteousness always retains its value, while sin is never the bargain it was purported to be. Weight-Watchers costs $16.95 per month, with a one-time sign up fee of $29.95, while righteousness costs nothing. It only has a

performance cost, not including tithing and fast offering. As Isaiah wrote: "He that hath no money; come ye, buy" a lifetime membership in the Lord's equivalent of the Weight-Watcher Program "without money and without price." (Isaiah 55:1).

Obedience to principles that mirror the Weight-Watcher Program will yield results that are evident when we study the mirror on our soul. With our finger on the pulse of our spirits, we will avoid behavioral binge-eating. We will distain the artificial sweetener of sin. The midriff bulge of poor spiritual nutrition will melt away before our eyes, and we will feel the satisfaction of being able to take in our priesthood pants a few inches because we are in such good shape. We "shall renew (our) strength; (we) shall mount up with wings as eagles; (we) shall run, and not be weary; and (we) shall walk, and not faint." (Isaiah 40:31). Through the Church-sanctioned Weight-Watcher Fitness Program, we will become and remain lean, mean, fighting machines, able to fulfil the measure of our creation. (See D&C 88:19).

Nevertheless, even Joseph Smith admitted that, from time to time, he lost his resolve. He was tempted by the sticky sweets of sin, just as we all are. He recalled that he "was left to all kinds of temptations; and mingling with all kinds of society, (he) frequently fell into many foolish errors, and displayed the weakness of youth, and the foibles of human nature." He was guilty of "levity, and sometimes associated with jovial company." (J.S.H. 1:28). In fact, he acted much as we all do. In the next few years, however, he helped to establish Weight Watcher Programs that ultimately would be franchised throughout the world.

Just as he did, we have the ability to reset our spiritual appestat when we notice it is out of whack. We can learn not to splurge on "food" that has no nutritional value, and we can condition ourselves to habitually resist temporal temptations. We can train ourselves to recognize the glistening qualities that are characteristic of the appearance of high fructose corn syrup telestial treats.

When we learn that "evils and designs (do) exist in the hearts of conspiring men in the last days," we will realize that low calorie beer is still beer. (D&C 89:4).

Reduced-fat Haagen Daaz ice cream still has 17 grams of fat in a 1/2 cup serving (290 calories, and 153 of those from fat). Warmed over pizza is still pizza. Too much of that, and we may as well don a hospital gown and climb up on a gurney in preparation for the liposuction of laziness. Better to be anxiously engaged in a good cause and to do many things of our own free will than to let someone hiding behind a mask suck out a couple of quarts of fat from our tummies with a straw designed by the Marquis de Sade, because we've been unwilling to sweat through a few crunches, and unable to resist the temptation to throw a few packages of Twinkies into our shopping cart every time we go to the market.

The reversal of years of spiritual neglect requires drastic action. The plastic surgery of repentance is always necessary. When a cancerous growth is removed, it has to have clean borders, but when it is gone, so too will be the soul scars that accompanied the surgery. These procedures need to be performed by a member of the American Society of Plastic Surgeons, just as bishops need to monitor the Lord's Weight Watcher Program.

The Stair Master of day-to-day perseverance can not only keep us in shape, but it can also become the mechanism to carry us to new heights. We can be "renewed" to "regain" our former spiritual stature, to "refresh" ourselves to begin once again, as we "redouble" our efforts, and "return" to our roots. As in the Weight-Watchers Program, we learn that "love-handles" don't really express love at all, that spiritual obesity is at epidemic levels, that Wonder Bread isn't what Jesus miraculously multiplied on the Mount of Beatitudes, and that a sedentary life-style is antithetical to the concept of eternal progression.

We need to be moving along the path and making steady progress. When we feel ourselves in bondage to the excess weight of unresolved sin, we need to increase our metaphysical metabolism, to go the second mile in order to burn as much of the fat of faithlessness as we can in the crucible of contrition, and to double our stride. When we move forward at an increased tempo, we will receive "a gift of spiritual independence that removes the veil of insensitivity to our destiny."

(Richard L. Gunn, "A Search for Sensitivity and Spirit").

We recall that in the Sacred Grove, Heavenly Father and Jesus Christ appeared to Joseph Smith as identical personages. One was indistinguishable from the other. We

104

wonder if this was because they didn't have an accumulation of the excess pounds that accompany improvident living and contribute to physical imperfection. We should not be surprised that when "the Savior shall appear, we shall see him as He is," a glorified, resurrected being of light. (D&C 130:1). The profound implication is, that if we are true to His Weight-Watcher Program, our appearance at that moment will reflect our true spiritual stature. Finally, we will be in both the image and the likeness of God.

"Whosoever repenteth,
and hardeneth not his heart,
he shall have claim on Mercy
through mine Only Begotten
Son, unto a remission of
his sins; and these shall
enter into my rest."
(Alma 12:34).

Chapter Ten

Cherubim and a flaming sword.

"What does the scripture mean, which saith that
God placed cherubim and a flaming sword
on the east of the garden of Eden, lest
our first parents should enter and
partake of the fruit of the
Tree of Life, and live
forever?"
(Alma 12:21).

Keep in mind the scriptural metaphors of cherubim and a flaming sword, as we explore the concepts of mercy and justice as they relate to repentance. Arguably, Alma Chapters 12 and 42 comprise the best explanations in all scripture regarding the mercy and justice of God. Mormon recognized that this was powerful doctrine, and when he abridged the records, he was inspired to transcribe the account of Alma's ministry in the first person tense on The Plates of Mormon. Thus, when we study his discourses verbatim, we feel as if Alma were speaking directly to us.

In Alma Chapter 11, we learned about the defection of a lawyer named Zeezrom, who lived in Ammonihah, and we were introduced to Antionah, a chief ruler in that city, who had taken up the gauntlet to confront Alma and Amulek. He was a child of the Devil who used a misrepresentation of the scriptures as ammunition to attack the missionaries. Wresting the scriptures is a standard tactic of Satan, that is frequently adopted by his disciples. Alma's encounter with Antionah illustrates that even when the wicked are familiar with the scriptures, their understanding is twisted and perverted.

In Alma 12, Alma answered the question posed by Antionah: "What does the scripture mean, which saith that God placed cherubim and a flaming sword on the east of the garden of Eden, lest our first parents should enter and partake of the fruit of the Tree of Life, and live forever?" (Alma 12:21 & Genesis 3:24). Then, in Alma 42, he taught his son about these same principles, because Corianton had been excusing his own behavior for similar reasons, claiming that it was unjust to punish sinners. Alma addressed the concerns of both Antionah and Corianton, basing his remarks on justice, which is the unalterable decree of God that declares that both righteousness and sin dictate their own consequences.

Fortunately, Alma was more familiar with the scriptures and with the doctrines of the kingdom than were either Antionah or Corianton. He was able to explain to both that there is another dimension to Genesis 3:24 that takes into consideration the pitfall that would have been created had Adam, in his unrepentant state, been permitted to stretch forth his hand and partake of the fruit of the Tree of Life. (See Alma 5:34). You see, in Ammonihah, Antionah's shallow Gospel scholarship had led him to the erroneous conclusion that the only way to live forever would be to partake of the fruit of the Tree of Life. (See Genesis 3:22).

Antionah reasoned that mankind had a justification for sinning because God had placed cherubim and a flaming sword on the east of the Garden of Eden to guard the way to the tree. He mistakenly thought that the key to eternal life was simply to partake of the fruit. It was his belief that with cherubim and a flaming sword

barring the way to the tree, he would have no chance to live forever.

Antionah was too literal in his private interpretation of scripture. He did not take into consideration the ramifications of what would have happened within the context of The Plan of Salvation should Adam in his fallen state have stretched forth his hand and partaken of the fruit of the Tree of Life. (See Alma 5:34). He did not consider that if he had done so, Adam would have been forever alienated from God's presence, for he had not yet been redeemed by the Atonement of Christ from the second death.

Thus, Antionah's taunting question provided Alma with a perfect teaching moment to explain to the people of Ammonihah that, rather than justifying wicked behavior, the referenced scripture should instead afford them a strong incentive to seek and embrace another way whereby they might live forever, not in sin, but in purity and glory. Antionah's ignorance gave Alma the opportunity to teach the people of Ammonihah about agency, atonement, justice, mercy, repentance, forgiveness, and redemption. It also allowed Alma to reveal to Antionah and his brethren how to proactively deal with the unalterable decrees of God relating to those who refuse to repent.

Alma correctly taught that, subtle though the symbolism might be, working out our salvation has less to do with cherubim and a flaming sword, and more to do with redemption. In the absence of repentance for our sins and without the benefit of the cornerstone principle of the Atonement within the framework of the Gospel Plan, we must ultimately be in a desolate state, living forever in our sins.

He told Antionah: "And now, behold, if it were possible that our first parents could have gone forth and partaken of the Tree of Life they would have been forever miserable, having no preparatory state; and thus The Plan of Redemption would have been frustrated, and the word of God would have been void, taking none effect." (Alma 12:26). Without the option of redemption from sin, if Adam and Eve were to have partaken of the fruit of the Tree of Life, which is eternal life or the

highest expression of the love of God, it would not have been possible for them to sustain a celestial existence. If they had forever remained in their filthy condition, stained by sin, they would have been incapable of maintaining strict obedience to celestial principles, nor would they have desired to do so. "By the temporal law they (would have been) cut off; and also, by the spiritual law they (would have) perish(ed) from that which is good, and become miserable forever." (2 Nephi 2:5). Thus, "The Great and Eternal Plan of Deliverance from Death" would have been frustrated. (2 Nephi 11:15).

The scenario Alma had outlined to the people of Ammonihah, and later to his son Corianton, demonstrated that this was not to be the case. The transgression of Adam resulted in alienation from God's presence, which is spiritual death, and the expulsion from the Garden resulted in mortality, making his eventual temporal death inevitable. However, Adam and Eve and their posterity were not created to live forever in the morally static vacuum of the Garden. In God's divine design, it is mortality that provides our best opportunity to become acquainted with evil as well as with good, with darkness as well as with light, with error as well as with truth, and with punishment for the infraction of eternal laws as well as with the blessings that follow obedience. As Ralph Waldo Emerson once asked: "What is the use of immortality to one who cannot wisely use half an hour?" This is why Alma and so many other parents have invested so much time and energy teaching their children correct principles, training them in their proper execution, and trusting them to consistently do so.

Alma told Antionah: "This is the thing which I was about to explain." (Alma 12:22). He then taught that we came into this world to die. This creates a host of potential problems, but The Plan offers elegant solutions to each one. For "we see that Adam did fall by the partaking of the forbidden fruit, according to the word of God; and thus we see, that by his fall, all mankind became a lost and fallen people. And now behold, I say unto you that if it had been possible for Adam to have partaken of the fruit of the Tree of Life at that time, there would have been no death, and the word would have been void, making God a liar, for he said: If thou eat thou

shalt surely die." (Alma 12:23).

This would have voided The Plan of Salvation. Death is our only exit from mortality; it is our golden ticket to immortality and eternal life, and it is the element of the Merciful Plan of our Father that caused us to shout for joy when it was first explained to us. (See Job 38:7). When Adam and Eve were placed in the Garden of Eden, it was with the understanding that they would violate one commandment in order to fulfil others. (See Genesis 1:28). When they were subsequently expelled from the Garden in consequence of their transgression, the cherubim and a flaming sword insured that they would be able to complete the mission they had accepted before the world was, to be fruitful, and multiply, and replenish the earth. (See Genesis 9:1).

Alma taught Antionah that the Fall was a key component of The Plan, inasmuch as it gave Adam and Eve and their posterity the opportunity to sojourn on the earth to prepare for a resurrection. "And we see that death comes upon mankind, yea, the death which has been spoken of by Amulek, which is the temporal death; nevertheless there was a space granted unto man in which he might repent; therefore this life became a probationary state; a time to prepare to meet God; a time to prepare for that endless state which has been spoken of by us, which is after the resurrection of the dead." (Alma 12:24).

The death of our physical bodies is a key element of the Gospel Plan. In fact, "it was appointed unto men that they must die; and after death, they must come to judgment, even that same judgment of which we have spoken, which is the end." (Alma 12:27). With broad strokes, Book of Mormon prophets paint a wonderfully vibrant portrait of The Merciful Plan of the Great Creator, and after our careful study of their teachings, the ultimate purpose of the Fall snaps into sharp focus. (2 Nephi 9:6). We can almost hear Father in Heaven explaining how Adam and Eve would transgress His law in order to become mortal so they and all of their posterity could die, and fill the measure of their creation. We can clearly see how the Fall allows us to prepare for the glorious resurrection to which Alma alluded.

The Spirit teaches us that through the Atonement, we may receive the kinds of immortal bodies that we will need in order to dwell in celestial fire. The beauty of the Last Judgment is that it will not come until after we have had the opportunity to conform our lives through repentance to the principles of The Great Plan of the Eternal God (Alma 34:9).

Alma hoped that as he taught the people of Ammonihah, they would receive a spiritual confirmation of these truths. "And after God had appointed that these things should come unto man, behold, then He saw that it was expedient that man should know concerning the things whereof He had appointed unto them; Therefore He sent angels to converse with them, who caused men to behold of His glory. And they began from that time forth to call on His name; therefore God conversed with men, and made known unto them The Plan of redemption, which had been prepared from the foundation of the world; and this He made known unto them according to their faith and repentance and their holy works." (Alma 12:28-30).

The children of God were to be instructed sufficiently and then to have the opportunity to act for themselves. Satan exerts a coercive influence, but the "perfect law of liberty" presupposes the vigorous exercise of free will. However, unless our behavior is in harmony with the laws of the Gospel, unbridled freedom will lead to tyranny. We are free to choose, but we cannot choose to escape the consequences of our poor choices. When we violate the commandments, as we all do, in conformity to the principle of opposition in all things, we are commanded to repent, for we have the power within ourselves to be "as Gods, knowing good from evil," and we are "in a state to act according to (our) wills and pleasures, whether to do evil or to do good." (Alma 12:31).

Adam and Eve were unequivocally taught about the penalty that would follow the violation of the commandments. "God gave unto them commandments, after having made known unto them The Plan of Redemption, that they should not do evil, the penalty thereof being a second death, which was an everlasting death as to things

pertaining unto righteousness; for on such The Plan of Redemption could have no power, for the works of Justice could not be destroyed, according to the supreme goodness of God." (Alma 12:32). Because God respects agency and honors law, He could not, in good conscience, summarily nullify the demands of Justice as they bore down on Adam and Eve following their transgression in the Garden. Nor would He desire to do so, because an elegant solution to Adam's conundrum had already been built into The Plan.

God provided another way for Adam and Eve to partake of the fruit of the Tree of Life, to gain knowledge of good and evil. (See Alma 5:34). He "did call on men, in the name of His Son, (this being The Plan of Redemption which was laid) saying: If ye will repent, and harden not your hearts, then will I have mercy on you, through mine Only Begotten Son. Therefore, whosoever repenteth, and hardeneth not his heart, he shall have claim on Mercy through mine Only Begotten Son, unto a remission of his sins; and these shall enter into My rest." (Alma 12:33-34).

Whoever would have faith in Christ and repent would gain a remission of their sins, because of their claim on Mercy through His Atonement. For obvious reasons, those who refused to repent because of the hardness of their hearts would not be able to enter into the Rest of God or receive the fulness of His glory. They could not comfortably inherit the glory of a celestial realm, if they had aforetime been willing to abide by only telestial or terrestrial principles.

"And now, my brethren," Alma urged the people of Ammonihah, "behold I say unto you, that if ye will harden your hearts ye shall not enter into the rest of the Lord; therefore your iniquity provoketh him that he sendeth down his wrath upon you." (Alma 12:36). The olive branch that Alma extended to the wicked people of Ammonihah would provide their last and only opportunity to avoid destruction.

Alma addressed the people of Ammonihah as his brothers and sisters in the Gospel. He held them to the same standard to which he adhered. He considered himself in need of repentance as much as those to whom he ministered. Therefore, he testified

of the truth and pleaded: "And now, my brethren, seeing we know these things, and they are true, let us repent, and harden not our hearts, that we provoke not the Lord our God to pull down His wrath upon us in these His second commandments which He has given unto us; but let us enter into the rest of God, which is prepared according to His word." (Alma 12:37).

After he had clarified the principles of agency, justice, atonement, mercy, repentance, forgiveness, and redemption in Ammonihah, Alma sat down with his son, Corianton. "I perceive there is somewhat more which doth worry your mind," he said, "which ye cannot understand - which is concerning the justice of God in the punishment of the sinner; for ye do try to suppose that it is injustice that the sinner should be consigned to a state of misery. Now behold, my son, I will explain this thing unto thee." (Alma 42:1-2). Just as he had for Antionah, (see Alma 12:23), Alma refreshed the memory of Corianton, reminding him that at the time of Adam and Eve's transgression, when they were driven into the lone and dreary world, God had "placed at the east end of the garden of Eden, cherubim, and a flaming sword which turned every way, to keep the Tree of Life." (Alma 42:1-2, see 1 Nephi 8:4).

This was done because "the man had become as God, knowing good and evil," and now the very real possibility existed that he would "put forth his hand, and take also of the Tree of Life, and eat and live forever" in his sins. (Alma 42:3 & Genesis 3:22).

As we have learned from our study of Alma's ministry in Ammonihah, were he to have done this without regard for The Plan of Salvation that had been designed for just such a scenario, The Plan itself would have been frustrated, because the Law of Mercy would have been powerless to satisfy the demands of the Law of Justice. In order to demonstrate for Adam and Eve the necessity of obedience to both of these laws, and to impress upon them the importance of the infinite and eternal Atonement that would reconcile the two, "the Lord God placed cherubim and the flaming sword, that he should not partake of the fruit." (Alma 42:2-3). He used this

notable symbolism to impress upon the mind of Adam the necessity of Atonement to reconcile the Law of Justice with the Law of Mercy.

Alma had very effectively used the same illustration ten years earlier when teaching the people of Ammonihah, explaining to them that it was imperative that the symbolism employed should focus their attention on the reality that eternal life is gained by redemption and not by the overpowering of cherubim who wield flaming swords. He had shown that by placing these to guard the way to the Tree of Life, Heavenly Father had prevented Adam and his posterity from inappropriately partaking of the fruit of that tree, and from living forever in their sins. Thereby, both the people of Ammonihah and Corianton were prevented from having any basis for justifying sinful behavior.

Satan, who was a liar from the beginning, had attempted to foil The Plan of Salvation by substituting his own counterfeit, unworkable alternative that would not require an Atonement. He must have thought his idea was brilliant, inasmuch as it would conveniently sidestep the Law of Justice and dismiss as inconsequential the Law of Mercy. His promotional efforts were thwarted, but not before significant ideological damage had been done.

Nevertheless, with the implementation of The Plan, mankind would be of provided with "a probationary time," a time testing, or of putting to the proof the question: "Will we serve God, when given the opportunity? Will we recognize Christ as our Savior, and exercise faith unto repentance?" The flaming sword would prevent Adam and Eve and their posterity from nullifying their opportunity to participate in this telestial tutorial, and the cherubim would guarantee that, though imperfect in their obedience, they could learn to be perfect in their repentance and in their service to God. (See Alma 42:4). Both the cherubim and a flaming sword were central to the successful execution of an Atonement, upon which the success of The Plan hinges.

"For behold, if Adam had put forth his hand immediately, and partaken of the

Tree of Life, he would have lived forever, according to the word of God, having no space for repentance; yea, and also the word of God would have been void, and the Great Plan of Salvation would have been frustrated." (Alma 42:5). The Plan of Salvation (Alma 24:14), has over a dozen names; it is variously called

The Merciful Plan of The Great Creator (2 Nephi 9:6), The Plan of Our God (2 Nephi 9:13), The Great and Eternal Plan of Deliverance from Death (2 Nephi 11:5), The Plan of Redemption (Alma 29:2), The Great Plan of the Eternal God (Alma 34:9), The Great and Eternal Plan of Redemption (Alma 34:16), The Great Plan of Redemption (Alma 34:31), The Plan of Restoration (Alma 41:2), The Great Plan of Salvation (Alma 42:5), The Great Plan of Happiness (Alma 42:8), The Plan of Mercy (Alma 42:15), The Plan of Happiness (Alma 42:16), and The Great Plan of Mercy (Alma 42:31), because it makes possible the resurrection of otherwise imperfect mortals to eternal lives of glory by harmonizing Justice with Mercy. "Now, if it had not been for The Plan of Redemption," Alma had told the people of Ammonihah, "which was laid from the foundation of the world, there could have been no resurrection of the dead; but there was a Plan of Redemption laid, which shall bring to pass the resurrection of the dead." (Alma 12:25).

The cherubim became involved in order to guarantee that The Plan of Salvation would not be frustrated in the sense that Mercy would be thwarted by the sword of Justice. Meanwhile, the issue of Adam's transgression in the Garden needed to be addressed, for "as they were cut off from the Tree of Life they should be cut off from the face of the earth." (Alma 42:6). In the absence of Mercy and the Atonement, Justice demanded that "man became lost forever, yea, they became fallen man. And now, ye see by this that our first parents were cut off both temporally and spiritually from the presence of the Lord." (Alma 42:6-7). So it was, that "they became subject to follow after their own will," which was a good thing, as long as an Atonement would be made for their anticipated failure to unvaryingly obey eternal laws. (Alma 42:7).

The supernal principle of agency was to be honored, even if it meant that Justice must be served. Thus, "it was appointed unto man to die" rather than to reclaim him

without redemption "from this temporal death, for that would (have) destroy(ed) The Great Plan of Happiness. Therefore, as the soul could never die, and the Fall had brought upon all mankind a spiritual death as well as a temporal, that is, they were cut off from the presence of the Lord, it was expedient that mankind should be reclaimed from this spiritual death." (Alma 42:6-9).

In our fallen state, we are subject to the influences of Satan. When we turn our backs on the invitation to establish a relationship with the Divine and are alienated from God by spiritual death, we become carnal, sensual, and Devilish, by nature. Alma explained to Corianton: "This probationary state became a state for them to prepare; it became a preparatory state. And now remember, my son, if it were not for The Plan of Redemption, as soon as they were dead their souls were miserable, being cut off from the presence of the Lord." (Alma 42:11). Justice would demand that the children of God eternally suffer the consequences of their own actions. (See Alma 42:12). They would be "in the grasp of Justice; yea, the justice of God, which (would consign) them forever to be cut off from His presence." (Alma 42:14).

This is why, from the Fall of Adam and Eve, God has provided His children with The Plan of Salvation, that mortality might become a preparatory state, where they might develop the qualities required for redemption from spiritual death. As Alma clarified: "And now, there was no means to reclaim men from this fallen state, which man had brought upon himself because of his own disobedience; Therefore, according to Justice, The Plan of Redemption could not be brought about, only on conditions of repentance of men in this probationary state, yea, this preparatory state; for except it were for these conditions, Mercy could not take effect except it should destroy the work of Justice." (Alma 42:12-13). The beauty of The Plan of Redemption, then, is that it meets the demands of perfect Justice through the infinite Mercy of a loving Heavenly Father. The Plan allows God to be both just and merciful at the same time because of the Atonement.

As Alma explained: "Now the work of Justice could not be destroyed; if so, God

would cease to be God. And thus we see that all mankind were fallen, and they were in the grasp of Justice; yea, the justice of God, which consigned them forever to be cut off from his presence. And now, The Plan of Mercy could not be brought about except an Atonement should be made; therefore God Himself atoneth for the sins of the world, to bring about The Plan of Mercy, to appease the demands of Justice, that God might be a perfect, just God, and a merciful God also." (Alma 42:13-15). In one brilliant stroke, the Atonement allowed God to satisfy Justice and still mercifully reclaim His children from physical and spiritual death. The Savior became the Master of the situation. In His sacrifice, the debt would be paid, redemption made, the covenant fulfilled, Justice satisfied, the will of Heavenly Father done, and all power given to the Son by divine investiture of authority.

"Now, repentance could not come unto men except there were a punishment, which also was eternal as the life of the soul should be, affixed opposite to The Plan of Happiness, which was as eternal also as the life of the soul. Now, how could a man repent except he should sin? How could he sin if there was no law? How could there be a law save there was a punishment? Now, there was a punishment affixed, and a just law given, which brought remorse of conscience unto man. Now, if there was no law given - if a man murdered he should die - would he be afraid he would die if he should murder? And also, if there were no law given against sin men would not be afraid to sin. And if there was no law given, if men sinned what could Justice do, or Mercy either, for they would have no claim upon the creature?" (Alma 42:16-21).

Alma had certainly studied the counsel of Father Lehi, recorded on The Plates of Lehi that were in his possession, and on it he based the next section of his remarks. He affirmed that "there is a law given, and a punishment affixed, and a repentance granted; which repentance, Mercy claimeth. Otherwise, Justice claimeth the creature and executeth the law, and the law inflicteth the punishment; if not so, the works of Justice would be destroyed, and God would cease to be God. But God ceaseth not to be God, and Mercy claimeth the penitent, and Mercy cometh because of the Atonement; and the Atonement bringeth to pass the resurrection of the dead; and

the resurrection of the dead bringeth back men into the presence of God; and thus they are restored into His presence, to be judged according to their works, according to the law and Justice." (Alma 42:22-23).

"Is Justice dishonored?" asked John Taylor. "No, it is satisfied, and the debt is paid. Is righteousness forsaken? No, this is a righteous act. All requirements are met. Is judgment violated? No, its demands are fulfilled. Is Mercy triumphant? No, she simply claims her own. Justice, judgment, mercy, and truth all harmonize as the attributes of Deity." ("Mediation and Atonement," p. 171-172). In the Atonement, our innate desire to be clean finds expression in the celestial spark that ignites our desire to repent.

These "great and eternal purposes ... were prepared from the foundation of the world. And thus cometh about the salvation and the redemption of men," and because of the preservation of agency and the right to deny the merits of Christ and the efficacy of the Atonement, "and also their destruction and misery." (Alma 42:26). President Taylor further taught: "To the Son is given the power of the resurrection, the power of the redemption, the power salvation, and the power to enact laws for the carrying out and accomplishment of the design. Hence, life and immortality are brought to light, the Gospel is introduced, and He becomes the Author of eternal life and exaltation." ("Mediation and Atonement," p. 171-172).

As Amulek had explained to the Zoramites: "Mercy can satisfy the demands of justice, and encircles (the repentant soul) in the arms of safety, while he that exercises no faith unto repentance is exposed to the whole law of the demands of Justice; therefore only unto him that has faith unto repentance is brought about The Great and Eternal Plan of Redemption." (Alma 34:16). Faith, without works of repentance made possible because of the Atonement, is dead, because it has insufficient power to save us from the demands of Justice. Anciently, the psalmist had explored this relationship between Justice and Mercy. "Justice and judgment are the habitation of thy throne: Mercy and truth shall go before thy face." (Psalms 89:14). Latter-day revelation sheds additional light on these foundation principles:

"Mercy hath compassion on mercy and claimeth her own; Justice continueth its course and claimeth its own; judgment goeth before the face of Him who sitteth upon the throne and governeth and executeth all things." (D&C 88:40).

"Do ye suppose that Mercy can rob Justice? I say unto you, Nay; not one whit. If so, God would cease to be God." (Alma 42:25). The Savior's mission on earth was principally to "redeem those who (would) be baptized unto repentance, through faith on his name." (Alma 9:27). In essence, Alma taught Corianton that the only payment required for the gift of salvation is "the heart and a willing mind." (D&C 64:34). The Atonement has purpose and meaning only for those who are willing to make their own sacrifice of a broken heart and a contrite spirit. (See D&C 59:8).

Ultimately, we are required to give up only our sins to merit salvation. Therefore, Alma counseled his son to "only let your sins trouble you, with that trouble which shall bring you down unto repentance." (Alma 42:29). The turning point for Corianton was the conscious recognition of his sins. When he had cleared this hurdle, and with a greater understanding of the operation of both Justice and Mercy and of the relationship and harmony between the two that was created with the introduction of The Plan of Redemption, his father warned him to cease excusing himself in sin. "O my son, I desire that ye should deny the justice of God no more. Do not endeavor to excuse yourself in the least point because of your sins, by denying the justice of God; but do let the justice of God, and his mercy, and his long-suffering have full sway in your heart; and let it bring you down to the dust in humility." (Alma 42:30).

In his discourse on opposition, Lehi had also weighed in on the relationship between Justice and Mercy: "For it must needs be that there is an opposition in all things," he said. (2 Nephi 2:11). Opposition may seem vexing, but it can lead to desirable results. In its absence, "righteousness could not be brought to pass, neither wickedness, neither holiness nor misery, neither good nor bad." Without it, there could be "no life neither death, nor corruption nor incorruption, happiness nor misery, neither sense nor insensibility." (2 Nephi 2:11). Without opposition, the

Law relating to the Savior's intercession for men "must needs have been created for a thing of naught; wherefore there would have been no purpose in the end of its creation." The very "wisdom of God and His eternal purposes, and also the power, and the mercy, and the justice of God" would have been destroyed. (2 Nephi 2:12).

Without law, there could be no sin, reasoned Lehi, and without sin, there could be no righteousness. "And if there be no righteousness there be no happiness. And if there be no righteousness nor happiness there be no punishment nor misery. And if these things are not there is no God. And if there is no God we are not, neither the earth; for there could have been no creation of things, neither to act nor to be acted upon; wherefore, all things must have vanished away." (2 Nephi 2:13).

Lehi's view of the Fall of Adam provides an interesting perspective on the basic claims of Christianity, and expands upon the principle of opposition with a wealth of information. (See 2 Nephi 2:14-17). In the beginning, "to bring about His eternal purposes in the end of man, after He had created our first parents, and the beasts of the field and the fowls of the air, and in fine, all things which are created," God presented Adam and Eve with "the forbidden fruit in opposition to the Tree of Life; the one being sweet and the other bitter." (2 Nephi 2:15).

"Wherefore, the Lord God gave unto man that he should act for himself. But man could not act for himself save it should be that he was enticed by the one or the other." (2 Nephi 2:16). Thus, in the Garden of Eden, God permitted the Lucifer to "tempt the children of men, or they could not be agents unto themselves; for if they never should have bitter they could not know the sweet. Wherefore, it came to pass that the Devil tempted Adam, and he partook of the forbidden fruit and transgressed the commandment, wherein he became subject to the will of the Devil, because he yielded unto temptation." (D&C 29:39-40). But Lehi understood that Adam had not been deceived. His was an intelligent, conscious decision, the result of a correct understanding of the requirements of the Gospel Plan.

The Fall resulted, and Adam and Eve "were driven out of the Garden of Eden, to till the earth." (2 Nephi 2:19). The scriptures clearly teach that Adam and Eve were

the first of Heavenly Father's children to live on this earth. "Father Adam (was) the Ancient of Days, and father of all, and (husband to) our glorious Mother Eve." (D&C 138:38-39). So began "the family of all the earth." (2 Nephi 2:20).

Lehi next taught that these first generations of mankind lived to great age so that they might have time to repent. "The days of the children of men were prolonged, according to the will of God, that they might repent while in the flesh; wherefore, their state became a state of probation, and their time was lengthened, according to the commandments which the Lord God gave unto the children of men: For He gave commandment that all men must repent, for He showed unto all men that they were lost, because of the transgression of their parents." (2 Nephi 2:21).

Lehi clearly taught that had Adam not transgressed the Law in the Garden, he would have vegetated there forever, in limbo, in a state of moral stagnation. "And now, behold, if Adam had not transgressed he would not have fallen, but he would have remained in the Garden of Eden, and all things which were created must have remained in the same state in which they were after they were created; and they must have remained forever, and had no end. And they would have had no children; wherefore they would have remained in a state of innocence, having no joy, for they knew no misery; doing no good, for they knew no sin." (2 Nephi 9:22-23). Life in Eden may have been idyllic, but it was not ideal. Our Father knew that Adam must fall if the curtain were to be raised on Act Two of the Three Act Play that is The Plan of Salvation, for "all things have been done in the wisdom of him who knoweth all things." (2 Nephi 9:24).

Thus, "Adam fell that men might be, and men are that they might have joy." (2 Nephi 9:25). In a grand summary of his discourse on opposition and the Fall of Adam, Lehi's simple aphorism speaks volumes and is one of the basic messages of the Restoration. When the Fall of Adam is considered in conjunction with the Atonement of Christ, it is clear that both are part of God's Plan of Eternal Progression for His children, who could only attain a fulness of joy in a personal, tangible, resurrection.

"For man is spirit, the elements are eternal, and spirit and element, inseparably connected, receive a fulness of joy." (D&C 93:33).

When Lehi returned to his original discussion after this lengthy parenthetical aside, he explained: "The Messiah cometh in the fulness of time, that He may redeem the children of men from the Fall. And because that they are redeemed from the Fall they have become free forever, knowing good from evil; to act for themselves and not to be acted upon, save it be by the punishment of the law at the great and last day, according to the commandments which God hath given." (2 Nephi 2:26). Thus, a way was provided for us to triumph as a direct result of the transgression of Adam and Eve that brought temporal and spiritual death into the lone and dreary world, or the world in which we now live; temporal death because of the separation of the body from the spirit at the close of mortal existence, and spiritual death because of the alienation of the Spirit from God in the absence of an Atonement, at the time of the Judgment. (See 1 Nephi 8:4).

"Wherefore, men are free according to the flesh; and all things are given them which are expedient unto man. And they are free to choose liberty and eternal life, through the great Mediator of all men." (2 Nephi 2:27). Heavenly Father always honors the eternal principle of agency. It is riskier this way, but it is the only way. Rather than enslaving us in good habits, He repeatedly gives us the opportunity to recommit ourselves to our covenants of obedience to true and eternal principles, and in particular to the Law of Mercy as it relates to repentance and forgiveness of sin through the Atonement.

On the other hand, men "may choose captivity and death, according to the captivity and power of the Devil; for he seeketh that all men might be miserable like unto himself." (2 Nephi 2:27). "The Spirit is pure," taught Brigham Young, and is "under the special control and influence of the Lord, but the body is of the earth, and is subject to the power of the Devil, and is under the mighty influence of that fallen nature that is of the earth. If the Spirit yields to the body, the Devil then has power to overcome the body and spirit of that man, and he loses both." ("Discourses of

Brigham Young," p. 69-70).

Jacob also had something to say about the same principles taught by his father Lehi, and that would later be emphasized by his descendant Alma. He urged his people to avoid spiritual sclerosis by repenting "with full purpose of heart." (Jacob 6:5). He knew that hardening of the spiritual arteries is a sign of a self-defeating illness that, left untreated, will effectively kill the Spirit. He posed questions loaded with powerful action verbs that were intended to rivet the attention of his listeners: "Will ye reject Christ," he asked, "and deny (His words), and the power of God, and the gift of the Holy Ghost, and quench the Holy Spirit, and make a mock of The Great Plan of Redemption?" (Jacob 6:8).

His message, like Lehi's and Alma's, was a call to repentance. If we do not repent, the Holy Spirit, which burns like a fire, will be quenched, and the Atonement of Christ will lose its power to save us. Without repentance and forgiveness, we will stand before the Bar of God with "shame and awful guilt" because, the Law of Mercy will not have been able to intervene and mitigate the exacting demands of the Law of Justice. (Jacob 6:9).

Jacob bluntly stated: "According to the power of Justice, ye must go away into that lake of fire and brimstone, whose flames are unquenchable, and whose smoke ascendeth up forever and ever, which ... is endless torment." (Jacob 6:10). So the logical path to follow is to "repent and enter in at the strait gate, and continue in the way which is narrow, until (we) shall obtain eternal life." (Jacob 6:11). This verse emphasizes the line of thought begun earlier, when Jacob asked: "I beseech of you in words of soberness that ye would repent, and come with full purpose of heart, and cleave unto God, as he cleaveth unto you." (Jacob 6:5).

Faith and repentance lead us to the strait gate of baptism. When we pass through its portal, our lives open up in an expansion of eternal opportunity as we obtain a remission of sins, gain membership in the Church, and are personally sanctified through the receipt of the Holy Ghost. We become at-one with our divine center. We

find ourselves on the path leading to the Celestial Kingdom. The way is strait and narrow, however, for the standard of the Gospel is undeviating. There is no room for compromise or rationalization. There is no latitude in God's declaration that He "cannot look upon sin with the least degree of allowance." (D&C 1:31).

After explaining The Great Plan of Redemption to his people, which solved the dilemma created by God's demand for perfection coupled with our inability to live sinless lives, Jacob simply stated: "O be wise; what can I say more?" (Jacob 6:12).

Actually, there is one more thing to be said, and it concerns the cherubim. "They are referred to in the Bible to designate sculptured, engraved, and embroidered figures used in the furniture and ornamentation of the Jewish sanctuary. The word "cherub" / "cherubim" is borrowed from the Assyrian kirubu / "to be near." Hence, it means "near ones," "familiar ones," "personal servants," or "bodyguards."

In ancient Israel, it was a term used to describe heavenly spirits who surround God and pay Him intimate service. Thus, over time it came to mean "angelic spirit." "As Jehovah was surrounded by figures of cherubim in His sanctuary on earth, so He is, according to scripture, surrounded by cherubim in heaven. The function ascribed to these servants is that of throne-bearers, or carriers, of His Divine Majesty." ("The Catholic Encyclopedia").

The Old Testament confirms that the word "cherub" / "cherubim" was used to designate angels, since Moses reported that God set cherubim to guard the way to the Tree of Life. (See Moses 4:31). These beings were angels who belonged to this world but who had not yet received mortal bodies. We know this because the Lord revealed to Joseph Smith: "There are no angels who minister to this earth but those who do belong to it." (D. &C. 130:5). Angels are ministering servants who carry messages from our Eternal Father and his Son Jesus Christ. Before men and women began to be translated, "angels coming to the earth were spirits belonging to this earth who had not yet obtained bodies of flesh and bones. After men and women had been translated as was Enoch, they, as translated beings, could and did come to minister unto the prophets." (Joseph Fielding Smith, Jr.)

References to cherubim are found in many places in the Old and New Testament: in visions, over the mercy seat in the tabernacle in the wilderness, as decorations on the curtains and veil of the tabernacle, embroidered on the veil and in the holy of holies in Solomon's temple, and as decorations upon which the molten sea rested. Generally, they are described as having wings. There are, however, no angels, cherubim included, who have wings. As a passage in The Doctrine & Covenants explains, the representation of wings is symbolical. As with certain beasts seen in vision by John, the presence of wings is simply "a representation of power to move, to act, etc." (D&C 77:4.) Just when it was that the notion arose that angels have wings is unclear, but I happen to like it. Pardon me if my Protestant background is showing.

As a footnote, there are cherubs and cherubim mentioned in the following scriptures: Exodus 25, 26, 36 & 37, Numbers 7, Ezekiel 9, 10, 11, 28 & 41, 1 Kings 6, 7, & 8, 2 Kings 19, 1 Chronicles 13 & 28, 2 Chronicles 3 & 5, 1 Samuel 4, 2 Samuel 6 & 22, Psalms 18, 80 & 99, Ezra 25. Nehemiah 7, Isaiah 37, & Hebrews 9.

"Only let your
sins trouble you,
with that trouble which
shall bring you down
unto repentance."
(Alma 42:29).

Chapter Eleven

Choices and worth.

Two conditions related to the exercise of agency, or free-will, are the opportunity to make choices in an atmosphere of opposition, and the necessity of personally facing the consequences that are related to those choices. The urgency of reconciliation to the laws of heaven through repentance and forgiveness through the Atonement is not so apparent, but is equally important. Chapters 2 and 9 of the Second Book of Nephi forthrightly address these issues, and comprise the theological core of The Book of Mormon. In fact, these chapters can be studied independently in order to capture these essential elements of The Gospel Plan as they relate to repentance.

In a patriarchal blessing given to his son Jacob, Lehi taught the fundamental truth that we are instructed sufficiently to know good from evil. (See 2 Nephi 2:5). It is for this purpose that the Light of Christ is given, to be our built-in beacon to guide us home to heaven. We were created with inherent goodness and the capacity to recognize and to cleave unto truth. This is why Joseph Smith was comfortable teaching the Saints correct principles, and then letting them govern themselves. He

knew that their knowledge of the truth would "forever govern ignorance," and that "a people who would be free must arm themselves with the power which knowledge gives." (James Madison).

But even in the best of circumstances, none of us is undeviatingly obedient to eternal law. This is why Lehi taught: "No flesh is justified." (2 Nephi 2:5). That is to say, no-one keeps the laws and commandments of God in perfection, for to be justified means to stand uncondemned before the Lord. Lehi emphasized that without a Redeemer, the conundrum in which we find ourselves would be hopeless. But, as he explained to his son, and as Jacob would later teach his own family, the demands of the Law of Justice have been satisfied by the Redeemer's infinite Atonement.

His mortal ministry, His agony in the Garden of Gethsemane, and His reconciliation with the will of His Father on the Cross of Calvary, bear witness that He died for our sins. In return, He only asks that we approach Him with the sacrifice of a broken heart and a contrite spirit. (See D&C 59:8). Our indebtedness to God, however, is completely beyond our ability to pay. But He does not ask us to settle our account with Him; He only asks that we keep His commandments. The marvel of His love is that the more we try to serve Him, the more He blesses us. Therefore, we become even more deeply indebted to Him and will remain so forever. We reveal how we feel about the Savior by repenting of our sins in an action that is much deeper than thanks. Our gratitude penetrates the deepest undercurrents of our lives, and is founded upon the grace of God.

Because of the intercession of Jesus Christ on our behalf, we will be briefly redeemed from spiritual death, which is estrangement from God. We will be allowed to come into His presence, perhaps for the last time, to see how much intrinsic light we have lost through wicked behavior. If we have not repented, the soul-stains of sin will be glaringly apparent, will noticeably tarnish the luster of our spirits, and will disqualify us from making a legitimate claim upon eternal life. For the unrepentant, the Last Judgment will be based on the legal demands of

Justice, for mercy will have no claim upon such creatures. (See Alma 42:31). Justice will dispassionately examine if we have met the conditions of our probation without reliance upon the Merciful Plan of The Great Creator. (See 2 Nephi 9:6).

Fourteen parenthetical verses in 2 Nephi 2 grow out of Lehi's remarks on the Atonement, and are set apart at their beginning and end by aphorisms that have become foundation scriptures in the liturgy of the Church. (See 2 Nephi 2:11-25). This section begins with Lehi's oft-quoted observation: "It must needs be that there is opposition in all things." (2 Nephi 2:11). The verses that follow demonstrate why that is so, illuminate the principle with examples, and caution that because of our exercise of agency in an atmosphere of opposition, undesirable consequences are likely to follow, that can only be mitigated by repentance.

Lehi also taught that there was opposition from the beginning, and that notwithstanding the idyllic atmosphere in Eden, Adam and Eve could not have had true moral agency until they had accepted the enticements of one who had been allowed by God to invade the sanctity of the Garden. Because everything has its opposite, the Atonement exists as the safety net that we all need, when we have exercised our agency unwisely, and have been unwilling or unable to resist the negative influences of the world.

By referencing opposition, Lehi implied that had Adam not transgressed the Law in the Garden, he would have vegetated there forever. Life in Eden before the Fall was not compatible with the concept of eternal progression; rather, it was morally static. Father knew that Adam must fall in order to initialize The Plan of Salvation, but Satan had no such knowledge, and so he pressured Eve to partake of the forbidden fruit. This was the very action necessary to bring about mortality and the opportunity for personal growth and eternal happiness that are critical to the successful implementation of The Plan.

Not knowing the mind of God, that opposition is necessary for the enjoyment of eternal happiness, Satan sought what he thought would be the misery of all

mankind, and with his congenital short-sightedness and his typical stratagem of promoting half-truths, he offered the forbidden fruit to Eve. "Ye shall be as God," he unwittingly promised, "knowing good and evil." (2 Nephi 2:18).

The Savior Himself explained: "It must needs be that the Devil should tempt the children of men, or they could not be agents unto themselves; for if they never should have bitter they could not know the sweet. Wherefore, it came to pass that the Devil tempted Adam, and he partook of the forbidden fruit and transgressed the commandment, wherein he became subject to the will of the Devil, because he yielded unto temptation." (D&C 29:39-40). But Adam was not deceived. His was an intelligent, conscious decision, the result of a clear understanding of the performance requirements of the Gospel Plan. Simply put, Adam fell that his family might come to know true happiness.

Without understanding all the ramifications of his decision to partake of the fruit of the Tree of Knowledge of Good and Evil, Adam still came to believe that it would be necessary to do so, even though it might come like a flash of lightning and a clap of thunder. In the end, though, he knew the storm would pass and that flowers would bloom. (See "I Ching," The Chinese Book of Changes).

The Fall set the stage for the creation of "the family of all the earth." (2 Nephi 2:20). The Doctrine & Covenants clearly teaches that Adam and Eve were the first of Heavenly Father's children to live on this earth. They are characterized as "Father Adam, the Ancient of Days, and father of all, and our glorious Mother Eve." (D&C 138:38-39). The Lord Himself commissioned them: "Teach it unto your children, that all men, everywhere, must repent, or they can in nowise inherit the kingdom of God. That by reason of transgression cometh the Fall, which Fall bringeth death, and inasmuch as ye were born into the world by water, and blood, and the spirit, which I have made, and so became of dust a living soul, even so ye must be born again into the kingdom of heaven, of water, and of the Spirit, and be cleaned by blood, even the blood of mine Only Begotten, that ye might be sanctified from all sin, and enjoy the words of eternal life in this world, and eternal life in the world

to come, even immortal glory." (Moses 6:57 & 59).

Spencer W. Kimball observed: We often try to "expel from our lives physical pain and mental anguish and assure ourselves of continual ease and comfort, but if we were to close the doors upon such sorrow and distress, we might be excluding our greatest friends and benefactors. Suffering can make saints of people as they learn patience, long-suffering and self-mastery." ("Faith Precedes the Miracle," p. 98). These are the very character traits that must have sustained Adam and Eve as they forged their new lives in the lone and dreary world outside the overly protective walls of the Garden. (See 1 Nephi 8:4).

President Kimball continued: "If we looked at mortality as the whole of existence, then pain, sorrow, failure, and short life would be calamity. But if we look upon life as an eternal thing stretching far into the premortal past and on into the eternal post-death future, then all may be put in proper perspective." ("Faith Precedes the Miracle," p. 97). This longitudinal view must have also reflected our first parents' outlook on life, for it explains why they so enthusiastically welcomed the opportunity to become mortal. "Blessed be the name of God," Adam declared, "for because of my transgression my eyes are opened, and in this life I shall have joy, and again in the flesh I shall see God. And Eve, his wife, heard all these things and was glad, saying: Were it not for our transgression we never should have had seed, and never should have known good and evil, and the joy of our redemption, and the eternal life which God giveth unto all the obedient." (Moses 5:10-11).

President Kimball pointed out: "If all the sick for whom we pray were healed, if all the righteous were protected and the wicked destroyed, the whole program of the Father would be annulled and the basic principle of the Gospel," which is the principle of free will, or agency, "would be ended. No man would have to live by faith. If joy and peace and rewards were instantaneously given the doer of good, there could be no evil, for all would do good, and not because of its rightness. There would be no test of strength, no development of character, no growth of

powers, and no (agency), but only satanic controls." ("Faith Precedes The Miracle," p. 97-98).

Oh, the wisdom of Lehi, when he declared: "It must need be that there is opposition in all things!" (2 Nephi 2:11). Thanks be to our Father in Heaven and to Adam and Eve for making it possible to have posterity in the stimulating testing center of mortality! It is for our benefit that we become acquainted with evil as well as with good, with darkness as well as with light, with error as well as with truth, with sorrow as well as with happiness, with pain as well as with pleasure, and with punishment for the infraction of eternal laws, as well as with the blessings that follow obedience. Our progression is dependent upon the principles of the Atonement, repentance, and forgiveness, which are the opposites of condemnation, damnation, and life without light.

The Plan was carefully crafted to create the conditions whereby we might come unto Christ within the crucible of our mortal experience. Perhaps there is sense, after all, in the seeming chaos of existence, and there is a common thread underlying all experience. Perhaps thee is a divine design that is related to our destiny. "For my thoughts are not your thoughts, neither are your ways my ways, saith the Lord. For as the heavens are higher than the earth, so are my ways higher than your ways, and my thoughts than your thoughts." (Isaiah 55:8-9).

In one of the few scriptural references to Lucifer's banishment from the presence of God for rebellion, Lehi described how an angel "had fallen from heaven; wherefore, he became a Devil, having sought that which was evil before God. And because he had fallen from heaven, and had become miserable forever, he sought also the misery of all mankind." (2 Nephi 2:17-18). Joseph Fielding Smith, Jr. taught that he and his angels were cast out because they had "lost the power of repentance, for they chose evil after having had the light." ("Doctrines of Salvation," 2:218-219).

Once again, through the illustration of opposites, we can see why cleanliness through repentance and forgiveness, founded upon the power of the Atonement,

is a central theme embedded within the doctrine of The Plan. The opposite of cleanliness is filthiness. Our failure to repent is a form of rebellion against our Heavenly Father that has eternally damaging consequences. Satan is the quintessential rebel whose efforts will come to naught. His counterfeit proposals are nullified every time a disciple looks to God, and lives. (See Alma 37:47).

To this end, Lehi next taught Jacob that since walking by faith and learning life's lessons by trial and error are vital to our growth and development, "the days of the children of men were prolonged, according to the will of God, that they might repent while in the flesh." Lehi knew that none of the children of our Heavenly Father could obey Him with exactness, "wherefore, their state became a state of probation, and their time was lengthened, (and) he gave commandment that all men must repent." (2 Nephi 2:21).

Mortality would thus become a time of testing and of putting to the proof our declared values. Agency and opposition are powerful forces that constantly refine us by pushing, pulling, and tearing at us within the crucible of experience. On our own, we can never eliminate the consequences of sin. As the dangling Sword of Damocles, they hang over our heads. Always at issue is the question whether we will take advantage of the Atonement of the Savior through repentance, so that we might enjoy eternal happiness in the Celestial Kingdom of God. If we do not do so, we must be lost because of the transgression of Adam and Eve, which brought temporal death because of the separation of the body from the spirit at the close of mortal existence, and the first spiritual death when, after we have reached the age of accountability, we sin without immediately thereafter repenting. Since the Law of Justice cannot be compromised, in the absence of Atonement we would experience not only physical death, but also suffer a spiritual death, which is alienation from God.

Alma taught that spiritual death occurs when we die "as to things pertaining unto righteousness." (Alma 12:16). For when Satan came among the children of Adam,

they "loved him more than God. And men began from that time forth to be carnal, sensual, and Devilish." (Moses 5:13). In the scriptures, this alienation from God is called "the first spiritual death." (D&C 29:41). This is why after repentance and baptism of water, we must be spiritually born again through the cleansing power of the Holy Ghost.

It is at the waters of baptism that we keep the commandment, and it is by the power of the Holy Ghost that our token of faith is justified. But it is in the atoning blood of Christ that we are sanctified, following purposeful repentance that has been catalyzed by our sacrifice of a broken heart and contrite spirit. (See D&C 59:8, Moses 6:60, & Psalms 34:18). When we stand before God at the Bar of Justice, we can thereby avoid the sentence of a second spiritual death, which is a permanent alienation from His presence. (See Jacob 6:9 & Alma 12:16). Those who have died without having had the opportunity take advantage of the oracles of God (see D&C 90:4-5) may accept in the Spirit World vicarious ordinances that have been performed on their behalf by faithful patrons in the House of The Lord. These proxies act as saviors on Mount Zion to their kindred dead. (See Obadiah 1:21). Thereby, the Atonement becomes both infinite and eternal. (See Alma 34:10).

"Teach it unto your children, that all men, everywhere, must repent, or they can in nowise inherit the kingdom of God." (Moses 6:57).

Chapter Twelve

Perfect in our repentance.

We are as buildings that are "fitly framed together," that "groweth unto an holy temple in the Lord," in order for our bodies to be the "habitation of God through the Spirit." (Ephesians 2:21-22). There is no room for dry-rot and there can be no skeletons lurking in the closet. We cannot superficially whitewash our sins to cover them up. The Savior called the scribes and Pharisees hypocrites, for they were "like unto whited sepulchres, which indeed appear beautiful outward, but are within full of dead men's bones, and of all uncleanliness." (Matthew 23:27).

Mortality was designed to be a life-long learning laboratory to give each of us the opportunity to mold our nature to more closely resemble that of our Father in Heaven. He negotiated with Justice and conceived the Atonement to make that metamorphosis possible. His Plan allowed for us to experience opposition, that our free will might be tried and tested in the fiery hot crucible of experience. But it also provided a Savior, Whose influence would become the only reasonable alternative to otherwise overwhelmingly negative forces competing for dominance in our lives.

When we fall short of obedience to all of God's laws, the Atonement stipulates that we go through a process of repentance. This requires that we Recognize our transgression, experience Remorse, Renounce the self-defeating behavior, Resolve to do better, make Restitution where possible, and then do our part to establish a

Reconciliation with the Spirit, in order to Receive a Remission of sin through the grace of God Who is our Redeemer.

Repentance thus becomes the catalyst that propels us upward toward the discovery of personal levels of experience with the Savior, for when He speaks of knowing Him, He must be referring to a special sense of the word. (See 1 Nephi 17:13). It is not enough that we know about Him by reading the Gospels, or by listening to others speak of Him. We must know Him through the bonds of common experience and common feeling. Repentance allows us to do this as we take halting steps toward our divine destiny.

The Plan provides for the blessing of repentance, that it might become a constructive exercise that is involved with both discovery and recovery. It allows our destiny to become a reunion with divine realities. Repentance opens the portal to religious recognition that is a re-learning of that which we have already known. In this context, the word religion may derive from the Latin root "ligare" - "to bind." Thus, religion means "to bind again." This fits nicely with the perspective linking repentance to a reunion with a divine purpose, or a Plan, for Heavenly Father's children.

Repentance represents so much more than the empty promises we make to ourselves that are generally kept for a few days or weeks at best, before they are abandoned in a return to our previously held lifestyle behaviors. Repentance has staying power. It has no bias, for its practice is anchored to doctrinal principles, nurtured within the rich culture medium of faith, validated by baptism, and witnessed in the fiery cauldron of the Spirit. (See the 4th Article of Faith).

Perfect repentance encourages us to consider the possibility that we might one

day be like the Savior. It give substance to our testimony that His grace consists of the gifts and power by which we may be brought to His perfection and stature, so that we may enjoy not only what He has, but also what He is. Repentance hinges upon His promise that by the grace of God we may be perfect in Christ, because we affirm His power to forgive sins. Then, we are "sanctified in Christ by the grace of God, through the shedding of the blood of Christ, which is in the covenant of the Father unto the remission of (our) sins, that (we) become holy, without spot." (Moroni 10:33). The repentance process commands the active participation of the Father, Son, and Holy Ghost, in addition to ourselves.

Our hope in Their mighty power to save is not wishful thinking, nor is it misguided trust in a promise that cannot be fulfilled. It is not a high stakes gamble based on a statistical improbability. Hope is the inevitable reward of well-founded faith that encourages us to grasp the horns of sanctuary, yield our hearts to the Savior of the world, and accept His invitation to come unto Him through repentance for our sins. By doing so, we draw upon the power of His Atonement which harmonizes the desires of our hearts with Gospel principles.

Our purpose in life is to grow in grace and to progress in stature until we have developed both the image and likeness of our Heavenly Father. (See 2 Peter 3:18 & 3 Nephi 28:10). But none of us is exact in our adherence to the learning curve scribed by the stylus of The Plan. It seems to be our nature to repeatedly violate the commandments; however, sin stops our progression, for no unclean thing can dwell with God. The contamination of sin is incompatible with the standard of spiritual hygiene that is required of those who would inhabit heaven.

As William Wordsworth observed: "Heaven lies about us in our infancy. Shades of the prison house begin to close upon the growing boy. But he beholds the light and whence it flows; he sees it in his joy. The youth, who daily farther from the east must travel, still is nature's priest. And by the vision splendid, is on his way attended. At length, the man perceives it die away, and fade into the light of common day." ("Ode: Intimations of Immortality"). God provided the principle

of repentance so that we may yet become holy through the sanctification of the Spirit. "By the water (we) keep the commandment; by the Spirit (we) are justified, and by the blood (we) are sanctified. (Moses 6:60). It is for this reason that the commandment is given: "All men, everywhere, must repent." (Moses 6:57).

Fading light is the consequence of the corrosive nature of sin, which is part of the brutal reality of the opposition in all things that is a necessary part of our mortal experience. Without repentance, which is the lynchpin of The Plan of Salvation, all must be lost. Fortunately, the Lord reveals truth to those who are spiritually prepared to receive it, and from the beginning, has provided repentance as a pathway to perfection, that all might be as the little children whom He most affectionately favored during His mortal and post-mortal ministries, and who, with the Savior Himself, become our role-models.

The beauty of repentance is that it can be a primer on midwifery, with the Savior our labor coach, as we begin the arduous process of our reunion with the Infinite. When we are dealing with weakness in our contractions that push the Lord's agenda, relying upon the power of the Atonement enables us to bear our witness with conviction, when we consider the efficacy of repentance.

Weakness can seed the atmosphere of our inspiration, that nurturing moisture might fall upon our tender testimonies and facilitate the germination of faith that is key to the transformation of our nature. When weakness is linked to faith and repentance, it can motivate us to positively respond to the invitation to do better, and to be kinder, to be more merciful and more forgiving. Following our purposeful repentance, with the sustained precipitation that is repetitively provided by the ordinance of the Sacrament, we can fulfil our destiny as spiritual beings having mortal experiences. (See Romans 8:13).

The Atonement may be hard for us to grasp because it was conceived in heaven. It is not of this world, and so if we try to wrap our finite minds around it, we will fail to do so. But, together with the companion principle of repentance, it must not be summarily dismissed just because it cannot be rationally explained or neatly

packaged. It is a gift that cannot be unwrapped with haste. Its power can only be experienced when we nurture a companionship with the Spirit, for when we are under its spell, we are at-one with the Savior. "The things which some men esteem to be of great worth ... others set at naught ... Yea, even the very God of Israel do men trample under their feet." (1 Nephi 19:7). The Atonement, together with repentance, are mysteries of the kingdom that can only be spiritually discerned. (See 1 Corinthians 2:14).

When we are born of God, our orientation is more toward the expansive laws of the eternal world than to the restrictive confines of our physical surroundings. Repentance brings us into a harmonious balance with the eternities. It helps us to overcome the world with a freedom from incarceration to the inexorable immutability of the destructive laws that govern the temporal world in which we now live. (See 1 John 5:3).

Repentance is the pinnacle of our experience, when through the Atonement of Christ we are liberated by independence from bondage to sin. This feeling is incalculable, indescribable, and inexplicable, and yet it is undeniable. It is not maturational, but is generational, as we become new creatures in Christ, when the Law of Mercy trumps the immutable Law of Justice through forgiveness because of the Atonement. (See 2 Corinthians 5:17).

Repentance, together with the Sacrament, fuels our actions, that the Atonement might charge our spiritual batteries and energize our vision with infinite perspective. These three affirmative actions bind us to heaven, and create a pulsing stream of inspiration whose flow has no temporal or spatial boundary. With them, we are swept up by quickening currents into the direct experience of a holy communion with our Father in Heaven, with the Savior Jesus Christ, and with the Holy Ghost.

Although the heavens will always be higher than the earth, through repentance Their thoughts will have somehow become our thoughts, and Their ways our ways. (See

Isaiah 55:8-9). We will be mesmerized by Their magic, Their work, and Their glory, as we are caught up in the process whereby the universe becomes "a machine for the making of gods." (Henri Bergson, "Two Sources of Religion and Morality").

Repentance is just the prescription we need for the religious fever that elevates our testimony temperature enough to get our juices flowing with an appreciation of the Savior's sacrifice. The Atonement helps us to see more clearly the potential of our position, and experience the earth-shaking and mind-bending theophany that, as the offspring of Deity, we enjoy a familial bond with the Redeemer of the world.

One of the risks of mortality is that temporal baggage can create imbalance that leads to confusion in our minds and in our hearts regarding the need for repentance. It is faith, the companion to repentance, that jars us out of our collective complacency. Faith repurposes the stagnation of the status quo. Faith unto repentance prods us to constructively expend our energy and to confidently put our agency to work. It inspires us with a settled conviction in our minds, in ways that were long ago creatively programmed by our Father in Heaven to touch our heart-strings. As they resonate with understanding, harmonic waves carry us to a greater appreciation of the Savior's declaration that His sheep know His voice, and follow Him. (See John 10:4).

Brigham Young taught: "The first principle that ought to occupy our attention and which is the mainspring of all action is the principle of improvement," and this requires us to balance the telestial trivia that constantly competes for our attention with the absolute necessity of regularly recurring repentance. (D.B.Y., p. 87).

What is at stake is nothing less than the riches of eternity. These are not tangible treasures, because they relate to our ability to see from the perspective of our Heavenly Father. Repentance brings these pearls of great price within our view, by expanding our vision beyond physical laws that pertain only to the temporal world, toward an appreciation of Gospel principles that relate to the eternities. Repentance endows us with the power to reach out and touch the face of God, not with our

unprincipled and ungovernable physical senses or with our hands, but with our incorruptible and unimpeachable spiritual sixth sense and our hearts.

We are immune from the corrosive influences of the world as long as our feet are firmly planted on Gospel sod. When we are assaulted by sounding brass and tinkling cymbals, those with a strong testimony of the gift of repentance have the ability to sift through the discordant cacophony of confusing voices. Repentance catalyzes a mystical and metaphysical transformation wherein we may be figuratively born of God, so that we may have ears that hear and respond to the word of the Lord, eyes that see clearly, and that are able to discern between truth and error, and noses that recoil at the stench of sin. (See Mosiah 5:7).

The process of repentance turns our thoughts to the Savior, so that, without distraction, we might feel His energy building within us, until it lifts us to the zenith of experience where the lines distinguishing mortality from eternity blur, and we find ourselves consumed in fires of everlasting burnings. (See Hebrews 12:29).

Repentance facilitates our reacquaintance with the sum of our existence and our experience. Recurring repentance teaches us to suppress the natural inclinations of the telestial world that surround us and continually encroach upon our spiritual stability. If we thwart that intrinsic light, "we are accountable, and to a degree, we condemn ourselves. We knew Christ before this life, we know Him here, and we will know Him hereafter. His sheep do indeed know His voice." (Truman Madsen). That voice commands all men and women, everywhere, and children also, to repent. (See D&C 18:9).

Repentance grounds us to practical belief, but its elements commit us to an upward thrust. However, our subsequent good works do not assure us of salvation, nor do they make us good; it is our faith unto repentance that does so. Wresting the scriptures, and suggesting that we are saved by works, twists holy writ from its true or proper signification, and perverts it from its correct application. Our faith notwithstanding, we are saved by the grace of God, after all we can do, and that is

primarily to repent. (See 2 Nephi 25:23).

Regarding sins for which we have repented, we will remember them only insofar as they increase our testimonies and strengthen our resolve to refrain from repeating them, but we will no longer fee the guilt associated with the transgression. The Spirit of the Lord Omnipotent will cause a mighty change to come over us, "that we (will) have no more disposition to do evil, but to do good continually." (Mosiah 5:2, see J.S.T. Romans 4:1).

Following repentance, we yearn to re-dedicate our lives to the Savior. We throw ourselves upon an altar of faith whose foundation is buttressed by a supernal display of divine direction. We are driven relentlessly forward with an unwavering confidence that His power to save will be unleashed in our behalf and flow over our wounds as a healing balm, that at the Pleasing Bar of God we might unflinchingly meet His penetrating gaze with clear eyes, and with hearts that are clean and pure. (See Proverbs 20:9, & Alma 3:7).

It can be challenging to muster faith unto repentance that leads us to the strait and narrow gate of baptism. In fact, "few there be that find it." (Matthew 7:14). Those who ultimately pass through this portal, however, find that the way before them has been clearly marked by the Atonement of Christ.

Our progression hinges largely upon what do we do with the Atonement, and upon what the Atonement does for us. Our imperfections may either hinder or enhance our progress. Fortunately, repentance laces our weakness with healthy measures of meekness and humility, so that the Atonement can amend our narrow perspective. Repentance redefines and redesigns what had heretofore been stumbling blocks; they are repurposed into the very stepping stones that are needed to reinforce our confidence, conquer our fears, and incapacitate the obstacles to our progression.

Because of repentance, we realize that "life is a sheet of paper white where each of us may write a line or two, and then comes night. Greatly begin. If thou hast time

but for a line, make that sublime. Not failure, but low aim is crime." (James Russell Lowell).

Repentance is complete when the Spirit of the Lord falls upon us, and we are

148

filled with joy and have peace of conscience. We use repentance as a springboard, that we might be capable of disciplined, controlled procedure and be receptive to flashes of insight and inspiration. Our desire to repent is amplified by the quiet spiritual stirrings that underlie our mortal experience because of the Light of Christ. Repentance sets us free to be creative, and sets us creative to become more free, by unleashing the doctrine of the kingdom to work its magic. It empowers the principles of the Gospel to become the perfect law of liberty.

The quality of forgiveness is really a celestial barometer, calibrated to a scale that measures the capacity of our hearts. Repentance gives form and substance to the visualization of our reunion with our Father. It expands the depth and breadth of His Plan to infinite proportion. It provides context to the familiar admonition to work out our salvation with fear and trembling before the Lord. (See Philippians 2:12). Repentance makes it a little bit easier to imagine stepping on shore, and finding it heaven; to sense ourselves taking hold of a hand, and finding it God's hand; to envision breathing deeply, and discovering it is celestial air that fills our lungs; to visualize feelings of invigoration, and finding it immortality; to create a vision of passing from storm and tempest to an unbroken calm. In our dreams of the night, we pre-play the self-fulfilling prophecy of awakening, and finding it Home. "For God speaketh once, yea twice, yet man perceiveth it not. In a dream, in a vision of the night, when deep sleep falleth upon men, in slumberings upon the bed; Then he openeth the ears of men, and sealeth their instruction." (Job 33:14-16). In our waking moments, we are preoccupied with our determination to make the journey to Christ. Even as we sleep, our dreams paint portraits that are bathed in Technicolor of our desire to follow Him. Thanks be to God for the principle of repentance to help us get through each day, and every night of darkness, of our lives.

"Repent ye, repent ye! Why will ye die? Turn ye, turn ye unto the Lord your God." (Helaman 17:7).

Chapter Thirteen

Wickedness never was happiness.

Even those who have been called to preach the Gospel risk falling into transgression in consequence of a shallow understanding of principles and doctrines. This can lead to marginalizing the true signification of the scriptures, twisting their intended meaning, and misapplying their application. As Alma declared to the inhabitants of Ammonihah: "Behold, the scriptures are before you; if ye will wrest them it shall be to your own destruction." (Alma 13:20). Picking apart the scriptures can distort doctrine and pervert principles until they become meaningless fragments that lack any coherent connection.

Alma's son Corianton was an example of one who suffered a stupor of thought as a result of doctrinal misinterpretation. Until he understood and was committed to the principle of repentance, Corianton could not rebuild his troubled life and could not perform the missionary labor to which he had been called. Therefore, his father sought to remedy the situation by explaining the doctrine of justice, as it relates to the Atonement and to repentance, that had been troubling him.

The contrasting states of the inhabitants of the Spirit World are typified by

happiness or misery. Justice, Alma explained, demands "all things shall be restored to their proper order, every thing to its natural frame, raised to endless happiness to inherit the kingdom of God, or to endless misery to inherit the kingdom of the Devil." (Alma 41:4).

The mortal mission of the Savior, together with His Atonement, was to "redeem those who will be baptized unto repentance, through faith on his name. (Alma 9:27). Therein lies the difference between immortality and eternal life. The Atonement is for those who desire eternal life by repenting and then entering into the covenants. This is the Gospel Plan, that all might have the opportunity to benefit from the Law of Mercy, thereby to be propelled into the Celestial Kingdom, because the Savior of the world satisfied the demands of the Law of Justice through His Atonement for sin.

Joseph Smith once declared: "Happiness is the object and design of our existence and will be the end thereof, if we pursue the path that leads to it; and this path is virtue, uprightness, faithfulness, holiness, and keeping all the commandments of God." ("Teachings," p. 255). But God will always grant to His children agency to choose their own path, "for behold, they are their own judges, whether to do good or do evil." (Alma 41:7).

We can choose our own actions, but we cannot choose to escape the consequences of those actions. "The decrees of God are unalterable; therefore, the way is prepared that whosoever will, may walk therein and be saved." (Alma 41:8). But we cannot "be restored from sin to happiness." (Alma 41:10).

For emphasis, Alma cited a Hebrew Hokmah: "Wickedness never was happiness." (Alma 41:10). In the words of Samuel the Lamanite: "Ye have sought all the days of your lives for that which ye could not obtain; and ye have sought for happiness in doing iniquity, which thing is contrary to the nature of that righteousness which is in our great and Eternal Head." (Helaman 13:38).

Moroni taught that "despair cometh because of iniquity." (Moroni 10:22). Every

law has both a blessing and a punishment affixed to it. When the law is obeyed, a blessing is given that is related to happiness, or joy. When that law is disobeyed, the natural consequence is punishment that is related to unhappiness, or misery.

Ultimately, despair is the feeling of hopelessness that accompanies entrenched disobedience in the absence of repentance.

As Alma explained: "All men that are in a state of nature, or I would say, in a carnal state, are in the gall of bitterness and in the bonds of iniquity; they are without God in the world, and they have gone contrary to the nature of God; therefore, they are in a state contrary to the nature of happiness." (Alma 41:11). The Savior taught that those who lack vision, and build "upon the works of men, or upon the works of the devil, verily I say unto you they have joy in their works for a season, and by and by, the end cometh, and they are hewn down and cast into the fire, from whence there is no return." (3 Nephi 27:11).

As Corianton listened to his father, he began to understand that "the meaning of the word restoration is to bring back again evil for evil, or carnal for carnal, or devilish for devilish, good for that which is good; righteous for that which is righteous; just for that which is just; (and) merciful for that which is merciful." (Alma 41:13). So important was this principle, that Alma constructed the message in the form of a chiasm that is preserved in verses 13-15:

A – "O, my son, this is not the case; but the meaning of the word restoration is to bring back again evil for evil, or carnal for carnal, or devilish for devilish — good for that which is good; righteous for that which is righteous; just for that which is just; merciful for that which is merciful.

B – Therefore, my son, see that you are merciful unto your brethren; deal justly, judge righteously, and do good continually; and if ye do all these things then shall ye receive your reward.

B1 – Yea, ye shall have mercy restored unto you again; ye shall have justice restored unto you again; ye shall have a righteous judgment restored unto you again; and ye shall have good rewarded unto you again.

A1 - For that which ye do send out shall return unto you again, and be restored; therefore, the word restoration more fully condemneth the sinner, and justifieth him not at all."

Sometimes, it is very difficult to tell just what brings happiness. Both poverty and wealth have failed miserably. Neither fame nor anonymity holds the key. Neither sickness nor health has the ability. Both principalities and the absence of worldly influence are inadequate. Neither beauty nor the beast has the advantage.

Sometimes, people forget that when they pray for rain, and their prayers are answered, they are also going to have to deal with some mud. "The weaver's skillful hand sews threads of gold and silver, in the pattern he has planned." (Benjamin Malachi Franklin). People can never hope to understand the answers they receive, if they continue to ask the wrong questions, or if they formulate their petitions based on desires rather than on needs.

In fact, without the Lord's fitness program that achieves spiritual symmetry through the Atonement and temporal balance through repentance, day-to-day life in the lone and dreary world lacks coherence and stability. (See 1 Nephi 8:4). This is why Moroni taught that "despair cometh because of iniquity." (Moroni 10:22).

Alma closed this portion of his exhortation to Corianton by applying the principle of restoration directly to his son: "Therefore, my son, see that you are merciful unto your brethren; deal justly, judge righteously, and do good continually; and if ye do all these things then shall ye receive your reward; yea, ye shall have mercy restored unto you again; ye shall have justice restored unto you again; ye shall have a righteous judgment restored unto you again; and ye shall have good rewarded unto you again." (Alma 41:14).

The fundamental truth he wanted to emphasize was that restoration is as personal as being "at-one" with the Savior, and that which we send out shall return unto us again, in accordance with the Law of Compensation. (See Alma 41:15). Alma wanted Corianton to understand that justice and mercy are inexorably tied to the Atonement and to repentance.

Repentance allows us to feel good about our honesty with ourselves and with others. It empowers us to remain true to proven principles, faithful to our covenants, and diligent in doing good to all men, in whatever circumstances we might find ourselves.

We receive a testimony of the principle of repentance when it has uplifted us, motivated us, and inspired us to reconnect with our intrinsic nobility. We are converted to the principle of repentance when it has called us out of darkness into the marvelous Light of Christ. When scales of darkness fall from our eyes, we see more clearly that we are a chosen generation, a royal priesthood, a holy nation, and a peculiar people. (See 1 Peter 2:9).

Alma sought to rekindle in his son a bright hope in the future. He knew that Corianton would be comforted in his trials if he would allow the Light of the world to become his Mentor. He would be empowered to endure in righteousness, thanks to the rejuvenating power of repentance. Alma encouraged his son to try the virtue of the word of God, because he knew that if there is anything at all in this vale of tears that is lovely, or of good report or praiseworthy, he should seek after these things. (See the 13th Article of Faith, & Philippians 4:8).

By exercising the principle of repentance, Corianton would be able to reestablish synchronicity with the divine design that had been fashioned for him by God. He would enjoy the innumerable small coincidences that we have all experienced, that are really manifestations of God working behind the scenes in our behalf. With perfect repentance, everything would snap into focus. Intelligence would

cleave unto intelligence, wisdom would receive wisdom, truth would embrace its own, virtue would love virtue, light would cleave unto light, mercy would have compassion upon mercy and claim her own, justice would continue its course and claim its own, and righteous judgement would go before the face of heaven. (See D&C 88:40).

The commandment to repent would become an invitation for Corianton to join his Heavenly Father in His work and glory, which is to bring to bring to pass our immortality and eternal life. (See Moses 1:39). Corianton's repentance would contribute to order in the cosmos, so that the universe itself could become "a machine for the making of Gods." (Henri Bergson, "Two Sources of Religion and Morality"). His repentance would set everything in order; it would make everything right in the world. It would clear the way for "the Great and Eternal Plan of Deliverance From Death" to work its magic, by influencing not only his life, but that of countless others, until the earth would be "full of the knowledge of the Lord, as the waters cover the sea." (2 Nephi 11:5 & Isaiah 11:9).

"Christ is our advocate with the
Father, if we repent.
(J.S.T. 1 John 2:1).

Chapter Fourteen

Purposeful repentance.

We might want to think about the following five dozen things, as we prepare to repent: Follow The Plan of Salvation, defend the faith, lay our lives on the altar of sacrifice, confess our sins, consistently repent, pattern our lives after the Savior, express our thanks in prayer, reconcile ourselves to occasional negative responses to our petitions, gain scriptural fluency, focus on the positive, confront evil courageously, forgive others, obey the commandments, endure to the end in righteousness, recognize the merits of the principles of righteousness, righteously exercise what power or authority we possess, appreciate God as the sole source of our protection, determine to serve Him, acknowledge His majesty and power and that of His servants, recognize His presence in the earth around us, validate the wisdom of our self-government by the righteous exercise of our agency, indicate by our actions that we understand the true value of things, refrain from coveting the profane things of the world, understand the relationship between commandments and blessings, multiply our talents, turn our weaknesses into strengths, use our means wisely, manage our time carefully, order our priorities, maintain our perspective even when our days seem purposeless, change our heart through faith on His name, accept responsibility for our actions, fervently

safeguard our agency, transform our failures into learning experiences, bear adversity well, distinguish between the detours that are distractions and those that are dead-ends, identify the challenges that are opportunities for personal growth, preserve an eternal perspective in times of adversity, keep our chin up, consecrate our time and talents, sacrifice (seemingly), be anxiously engaged, perform acts of quiet Christianity, open our arms to those around us, love our neighbors, teach others what we have learned, perform missionary service, acknowledge the qualities of goodness in others, express appreciation, recognize how precious our divine attributes are, read the scriptures, promote the cause of Zion, magnify our callings, shout Hosannas to the Lord, remain valiant in our testimonies of Jesus, worship God in the temple, honor our covenants, observe the Word of Wisdom, be temperate and not easily provoked to anger, cultivate integrity, view education as a life-long process, know how to work, nurture family relationships, and take our responsibilities as teachers and as mentors seriously.

"Repent, and prepare
ye the way of the Lord, and
make his paths straight;
for the kingdom of
heaven is at hand."
(D&C 33:10).

Chapter Fifteen

Have I been forgiven?

Following repentance, how can we know if we have received forgiveness of our sins? In Mosiah 5:1-4, Mormon identified three key factors.

"And now, it came to pass that when king Benjamin had thus spoken to his people, he sent among them, desiring to know of his people if they believed the words which he had spoken unto them. And they all cried with one voice, saying: Yea, we believe all the words which thou hast spoken unto us; and also, we know of their surety and truth, because of the Spirit of the Lord Omnipotent, which has wrought a mighty change in us, or in our hearts, that we have no more disposition to do evil, but to do good continually. And we, ourselves, also, through the infinite goodness of God, and the manifestations of his Spirit, have great views of that which is to come; and were it expedient, we could prophesy of all things. And it is the faith which we have had on the things which our king has spoken unto us that has brought us to this great knowledge, whereby we do rejoice with such exceedingly great joy." (Mosiah 5:1-4).

<u>First, the Spirit of the Lord comes upon us.</u>

When we have His Spirit, our lives are dramatically quickened and we are as white-hot sparks struck off the divine anvil of God. When we are in harmony with God's purposes and His Spirit envelops our lives, they can become almost sacramental.

"I said to the man who stood at the gate of the year, 'Give me a light, that I may tread safely into the unknown.' And he replied, 'Go out into the darkness, and put your hand in the hand of God. That shall be to you better than a light, and safer than the known way.' (Minnie Lou Haskins, "A Dialogue Between a Man, and The Keeper of The Gate of The Year").

<u>Secondly, we feel a mighty change in our hearts and we are filled with joy.</u>

The people understood what Benjamin meant, when he described their feelings: "For behold, this day he hath spiritually begotten you; for ye say that your hearts are changed through faith on his name; therefore, ye are born of him and have become his sons and his daughters." (Mosiah 5:7).

Lehi had taught: "Adam fell that men might be, and men are that they might have joy." (2 Nephi 2:25). This is one of the basic messages of the Restoration. When the Fall of Adam is considered in conjunction with repentance through the Atonement of Christ, it is clear that both are part of God's Plan of Eternal Progression for us, and that its intended goal is our happiness. In fact, Joseph Smith said: "Happiness is the object and design of our existence and will be the end thereof, if we pursue the path that leads to it; and this path is virtue, uprightness, faithfulness, holiness, and keeping all the commandments of God." ("Teachings," p. 255). For we are "spirit, the elements are eternal, and spirit and element, inseparably connected" through obedience to the principles of the Gospel "receive a fulness of joy." (D&C 93:33).

<u>Lastly, we have peace of conscience. We have no more disposition to do evil, but to do good continually.</u>

The desired result of all Gospel-oriented teaching is achieved when a mighty

change has been wrought in our hearts and our dispositions have changed. We have the spirit of prophecy, the testimony of Jesus, and great knowledge of the mysteries, all gained by personal revelation. We have been born again, not by maturation, but by generation. As Paul wrote: "If any man be in Christ, he is a new creature. Old things are passed away; behold, all things are become new." (2 Corinthians 5:7). Joseph Smith showed us the way in his last hours of mortality, when he declared: "I have a conscience void of offense towards God, and towards all men." (D&C 135:5).

"Those
who harden their
hearts will not be saved;
those who repent will enter
into the Lord's rest."
(J.S.T. Hebrews 4:3).

Chapter Sixteen

Father, forgive them.

Through the mouth of His prophet Isaiah, the Lord reassured Israel: "Fear not, for" not just with fickle favoritism, but "with <u>everlasting kindness</u> will I have mercy on thee." (3 Nephi 22:4 & 8, underlining mine). Not only would the Lord be merciful, but He would be so perpetually, ceaselessly, permanently, and interminably. His forgiveness would be endless and eternal.

He further promised His covenant children: "No weapon that is formed against thee shall prosper, and every tongue that shall revile against thee in judgment thou shalt condemn." (Isaiah 54:17). The Lord knows firsthand what weapons are most effective in the battle that is raging in our hearts. He knows that philosophical, conceptual, moral, ethical, and sociopolitical weapons that are unleashed by the tongue are far more destructive than bombs and bullets, for they can kill the spirit, rather than just the body.

In the courtyard of Pilate, the Jews raised their voices to condemn the Bridegroom to whom they had been betrothed. Contrasted against His infinite capacity to forgive

sin when it is followed by heart-felt repentance, their words must have stung His ears, when He heard them cry out with awful self-incrimination: "His blood be on us, and on our children." (Matthew 27:5).

If there were ever justification for the Savior to harbor bitter feelings toward those who had wronged Him, it would have been as He staggered under the weight of His cross along the Via Dolorosa, the "Way of Grief, Sorrow, and Suffering," or simply the "Painful Way." Knowing that every step would bring Him closer to Calvary, anguish must have rolled over Him in waves as He grappled with the fact that His suffering in the Garden of Gethsemane had been the result of betrayal by those who had no inclination to repent, or in any other way to take advantage of the Atonement. Nevertheless, although the Revelation of God (see John 1:1) had fallen upon deaf ears, and the foundation of faith had been eroded, the hope of salvation had been destroyed, and there was neither root nor branch upon which the guilty could stand, not a word of recrimination ever fell from His lips. "And He answered (Pilate) to never a word, insomuch that the governor marvelled greatly." (Matthew 27:14).

Then, on the Cross at Calvary, just as the curtain was about to be drawn upon His mortal ministry, the Savior looked down upon the Roman soldiers who had crucified Him, and uttered these ten remarkable words: "Father, forgive them, for they know not what they do." (Luke 23:34).

Just three days later, "Mary Magdalene, and Joanna, and Mary the mother of James, and other women that were with them," found the Apostles gathered together, and told them about their experience before an empty tomb. (Luke 24:10). At first, the words of the women seemed to the Apostles "as idle tales, and they believed them not. (But) then arose Peter, and ran unto the sepulchre; and stooping down, he beheld the linen clothes laid by themselves, and departed, wondering in himself at that which was come to pass." (Luke 24:11-12). Not long thereafter, the resurrected Savior appeared to His repentant Apostle, and doubtless comforted him. (See Luke 24:34 & 1 Corinthians 15:5).

Long before any of these events transpired, and even before the foundation of the world, the Savior had begun to consistently accumulate reserves in His spiritual bank account to be used against the day when He would need them most. He knew from the beginning, even before The Great and Eternal Plan of Deliverance from Death (2 Nephi 11:5) had been explained to His Father's children, that His was to be an infinite and eternal Atonement for every sin that would ever be committed by His brothers and sisters. Thus, when the critical hour came in the Garden of Gethsemane, followed by the mockery of his trial before Pilate and His crucifixion on Calvary, He was able to plumb the limitless depths of His mercy and extend His magnificent forgiveness to those who had so grievously offended Him. "

He was wounded for our transgressions, (and) he was bruised for our iniquities. The chastisement of our peace was upon him, and (yet) with his stripes we are healed." (Isaiah 53:5). Thus, did His prophet Isaiah describe the reach of the Atonement, over 700 years before the mortal ministry of the Savior. His sacrifice extends to neutralize the sins of the best of us and the worst of us; it was infinite in both its temporal and eternal influence, and it only waits upon our initiative to manifest its power.

As Alma declared about 125 years before Christ's agony in Gethsemane: "The Atonement (was) prepared from the foundation of the world, that thereby salvation might come to him that should put his trust in the Lord, and should be diligent in keeping His commandments, and continue in the faith even unto the end of his life." (Mosiah 4:6). The Atonement to which Alma referred took into account every sin that would be individually or collectively committed by the family of man, beginning at the foundation of the world and only ending after the Lord has come a second time to usher in His millennial reign on earth. The Atonement anticipated the shortcomings, the sins of omission, and the sins of commission that would be frustratingly, repetitively, and painfully committed by every generation of the children of men, from the beginning to the end of time. It is all the more remarkable to realize that the Atonement is so comprehensive in its scope that

it anticipated sins that had not yet been committed, for the Lord knows us; He knows what is in our hearts, whether we will keep His commandments, or not. (See Deuteronomy 8:2).

When the Savior stood before the Council and said to His Father: "Here am I, send me," (Abraham 3:27), He knew full well the price that would be required to satisfy Justice in order to obtain mercy. He had the spiritual capacity to make such a statement, but even his maturity as a God in Heaven could not take away the anticipatory pain He must have felt, even then, for the scriptures describe Him as the "lamb slain from the foundation of the world." (Revelation 13:8).

We, who participated in the Council, easily and enthusiastically raised our arms to the square when our Father's proposal was brought to a vote. (See Job 38:7). But could we have truly felt the import of the moment? He was not only making history, but He was also creating a binding foundation and precedent to re-write history itself. We were eyewitnesses to the vitalization of "The Merciful Plan of The Great Creator." (2 Nephi 9:6).

As the poet wrote: "There was a little girl who had a little curl right in the middle of her forehead. When she was good, she was very, very good. And when she was bad, her Heavenly Father loved here anyway." (Kristen McKee, "Nursery Rhymes for the Unconditional and Unschooled").

In our pre-mortal life, we must have palpably sensed the enveloping reach of the Savior's love for us. We must have understood His quintessential example of humility, His supreme act of selflessness, and His superlative expression of altruism. He had just become our personal Redeemer, and had activated in our behalf the power of the Atonement. The key to our happiness was the plain and precious reality of the sacrifice of the Savior of the world, the doctrine of Christ. (See 2 Nephi 21:31). Forgiveness of sin through repentance would be based upon our correct understanding of the Atonement, which was why it was surely the foundation of the curriculum that prepared us for mortality.

Still, we wonder how we could have comprehended the profound significance of the events that were unfolding before us; that the exercise of our free will had just been guaranteed, the principles of The Plan certified, the price of our future offenses successfully negotiated, the guarantee of payment to satisfy the debt made in advance, and the demands of Justice equally balanced against Mercy. We even witnessed the preparation of cherubim and a flaming sword that would guard the way and insure our hope of eternal progression.

Our Heavenly Father's work and glory had been confirmed. According to His Plan, all the world would become a stage, and we would become the players thereon, with our entrances and our exits predetermined by divine design. (See Shakespeare, "As You Like It," Act 2, Scene 7). His work and glory would influence us to become method actors so immersed in our parts, and so determined to learn our lines, that immortality and eternal life would flow as the natural consequence of our active engagement in the theater of life. (See Moses 1:39).

As Aaron taught King Lamoni's father around a hundred years before the mortal ministry of the Savior: "Since man had fallen, he could not merit anything of himself; but the sufferings and death of Christ atone for their sins, through faith and repentance, (and) he breaketh the bands of death, that the grave shall have no victory ... that the sting of death should be swallowed up in the hopes of glory." (Alma 22:14, see Colossians 1:27).

Today, we repent that the God of our Lord Jesus Christ, the Father of glory, might give unto us the spirit of wisdom and revelation, that the eyes of our understanding might be enlightened, that we might embrace the hope of the high calling of Jesus Christ, and that the riches of glory might abide as an inheritance in for those who are faithful to the teachings of The Church of Jesus Christ of Latter-day Saints. (See Ephesians 1:17-18).

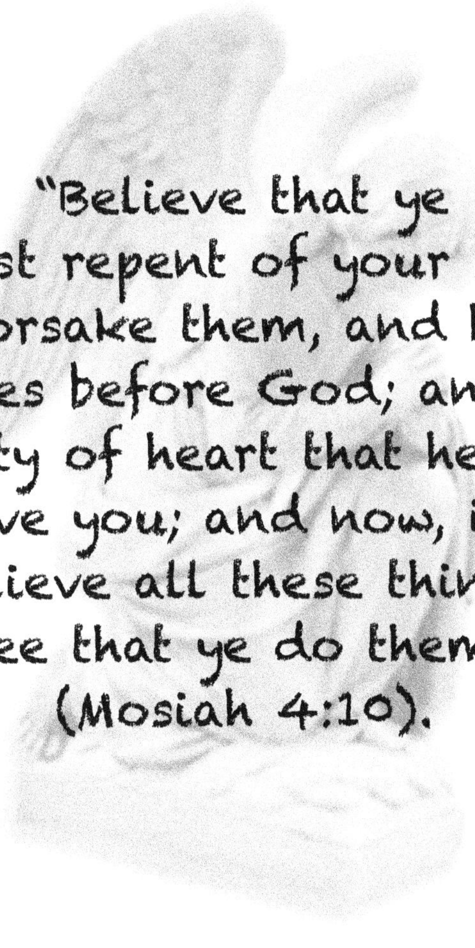

"Believe that ye
must repent of your sins
and forsake them, and humble
yourselves before God; and ask in
sincerity of heart that he would
forgive you; and now, if you
believe all these things,
see that ye do them."
(Mosiah 4:10).

Chapter Seventeen

Before a wound can heal.

"Repentance is the first pressure we feel, when
we are drawn to the bosom of God."
(Jeffrey R. Holland)

"The first condition of happiness is a clear conscience. (David O. McKay, "Gospel Ideals," 1976). In physical terms, before a wound can heal, it has to be clean. Anyone who has had a physician vigorously scrub out a wound knows how carefully and thoroughly the task must be accomplished before sterile dressings may be applied to allow the healing process to begin. The same principle applies to character development.

The purpose of life is to grow and progress in stature, until we have developed the image and likeness of our Heavenly Father. (See 2 Peter 3:18 & 3 Nephi 28:10). During the process, we will fail to measure up again and again. This creates a problem because "no unclean thing can dwell with God," and yet it is human nature to repeatedly violate eternal law. (1 Nephi 10:21). Unfortunately, sin stops our progress. God, however, has provided the principle of repentance so that we may

yet become holy. Therefore, we are commanded: "All men, everywhere, must repent." (Moses 6:57).

David O. McKay taught: "Spirituality is the consciousness of victory over self, and of communion with the infinite." (C.R., 10/1969). The Spirit invites us to try the virtue of the word of God, and leads us to sainthood through repentance and forgiveness because of the Atonement of Christ. As we submit to His will, we develop His nature and character. His gentle counsel is: "All that I have, I could give to you, but what I am, you must earn for yourself, line upon line, and precept upon precept. (See D&C 98:12).

The great blessing of repentance is that it allows us to become clean in the sight of God, and to get moving again on the pathway to perfection. After our repentance, God will forgive us, and remember our sins no more. It is true that we might retain a remembrance of them, insofar as they increase our testimonies and strengthen us to become more stalwart soldiers in the Army of Christ. But we will no longer feel the guilt or suffer the consequences of disobedience that include withdrawal of the Spirit.

Repentance, then, can satisfy a two-fold purpose. First, it allows us to be justified by the Spirit, to become holy, sanctified, and qualified to enter the Presence of the Lord. Secondly, it serves to strengthen existing testimony, which makes it more unlikely that we will yield to temptation in the future. For example, after his exhortation to them, King Benjamin's people "cried with one voice, saying ... the Spirit of the Lord Omnipotent ... has wrought a mighty change in us, or in our hearts, that we have no more disposition to do evil, but to do good continually." These people made a covenant to forsake their sins, and to keep the commandments, in order to avoid the otherwise inevitable consequences of disobedient behavior. (Mosiah 5:2 & 5). They knew that their repentance was complete when the Spirit of the Lord fell upon them, for they were filled with joy, and they had peace of conscience.

In his last hours of mortality, Joseph Smith was similarly able to declare: "I have

a conscience void of offense towards God, and towards all men." (D&C 135:5). He gave us all the confidence to walk in the valley of the shadow of death and yet to fear no evil. (See Psalms 23:4). "Life actually has no significance except as a preparation for the ultimate goal of death. In Christianity, the meaning of existence is consummated in its end." (Carl Jung). For Latter-day Saints, "one of the greatest contributions of Joseph Smith was his knowledge of what is to come after death. He did much to clarify our understanding of heaven, and to make it seem worth working for." ("My Religion and Me Lesson Manual").

The sons of Mosiah had a similar effect upon those whom they taught in the Land of Nephi. (See Alma 23). Their Lamanite converts left behind their former lives, giving up all their sins to know the Savior. They changed their names and became Saints, promising to never again return to their wicked ways. They embraced the cultural lifestyle and traditions of the Nephite missionaries, and opened up a lasting correspondence with them. As the scales of darkness began to fall from their eyes, they become a pure and delightsome people. This remarkable transformation was accomplished in a very short time under the cleansing influence of the Spirit. When the Light of Christ is given the opportunity, it does the same thing today for all the people of the earth, for it is "the power of God unto salvation." (Romans 1:16).

Repentance that brings about such change requires great courage, much strength, many tears, unceasing prayers, and untiring efforts. It also requires a Redeemer to provide an Atonement to satisfy the demands of Justice. "There is no royal road to repentance, no privileged path to forgiveness. We must all follow the same course whether we are rich or poor, educated or untrained, tall or short, prince or pauper, king or commoner. There is only one way. It is long road, spiked with thorns and briars and pitfalls and problems." (Spencer W. Kimball, "The Miracle of Forgiveness," p. 149). It may require that we travel a path leading to our own personal Gethsemane, on to Calvary, and then to a quietly empty Garden Tomb. But reaching our destination makes the journey worth the effort.

In order to repent, we must recognize our sins. This might at first sound like a trivial point, but we should remember Alma's wise counsel to his son that applies to us all: "Let your sins trouble you," he urged Corianton, "with that trouble which shall bring you down unto repentance. Do not endeavor to excuse yourself in the least point." (Alma 42:29-30).

We must feel sorrow for our sins. We must feel remorseful, even terrible about them. We must feel profoundly filthy. We must want to unload and abandon them. We must be almost obsessive-compulsive about cleansing our souls. We must be broken in heart, and have the spirit of contrition. (See D&C 20:37). A broken heart is softened to receive the things of the Spirit, and is teachable. It is "to be broken down with deep sorrow for sin, to be humble and thoroughly penitent." (Bruce R. McConkie, "Mormon Doctrine," p. 161). At that level of spiritual preparation, when our faith has convicted us of our sins, we must be prepared to ask, as did those on the Day of Pentecost: "What shall we do?" The answer is straightforward: "Repent and be baptized every one of you in the name of Jesus Christ for the remission of sins." (Acts 2:37-38).

We must acknowledge and abandon our sins. "By this ye may know if a man repenteth of his sins - behold, he will confess them and forsake them." (D&C 58:43). Confession removes a heavy burden from our backs. The Lord has promised, "I, the Lord, forgive sins, and am merciful unto those who confess their sins with humble hearts." (D&C 61:2).

All sins must be confessed to God, but those that might affect our standing in the Church should be confessed to the proper priesthood authority, as well. In our day, the bishop and others in comparable positions can forgive in the sense of waiving the penalties. In this capacity, the bishop represents the Lord. This is why it is proper that members confess their sins to the Bishop, when those sins might jeopardize their standing in the Kingdom. Church judicial action as it relates to members is required for three reasons: to preserve the good name of the Church, to help the

sinner on the pathway to repentance and forgiveness, and to insure impartiality when priesthood leaders deal with Church members.

However, only the Lord "hath power on earth to forgive sins." (Matthew 9:6). But He recognizes that even the righteous do not become perfect overnight. Therefore, He has promised: "As often as my people repent will I forgive them their trespasses against me." (Mosiah 26:30). Of those who will not repent, however, He said: "The same shall not be numbered among my people." (Mosiah 26:32). The removal of one's name from the records of the Church is the extent of the penalty.

"We believe that all religious societies have a right to deal with their members for disorderly conduct, according to the rules and regulations of such societies; provided that such dealings be for fellowship and good standing; but we do not believe that any religious society has authority to try men on the right of property or life, to take from them this world's goods, or to put them in jeopardy of either life or limb, or to inflict any physical punishment upon them. They can only excommunicate them from their society, and withdraw from them their fellowship." (D&C 134:10).

We must make restitution, if possible, when we have sinned against another. Wrongs must be righted and fences mended. The truth is that restitution can be therapeutic for the transgressor, as well as for the offended party, for "that which ye do send out shall return unto you again." (Alma 41:15).

We must forgive others. "Wherefore, I say unto you, that ye ought to forgive one another; for he that forgiveth not his brother his trespasses standeth condemned before the Lord; for there remaineth in him the greater sin." (D&C 64:9). We may find that "enduring to the end" simply involves mastery of two principles: repentance for our own sins, and forgiveness of others. The Savior obtained forgiveness for the sins of mankind only after the most excruciating suffering on His part. Is it, then, too much for Him to ask us to forgive each other? He recognized that The Plan of Redemption breaks down without our forgiveness, which is really

a celestial barometer that measures our testimony temperature. Christ requires forgiveness by those who would be obedient to the Laws of His Kingdom simply because they must do so in order to feel comfortable living there. He commanded Joseph Smith: "I, the Lord, will forgive whom I will forgive, but of you it is required to forgive all men." (D&C 64:10). Brigham Young is reported to have put it a little more bluntly, when he declared: "He who takes offense when none was intended is a fool, and he who takes offense when one was intended is usually a fool." Someone once observed that if someone who has offended you is standing between you and the Lord, it is he who is still closer to heaven.

When we withhold our love, we repudiate the Spirit of Christ in a brazen confirmation that we never really knew Him, and that for us He lived in vain. It means that His teachings suggested nothing to us, and that in all our thoughts we were never really near enough to Him to be seized with the spell of His compassion for the world. We are only fully repentant when we have charity or the pure love of Christ, and are strictly obedient to the principle of forgiveness, and that door swings both ways.

Only when the process of repentance has been completed, does the Atonement become fully effective in our lives. "My soul was harrowed up to the greatest degree and racked with all my sins," Alma recalled. "Yea, I did remember all my sins and iniquities, for which I was tormented with the pains of hell; yea, I saw that I had rebelled against my God, and that I had not kept his holy commandments. So great had been my iniquities, that the very thought of coming into the presence of my God did rack my soul with inexpressible horror. It came to pass that as I was ... harrowed up by the memories of my many sins, behold, I remembered also to have heard my father prophesy ... concerning the coming of one Jesus Christ, a Son of God, to atone for the sins of the world.

Now, as my mind caught hold upon this thought, I cried within my heart: O Jesus, thou Son of God, have mercy on me. And now, behold, when I thought this, I could remember my pains no more. And oh, what joy, and what marvelous light I did

behold; yea, my soul was filled with joy as exceeding as (had been) my pain! There can be nothing so exquisite and sweet as was my joy." (Alma 36:12-14, 17-21).

What a great Plan of our Father! Live our lives, push the envelope, and dare to take risks. After the Plan has been explained to us, if we fail to abide by its laws, Jesus Christ will take the heat. The beauty of The Plan is that if we Recognize our mistakes, if we experience Remorse for having made them, if we attempt to make Restitution if our behavior has wronged others, if we learn from the mistake and Reform our ways, and Resolve to Refrain from repeating it, we will be free to continue the path of progress, with a complete Resolution of what would have otherwise been an incapacitating short-coming.

The unique source of that peace is our complete and all- encompassing repentance, the power of the Savior's Atonement that transforms us, and Heavenly Father's consequent forgiveness of our sins. Such is our cleansing that we may "manifest unto the people," as did Alma, that we have "been born of God." (Alma 36:23). As Parley P. Pratt declared: "I have received the holy anointing, and I can never rest until the last enemy is conquered, death destroyed, and truth reigns triumphant." ("Deseret News," 4/30/1853).

Each of us may share that intensity of feeling when we have conquered those self-defeating behaviors and character traits that limit our progression. The Prophet Joseph Smith is reported to have declared: "Salvation consists in a man's being placed beyond the power of his enemies, meaning the enemies of his progression, such as dishonesty, greediness, lying, immorality, and other vices." On another occasion, he taught: "Salvation consists in the glory, authority, majesty, power and dominion which Jehovah possesses and in nothing else; and no being can possess it but himself or one like Him." ("Lectures on Faith #7).

We should repent now, in order to become like Him; in order "to prepare to meet God." (Alma 34:32). It is difficult to learn a skill all at once, but it is easy if we repetitively practice each day until we gain mastery. We are past repentance only

when we no longer have the will or the desire to do so. As Spencer W. Kimball wrote: "It is true that the great principle of repentance is always available, but for the wicked and rebellious there are serious reservations to this statement. For instance, sin is intensely habit forming, and sometimes moves us to the tragic point of no return. Without repentance there can be no forgiveness, and without forgiveness all the blessings of eternity hang in jeopardy. As the transgressor moves deeper and deeper in his sin, and the error is entrenched more deeply and the will to change is weakened, it becomes increasingly near hopeless and he skids down and down until either he does not want to climb back, or he has lost the power to do so." ("The Miracle of Forgiveness," p. 117).

The Savior said that we must be perfect, for otherwise we cannot inherit the Kingdom of God. Perhaps He meant that we must be perfect in our repentance. After explaining to his people the great Plan of Redemption that solved the dilemma created by God's demand for perfection coupled with our inability to live sinless lives, the prophet Jacob simply stated:" O be wise; what can I say more?" (Jacob 6:12). Moroni offered the same message: "Be wise in the days of your probation: strip yourselves of all uncleanness ... Ask with a firmness unshaken, that ye will yield to no temptation, but that ye will serve the true and living God." (Mormon 9:28).

"Repent, all ye ends of the earth, and come unto me, and be baptized in my name, that ye may be sanctified by the reception of the Holy Ghost, that ye may stand spotless before me at the last day."
(3 Nephi 27:20).

Chapter Eighteen

Just get back on the bike.

"The race is not to the swift."
(Ecclesiastes 9:11).

When my grandson Parker Edwards was 10 years old, his interest in dirt bikes reached an almost feverish pitch. For a time, his excitement exceeded his skill, and he consequently took his fair share of spills. Motorcycling can be a lot of work, and for a ten-year-old it can be exhausting, especially in the aftermath of a yard-sale crash. Fortunately, our motorcycling experiences have been (for the most part) free of serious injury, 1) because of Parker's skill, 2) because of his ability to carefully follow instructions, 3) because of attentive parental control, and 4) because of a serious investment in protective equipment.

Nevertheless, after an especially grueling morning at the ORV Park in the Coast Range west of Portland, Oregon, Parker was ready to hang it up right there on the trail, and just walk away from his (upside-down) bike. The only problem was that we were miles from the parking lot, and slinking away to lick his wounds was not really a viable option. I was impressed with the simple wisdom and broad

application of the counsel given to Parker by his father, when he gently said: "Just get back on the bike."

I think dirt biking is similar to our life experiences. Maybe that's why I enjoy it so much. We can be zooming along standing on our foot-pegs without a care in the world, with the wind in our face, and enjoying the freedom of the trail. Then, almost without warning, we might hit a rock that jerks the handlebars sideways, causing us to lose our sure grip, and we suddenly find ourselves one with mother earth. (Maybe that's why we call it "dirt-biking!").

When life throws us a curve, and we go south when the trail goes north, we need to remember to "Just get back on the bike." When we do, and I think of Parker when I say this, we'll find that in no time, we'll forget the spill, as we twist the throttle to get back up to speed, looking with eager anticipation for the next opportunity to get serious air. Then, when the next rock in the trail looms before us, we'll be the wiser for our experiences, we'll be less intimidated, and we'll be better prepared to avoid another close encounter of the dirt kind.

"As many of the Gentiles as will repent are the covenant people of the Lord; and as many of the Jews as will not repent shall be cast off; for the Lord covenanteth with none save it be with them that repent and believe in his Son, who is the Holy One of Israel."
(2 Nephi 30:2).

Chapter Nineteen

Removing the barnacles of life.

Portland, Oregon lies on the Columbia River, over 75 miles from the Pacific Ocean. Yet, ocean-going ships regularly cross the treacherous Columbia Bar at the mouth of the river, to steam upstream to deliver and take on cargo at Portland's bustling wharves. There are easier ports of call, but a trip to Portland every now and then is worthwhile for at least one special reason.

The barnacles that attach to the hull can proliferate and create significant drag as ships makes their way through the water. This creates inefficiency that translates into increased fuel costs that can become prohibitively expensive. Additionally, if the barnacles work their way onto the rudder mechanism, they can seriously compromise the ability of the captain to smoothly move the ship forward toward its intended destination.

But those barnacles thrive only in salt water. Fresh water kills them, and when they die, they lose their grip on the ship's hull and fall off in the water. Thus, the accumulation from months or years of contamination can be eliminated in just a few days as the ship moves through fresh river water, leaving it "as good as new."

In a similar fashion, we can rid ourselves of "the barnacles of life" that would otherwise compromise our life's mission or purpose. This can be done by completely immersing ourselves in living water that leave us afresh and anew, and with a feeling afterward that can be almost indescribable.

"Neither did they receive
any unto baptism save they
came forth with a broken heart
and a contrite spirit, and witnessed
unto the church that they truly
repented of all their sins."
(Moroni 6:2).

Chapter Twenty

The door swings both ways.

"God so loved the world that He gave his Only Begotten Son, that whosoever believeth in Him should not perish, but have everlasting life." (John 3:16). He is involved in our lives in the most intensely personal way possible, for He sent His Firstborn Son to be our Savior. (See D&C 88:5). When we are at one with Him, we are quickened, filled with joy, and are at peace. We are able to declare, as did Joseph Smith: "I have a conscience void of offense towards God, and towards all men." (D&C 135:5).

The Savior died to loose the bands of death that bind us. (See Alma 7:12). In Gethsemane, he accepted our weaknesses in order to know "how to succor his people according to their infirmities." (Alma 7:12). The crucified Christ is the primary focus of Christianity today, but if we fail to understand the Mortal Messiah, we receive only a one-dimensional view that ignores the wonderful symmetry of His humanity and divinity. His example teaches us that in spite of our own hardships we may look to Him for understanding as we develop empathy to put our own trials into perspective. He taught us to be patient even in the face of challenges whose portion seems unfair, whose difficulty seems unreasonable, and

whose proportions seem insurmountable. In addition to forgiveness for our sins, one of the blessings of repentance is that we will receive the strength to endure suffering that is not of our own making. "If we can bear our afflictions with understanding, faith, and courage, we shall be strengthened and comforted and spared the torment which accompanies the mistaken idea that all suffering comes as a chastisement for transgression." (Marion G. Romney, C.R., 10/1964).

Latter-day Saints tend to emphasize the Savior's suffering in Gethsemane as the pivotal experience circumscribing His sacrifice, but it was really a many-faceted drama played out on different stages.

It began even before the creation of the earth, for the scriptures identify Jesus Christ as "the Lamb slain from the foundation of the world." (Revelation 13:8). It will only end when the Redeemer has interceded for the last repentant sinner. Alma said of the Savior's ministry: "And he shall go forth, suffering pains and afflictions and temptations of every kind; and this that the word might be fulfilled which saith he will take upon him the pains and the sicknesses of his people." (Alma 7:11). It seems that the work in which He was engaged followed a natural progression until His preparation was complete and every necessary detail relating to the Atonement had been worked out. Early in His ministry, Jesus said: "My time is not yet come." (John 7:6). But later, when all had been accomplished, He confirmed: "My time is at hand." (Matthew 26:18). Gethsemane, Calvary, and the empty tomb validate His thorough preparation. Ours generally needs some more time. For example, we may be perfect in our repentance, but we may need to hone our capacity to forgive others.

As we struggle to deal with their trespasses, it is well to remember that we are all unprofitable servants. That is because we can do nothing that puts God in our debt. The Sacrifice of His Son is completely beyond our ability to pay. But He does not ask us to settle our account with Him; He only asks that we keep the commandments. These include perfect repentance leading to forgiveness, and perfect forgiveness of others leading to peace of mind. The marvel of His love is that the more we try to

do this, the more He blesses us. Therefore, we become even more deeply indebted to Him and remain so forever. Ultimately, when we are redeemed by the precious blood of Jesus Christ, it will be by His grace alone that we enjoy salvation. (See Ephesians 2:5 & 2 Nephi 25:23).

We are as the dust of the earth and are as nothing in comparison to our debt to God. (See Mosiah 2:5 & Helaman 12:7). In this sense, Brigham Young declared: "There is no man who ever made a sacrifice on this earth for the kingdom of heaven except the Savior. I would not give the ashes of a rye straw for that man who feels that he is making a sacrifice for God. We are doing this for our own happiness, welfare, and exaltation, and for nobody else's. What we do, we do for the salvation of the inhabitants of the earth, not for the salvation of the heavens, the angels, or God." (J.D., 16:114).

Learning to forgive another can be a lifetime process and drawn out struggle. God knew this might be the case, so He said: "I will give unto the children of men line upon line, precept upon precept, here a little and there a little; and blessed are those who hearken unto my precepts, and lend an ear unto my counsel, for they shall learn wisdom." (2 Nephi 28:30). It may take time and the experience may feel like our own personal Gethsemane, but the reward will be wisdom and increased capacity, understanding, knowledge, insight, and perception. Our experiences with others are designed to try us and prove us (D&C 98:12), and they give us "consolation by holding forth that which is to come, confirming our hope!" (D&C 128:31).

As we go through life, "enduring to the end" includes intimate mastery of two principles: repentance for our own sins and forgiveness of others. The Savior obtained forgiveness for the sins of mankind only after the most excruciating suffering on His part. Is it, then, too much for Him to ask us to forgive each other, even though it might be staggeringly painful to do so? He recognized that unless this frequently overlooked dimension of forgiveness is a part of our daily lives, The Plan of Redemption will fail and our souls will be lost. The depth and breadth of our forgiveness, then, is a celestial sphygmomanometer that measures the way

we deal with the high blood pressure of self-inflicted pain and the telestial trauma seemingly exacted by others. Its quality is a cosmic compass, pointing us toward eternal life. It is a stethoscope, gauging the vital capacity of prideful hearts that must be broken in contrition in order to exhibit the steady sinus rhythm that confirms perfect harmony with the proven principles of perfection.

Our forgiveness acts as a pacemaker, measuring out therapeutic doses of doctrinal energy. If we are to have a stable heart rate and avoid the angina of anguish we must be absolutely and unconditionally forgiving. If we want to one day live comfortably with our Heavenly Father in His Celestial Kingdom, we must first put the nitroglycerin tablets of tenderness under our tongues to temper the urge to use them as weapons to lash out at others who may have offended us. Taking 81 mg. tablets of the aspirin of acceptance of others will assuage our annoyance with them and reconcile us to those whom we feel may have taken advantage of us. The Lord commanded Joseph Smith: "I, the Lord, will forgive whom I will forgive, but of you it is required to forgive all men." (D&C 64:10). Brigham Young is said to have put it a little more bluntly: "He who takes offense when none was intended is a fool, and he who takes offense when one was intended is usually a fool." We are only fully repentant when we endure to the end in righteousness by being strictly obedient to the principle of forgiveness, and that door swings both ways.

"Concerning the holy order,
or this high priesthood, there were
many who were ordained and became high
priests of God; and it was on account of their
exceeding faith and repentance, and their
righteousness before God, they choosing
to repent and work righteousness
rather than to perish."
(Alma 13:10).

Chapter Twenty One

You are a work in progress.

"Even the humblest human beings, Pope John Paul II observed, are naturally philosophic, asking themselves such questions as Who am I? Where do I come from, and where am I going? Religious revelation provides answers to these questions, the Pope acknowledged." ("Uniting Faith and Reason," Time Magazine, 10/26/1998). Truly did Shakespeare muse: "All the world's a stage," for life is a Three Act Play and we are willing participants in a drama whose script was written long before the earth fell into existence. ("As You Like It," Act 2, Scene 7).

The First Act took place during our pre-earth life, where our Father nurtured us by His side. The Second Act takes place here on the earth, where we have come for a brief sojourn to have experiences that only mortality can offer. The Third Act will take place after physical death overtakes us and on the wings of angels we are carried back home. The name of the three-act play is The Plan of Salvation. (See Moses 6:62).

We pay dearly for our secular education and expect a handsome return on our investment. But our reintroduction to the elements of The Plan is equivalent to

matriculating in a bachelor of independent study fine arts program. Its only entrance requirement is a ready heart and a willing mind, and there is no temporal tuition. Its far-reaching design and sole purpose is to shepherd us back to our heavenly home. In the course catalogue, primarily The Pearl of Great Price and

The Book of Mormon, it is variously called The Plan of Salvation (Alma 24:14), The Plan of Salvation Unto all Men (Moses 6:62), The Great Plan of Salvation (Alma 42:5), The Plan of Our God (2 Nephi 9:13), The Plan of Restoration (Alma 41:2), The Great Plan of the Eternal God (Alma 34:9), The Plan of Redemption (Alma 29:2), The Great Plan of Redemption (Alma 34:31), The Great and Eternal Plan of Redemption (Alma 34:16), The Plan of Mercy (Alma 42:15), The Great Plan of Mercy (Alma 42:31), The Great and Eternal Plan of Deliverance from Death (2 Nephi 11:5), The Merciful Plan of The Great Creator (2 Nephi 9:6), and those two perennial favorites, The Plan of Happiness (Alma 42:16), and The Great Plan of Happiness (Alma 42:8).

The Plan is mentioned by name in neither the Doctrine & Covenants nor in the Old or New Testament, although Paul came tantalizingly close when he wrote that Christ "became the author of eternal salvation unto all them that obey him," and "the author and finisher of our faith." (Hebrews 5:9 & 12:2). Paul indirectly referred to God as the author of peace. (1 Corinthians 14:33). Whatever the name it goes by, The Plan embraces God's ordained core curriculum leading to family exaltation.

The Plan diagrams safe passage through the minefields of mortality, documents potential perils and pitfalls, charts the recommended route that leads to refuge, maps out success strategies for abundant living, and measures our progress on the pathway to perfection. Its elements are similar to the World Wide Web that requires only computer literacy, an I.P. address with a network, and relevant hardware and software. The mainframe of The Plan must exist somewhere, although its exact location is very hazy. A best guess is that it is somewhere in the neighborhood of Kolob. The storage of its data certainly exceeds that of the internet, which in 2019 was estimated to be in the neighborhood of 1,200 petabytes. One way to determine the number is to consider the sum total of data held by online storage and service

companies like Google, Amazon, Microsoft and Facebook. Estimates are that the big four store at least 1,200 petabytes between them. That is 1.2 million terabytes, or 1.2 billion gigabytes. (One terabyte is 1,000 gigabytes).

The mind-boggling storage capacity of The Plan has the potential to order our chaotic world, to bless us with clarity rather than confusion, to teach us fluency in the language of the spirit, and to educate those who are functionally illiterate so that they might be mesmerized by the power of the Word. In simple binary terms, the Atonement is the Savior's user name, and repentance is the password that grants us access to happiness.

The operating system of The Plan first reviews what life must have been like in the pre-earth existence, and secondly it explains the purpose of mortality, while lastly it opens our hearts and our minds to expanding eternal opportunities. When we conform to The Plan's overall strategy for success, we become better friends, neighbors, and missionary representatives of Christ, and we are also better equipped to find true happiness. It is within the elements of The Plan that we discover that "while thousands of candles can be lighted from a single flame, the life of the candle will never be shortened." (Buddha).

In our busy and complex world, we often see through a glass darkly, making it very difficult to discern how to harness the power of the elusive equations found within The Plan. Its permutations do not reveal if our passage through its portals is found with fame or anonymity, discovered by poverty or wealth, realized in sickness or health, undertaken with influence or obscurity, or if it is better accomplished by beauty or the beast. We sometimes forget that it promises both nurturing rain along with the mud that inevitably follows, and that it is our lot in life to dutifully trudge along past potholes and other obstacles on rocky roads that are uphill most of the way and that face a steady headwind. Within the fabric of The Plan, there are sometimes "dark threads that are as needful in the Weaver's skillful hand as the threads of gold and silver, in the pattern He has planned." (Benjamin Malachi Franklin, "The Weaver").

We cannot hope to find meaning in our lives if we treat the elements of The Plan superficially or carelessly. A conscious appreciation of their value must be earned. If we take them for granted or if we abandon their core principles, their power to bless our lives may slip away and be lost forever. While The Plan guarantees free will, it also gives us wide latitude to use our agency inappropriately to make poor choices. It gives us enough rope to either hang ourselves, or to lasso the stars and "hitch our wagons" to eternity. (Ralph Waldo Emerson, "American Civilization").

The Plan provides us with currency sufficient for our needs, but it also allows us, if we choose to do so, to substitute its legal tender for wads of counterfeit cash with which late payments may be made with interest and penalties tacked on for bad behavior. If we attempt to subvert The Plan in futile efforts to gain, obtain, and retain blessings we do not deserve, our destabilizing efforts will reward us with a pyrrhic victory at best.

If we never learn the hard lessons of life that The Plan throws our way with frustrating frequency, we will continually look elsewhere for gods of wood and stone that may temporarily soothe our temporal trauma but can never permanently redeem us from our misery. Our worldly ways will leave us vulnerable to a spiritual sickness that mimics the symptoms of those with advanced diabetes. When our peripheral circulation has been compromised, we will become numb to "the better angels of our nature" as we lose our capacity to touch and feel the power of the Atonement. (Abraham Lincoln).

If we become isolated from the sensitivity to our surroundings that is nurtured by The Plan, we may become inured to our condition in the sense that we are "past feeling." We may overcompensate with knee-jerk reactions, and without conscious awareness develop a "lead foot" that puts the pedal to the metal. Although life in the fast lane may be thrilling and provide a brief rush of adrenaline and a heady feeling from the release of other brain chemicals, when it finally "takes our breath away" we may not realize that our reduced lung capacity has robbed us of the

vibrancy and joie de vivre that could have been ours without chemo-therapeutics.

Nothing can compensate for the dogged and determined discipline required by The Plan. Cheap thrills will never replace its lofty rewards. The titillation of novelty and the counter-productivity of spectacle cannot defeat, but only delay, implementation of The Plan's noble principles. The universal influence of the Light of Christ encourages us to fix our attention on a Pole-star that has been designed to lift us to higher plateaus of personal progress.

The Plan allows us to become engaged and energized as we journey through Idumea at an unhurried and yet productive pace. It even allows us to be captivated by its complexity, immersed in its intricacies, riveted by its rewards, and wrapped up in its wonders, without being dragged down by its deficiencies. Repentance stands at attention before the portals of heaven, patiently waiting for us to acknowledge the power of the to transform our lives.

In a sense, we must return to the secret garden of our childhood in order to fully mature because, as William Henry Wordsworth wrote: "Heaven lies about us in our infancy. Shades of the prison house begin to close upon the growing boy, but he beholds the light and whence it flows. He sees it in his joy. The youth, who daily farther from the east must travel, still is nature's priest, and by the vision splendid, is on his way attended. At length the man perceives it die away, and fade into the light of common day." ("Ode: Intimations of Immortality").

Fortunately, the Haz-Mat Protocol of repentance has been written into The Plan that detoxifies us from the cares and conditioning influences of the world and from the homogenization process that occurs as we are worn down by the vicissitudes of life. It allows us to be born again and to be repetitively re-vitalized, as we are re-introduced to that Magical Kingdom where dreams really do come true. In between the sights and sounds, rides and attractions, and thrills and spills of our earthly theme-park experience, the inherent stabilizing influence of repentance draws our attention to personal spiritual hygiene practices including bathing in fonts that have

been designed for the specific purpose of removing the grit and grime that would foul our inner-workings.

The Plan mandates the need to make frequent changes out of soiled clothing into clean garments, and even requires occasional physical therapy and spiritual massage for relief from the bumps and bruises that we'll surely receive during our journey.

The Plan provides for sanctuaries into which we may retreat, but these will have drafty windows and doors, leaky pipes, faulty fixtures, and hot water heaters that are overwhelmed with calcium deposits. It will be up to us to learn to be become handy with the tools that are provided for home repairs. But we cannot hope to attend to our personal needs so successfully that, on our own, we maintain ideal form and function. Grandma's home remedies, although useful, will not be equal to the task, and if we eagerly embrace the elixirs peddled by the world's snake-oil salesmen we will just be grasping at straws.

So we must embrace The Plan, its therapies, and its gurneys upon which we will be given transfusions of the spiritual element to keep us going, at least until it's time to repeat the process in a weeks' time. When we frequent the blood-bank that has been created in our behalf, we will be on both the receiving and the giving end of transfusions. Those who go to dialysis centers have similar experiences where contaminants are removed from their blood because their kidneys cannot accomplish the task on their own. But there will be some who will not seek help, because they are so caught up in the celebration of their so-called autonomy.

The Lord has characterized those who have been enemies of God from the Fall of Adam, "and will be, forever and ever, unless they yield to the enticings of the Holy Spirit … and becometh as (children), submissive, meek, humble, patient, full of love, willing to submit to all things which the Lord seeth fit to inflict upon (them), even as a child doth submit to his father." (Mosiah 3:19).

It's great to strike out on our own, get our own apartment, earn a living, and pay our own bills. But The Plan anticipates that eventually we'll all return Home to move back in with our Heavenly Parents and live under one roof as we did at first, that we might be one big happy family again.

In contrast to the hectic pace demanded by our technologically oriented world, the elements of The Plan generate repetitive opportunities to stop and smell the roses along the pathway that leads Home. In fact, Heavenly Father created the roses in the first place, as love letters to His children. Of these subtle, positive reinforcements, the poet wrote: "Earth is crammed with heaven, and every bush with fire of God. But only those who see, take off their shoes. The rest stand around picking blackberries." (Elizabeth Barrett Browning).

The ingenuity, originality, and resourcefulness of the is such that it creates redundant mechanisms designed to give us repetitive opportunities for self-reflection, self-analysis, self-renewal, self commitment, and self-actualization, while minimizing our tendency to focus inward. When we conform our lives to its dependent principle of repentance, we find our greatest expression, and room for self-doubt or second-guessing is eliminated.

Repentance sets us free to be creative, and our creativity sets us free to plan properly prior to the time when we come face to face with the crises of life, so that we can prevent poor performance or mitigate its consequences. When we learn to rely upon the doctrine of Christ, internalize its elements, and freely surrender ourselves to its infinite possibilities without reservation, we find our greatest individuality, personal expression, and freedom. Our progress along the pathway to perfection assumes self-shaping, self-supporting, self-sustaining and self-renewing characteristics. At its core, the doctrine of Christ becomes a perfectly liberating law that allows us to reach our potential in a mutually supportive atmosphere of inter-dependency with the Savior.

Those of weak character frequently think that they can side-step or somehow bypass the requirements of The Plan, but this is because they have never enjoyed

the experiences of those who live on the strait and narrow path, thanks to the liberating influence of the Atonement. They mistake wickedness for happiness, confusing nature with nobility. When their behavior reflects worldliness rather than illumination from the Source of all light, when their activities harmonize more with secular standards and less with spiritual certainties, or when they are with their peers but without God, the resulting false sense of security generates instability and is unsustainable. Young people talk about "Best Friends Forever," but Heavenly Father would rather have us "Be Forever Faithful" through bonds of obedience to the principles of The Plan.

Opposition allows us to gauge the success of our internalization of The Plan's provisions and gives us a sense of how we are doing in our efforts to consciously and energetically participate without deviation in purposeful programs of personal progress that carry us forward on proven pathways. Conformity has the capacity to provide significant sustainable support within the embrace of The Plan, even as it carries us upward "as upon eagles' wings." (D&C 124:99). Without the consistency that is one of the greatest blessings of The Plan, our lives would become cruel jokes with punch lines that would pierce our hearts without pity. Such is the condition of those who are confronted by the sense of utter futility that accompanies their failure to focus on the innate upward reach of The Plan.

Without its light-generating capacity, we would be doomed to dance in flickering shadows that are only illusions and caricatures of reality. The blind who lead the blind flutter about in the dark until the discrepancy between their marginalized behavior and the ideals of The Plan become so great that their short-lived pleasure in worldly ways evaporates as the morning dew in the full light of day. Sooner or later, when this disparity becomes so great that it reaches "critical mass," a requisite readjustment will tear down the façade of corruption and the accretions of hypocrisy, to allow the cultivation of more nurturing lifestyles made possible by obedience to the principles of The Plan.

We see this happening quickly in scripture, because historical narrative artificially

compresses the passage of time. In fact, the obligatory alterations occur more gradually. In any event, time is an integral component of The Plan, and was created as an elegant matrix to provide us with the gift of perspective.

"They say time is the fire in which we burn." (Delmore Schwartz, "Calmly We Walk Through This April's Day"). This is true, in the sense that it is "with fire and with the Holy Ghost" that time becomes the element we use to work out our own salvation with fear and trembling before the Lord. (3 Nephi 9:20, see Mormon 9:27).

The invention of time allowed for the construction of a probationary state within which we could prove ourselves. The early learning center of life demanded a contextual environment into which the element of time could be inserted. An Atonement was provided, taking into account the probability that we would blow up the chemistry lab a time or two, as we experimented with the permutations and combinations of the volatile elements of eternity.

Enough time was built into The Plan for us to recognize our failure to be obedient to its principles, and for subsequent correction through repentance, forgiveness, renewal, and recommitment. The brilliantly crafted characteristic of repentance was designed as a celestial barometer that could easily measure the intensity of the telestial tempests that would regularly sweep across our landscapes. At the same time, our exercise of repentance would trigger alarm bells in heaven, and get our Father's immediate and undivided attention. It would alert Him to our on-going efforts to rely upon the Atonement as the only moderating influence that could mitigate the damage of telestial and celestial trauma caused by the repetitive explosions within the temporal test tubes that are tailored to the curriculum of The Plan and that are scattered about in life's laboratory.

The Plan provides for a recalibration through repentance, that allows us to become reinvigorated by the refreshing breeze of celestial air. The Plan also gives us the opportunity to live our lives in an atmosphere of free-will, to push the envelope, and to take risks. If, in our efforts, we fail to measure up to its laws, Jesus Christ

will intervene in our behalf. If we Recognize a mistake, if we experience Remorse for having made it, if we attempt to make Restitution if our behavior has wronged others, if we learn from our blunders and Reform our ways, Resolving to Refrain from Repeating them, Repentance will encourage us get back on the bike and to continue our wobbly journey along the path of progress, with a complete Resolution through the Atonement of what would have otherwise been incapacitating short-comings and irreconcilable inadequacy. By following this process, our powers will expand as we experience the glittering facets of the life of the Spirit wherein we are receptive to flashes of insight. We will be cast off into streams of revelation and carried along in the quickening currents of direct experience with God.

The Plan releases our energies to be creative and fosters creativity to allow us to experience greater capacity. In its design, is the perfect law of liberty. (See James 1:25). Our eternal welfare is thoroughly integrated into the success strategy of The Plan. Spencer W. Kimball recognized its nurturing potential when he urged us to lengthen our stride. In doing so, he knew that we would be lifted to spiritual independence and to an awakening sensitivity toward our divine destiny.

However, it is not the purpose of The Plan to give us our second wind in the first mile of the race, when we have only just begun our journey. We only feel its rejuvenating energy after we have warmed up our muscles with spiritually aerobic exercise, when we have loosened up our ligaments in compassionate service, when we have stretched beyond our perceived capacity and have gained the flexibility that comes with experience, when we have worked out the "nots" in our physical and spiritual muscles by pushing ourselves to the breaking point and beyond through purposeful repentance, when we have cleared our vision to see beyond our supposed limitations, have raised our sights to fix our mind's eye on a finish line that rises up to meet a celestial horizon, and when we have finally settled in to a reasonably comfortable pace to see ourselves through to the end.

While The Plan envisions a Utopian society, it still contains provisions for those whose agency has led them away from the rod of iron. It has built-in breakers that

will trip our circuits when they are overloaded, and it has the means to improve our circumstances when they seem to be stymied. If we are caught in the trauma of temporal traps, if our faith is flawed and we are blinded to the impotence of our false gods, sooner or later, our misery will catch up to us. Without The Plan, those

212

who feel confusion, abandonment, disillusionment, or despair as a consequence of their focus on worldly pleasure, will "perish in Babylon, even Babylon the great, which shall (surely) fall." (D&C 1:16).

If we want The Plan to work to our benefit, we cannot at the same time purchase a vacation home in Idumea as a refuge from life on the strait and narrow path. Such diversions are only detours from life's journey. They will only cause us to lose traction, slow our forward momentum, derail us from our sure footing on Gospel sod, and delay our progress toward our determined destination. When we succumb to temptation and delve into these distractions, we lose power, purpose, and focus. For example, if we depend more upon economic security than on spiritual preparedness, we are more inclined in times of crisis to grasp at the world's goods rather than rededicate ourselves to the proven principles of The Plan. If we put our trust in "idea gods," we will have no-where to look for help when the hot winds of change melt the foundations of our misplaced faith in the "flavor of the day."

The Plan is frequently ignored because it is easy to be infected by the desire to obtain what we do not need, to hoard what we have not earned, to amass what we do not deserve, and to stockpile what we cannot ultimately control. Each fall and winter, several million unvaccinated people worldwide succumb to the effects of an influenza virus that manifests itself in frustratingly mutated forms, but more die spiritually because they are infected by avarice and greed, covetousness and lust, and pride and prejudice.

People think that they can be happy if they wander and play, never considering that a key feature of The Plan is to ponder and pray, and to study and apply the principles of its playbook. If we disregard The Plan, we may fall into activities that dull our senses and make us vulnerable to Satan's enticements. Life is all a stage,

but when the bouquets are thrown at our feet when we are summoned for a final curtain call after the last act has been played out, it will be only those of us who have been obedient to the principles of The Plan who receive standing ovations. This is why Samuel the Lamanite charged the people of Zarahemla: "Ye have sought all the days of your lives for that which ye could not obtain, and ye have sought for happiness in doing iniquity, which thing is contrary to the nature of that righteousness" which is inherent in The Plan. (Helaman 13:38).

The adversary finally betrays his followers because they can only live in opposition to their covenant consciousness for so long before his cunning caresses lead them into conceptual cul-de-sacs. These are doctrinal dead-ends, in which all exits lead to confusion, uncertainty, doubt, ambiguity, hesitation, and a retreat that plunges them headlong into a perceived freedom that is on closer inspection a bottomless pit of misery. In a perverted and twisted way, he "seeks that all men might be miserable like himself." (2 Nephi 2:27). Never does he promise happiness, but instead manipulates us to think that we can circumvent the principles of The Plan by engaging in a warped reasoning that encourages rationalization that is only a reinvention of happiness in its mutated forms.

The meager substitutes for the rewards of The Plan include affluence, authority, comfort, dominion, fashion, influence, position, style, and wealth. Lumped together, these are the Holy Grail of those who engage in a blind quest for the power and control that are the antithesis of the principles of The Plan. To be sure, Heavenly Father wants us to reach our potential, and He could easily give us what He has. But instead, His Plan foreordains us to become all that He is, by incorporating His image and likeness within our own being and nature. (See 2 Peter 3:18 & 3 Nephi 28:10). For The Plan to succeed, it is critical that the bodies we were given be kept in good working condition, because they are the earthly tabernacles of our eternal spirits. Repentance allows our corruptible bodies to become clean, pure, and full of light.

Our healthy bodies invite spirituality and happiness, and lead to eternal life in the

Celestial Kingdom of God. For we are "spirit, the elements are eternal, and spirit and element, inseparably connected, receive a fulness of joy." (D&C 93:33). "When health is absent, then wisdom cannot reveal itself, culture cannot become manifest, strength cannot fight, wealth becomes useless, and intelligence cannot be applied." (Heraclitus - Philosopher of the Golden Age of Greece).

This key Plan provision relating to physical and spiritual health dictates that we will inherit our bodies in the resurrection and be reunited with our spirits, never again to be separated. "The spirit and the body shall be reunited again in its perfect form; both limb and joint shall be restored to its proper frame." (Alma 11:43). Therefore, our bodies must be kept as pure and as holy as are our spirits, in order for The Plan to work optimally.

It is only natural, then, that Satan would tempt us to misuse our bodies. He is miserable because he was never permitted to enjoy corporeal form. Because misery loves company, he wants each of us to be wretched also. Thus, "the wicked one cometh and taken away light and truth, through disobedience." (D&C 93:39). Those who experience the worst manifestation of misery are Sons of Perdition. They are utterly ruined, because The Plan provides that in the resurrection they will inherit bodies in a kingdom without glory. Tragically, their bodies and spirits will be perfectly matched to each other. They will be incorruptible, yet they will be without light. Their darkness will be a sinister and impenetrable gloom, and a nightmare from which they may never awaken.

The Lord has specifically protected us against this risk, by giving us a codicil to The Plan known as Doctrine & Covenants Section 89 - The Word of Wisdom. This revelation was given "in consequence of the evil and designs which do and will exist in the hearts of conspiring men in the Last Days." (D&C 89:4). Evidently, more so than in former times, evil now has a well entrenched and particularly pervasive and persuasive influence. The Lord's Law of Health has never been more important than it is today. So that the deck is not stacked against us, the Lord has leveled

the playing field by giving us this addendum. We may still enjoy our moral agency, even as we have been given pointed and specific instruction identifying what we ought to do to avoid deviation from the pathway to happiness dictated by The Plan.

Our finest hours are those when unexpected challenge is met with extraordinary response. Like the Seven Dwarfs, when we embrace the tenets of The Plan we whistle while we work, because we have learned that, because of the Atonement, our efforts are linked to happiness. The virtue of The Plan, and particularly of the principle of repentance, is its incredible power to touch our hearts, to change our nature, to soften us and to humble us, to make us as pliant clay in the hands of the Master Potter, to mold us as children, and to secure us in our happiness.

But the more we chase the caricatures of The Plan, the more "The Right Stuff" eludes us. However, if we plan our work and work The Plan, "that happiness which is prepared for the Saints" will come and sit softly on our shoulders. (2 Nephi 9:43). Lehi simply stated: "If there be no righteousness there be no happiness." (2 Nephi 2:13). Satan's direct frontal assault on The Plan, consisting of customs, rituals, social conventions, traditions, and institutions, works tirelessly to sabotage our best efforts to embrace it. Even technology gets in the way, substituting the electronic media for the direct interpersonal relationships, the skin to skin contact, that is fundamental to its operation.

"Reach out and touch someone" becomes a euphemism for "Use technology to isolate yourself from others." We see each other's Faces in Books and nurture on-line relationships to the exclusion of conventional real-time social interactions. Computers assess compatibility, talking heads provide commentary, sound-bites substitute insensibility for substance, and spin-doctors use the internet to twist the news and promote hidden agendas.

It is precisely because of the threat of behavioral instability that God has provided us with the covenants that are integral to The Plan. Therein lies the power of reorientation to a lifestyle that pertains to righteousness, and a recalibration of

the moral compass that leads to happiness. Our covenants provide unequivocal understanding and clear definitions of eternal truth. They allow us to learn from the events within which we are swept up, to derive mutual benefit from our relationships with others, to grow within our environment no matter how unique or difficult it might seem, and to protect us from the worldly influences that encroach upon the fortress of our spiritual security, sanctuary, and symmetry.

The principle of repentance softens our telestial tendencies and creates an impenetrable shield of faith. It provides a sounding board against which we can discern between the polarized opposites that clamor for our attention. The fruits of repentance, or forgiveness through the Atonement of Christ, defines the difference between happiness and its worldly counterfeits, and strikes familiar chords within our hearts and souls. Applying the principle of repentance in our lives is the spiritual equivalent of dusting for Satan's dirty fingerprints on the idols with which he teases, taunts, tempts, torments, and tortures us. If we fail to do so, he can turn and twist our attention from the truth.

Our covenants are like chiropractic adjustments that treat spiritual scoliosis. The sturdiest plants that bear the best fruit are those that have deep roots in good, rich, nurturing soil. The Plan encourages us to surround ourselves with a loam that is rich in art, conversation, decency, example, honor, music, and virtue. Its objective is to allow our spirits to grow freely beyond narrow confines that are equivalent to one-pint nursery containers. Instead, we send down taproots into Gospel soil and are anchored to the Infinite.

As we do so, we commit the 13th Article of Faith to memory as well as to our lifestyle. "If there is anything virtuous, lovely, or of good report or praiseworthy, we seek after these things." (See Philippians 4:8). To the extent that we do this, we are ignited with the "fire of God." (2 Kings 1:12). If we don't, we may experience hell while yet on earth, for that mental anguish may simply be the conscious recognition of lost opportunities and the unconscious sense of dread that accompanies the stupor of thought when our decisions, or our indecision, precipitates a subtle revolt

against The Plan.

Our obedience to the elements of The Plan gives us the opportunity to enjoy heaven while yet on earth. The Savior revealed: "Abundance is multiplied unto (us) through the manifestations of the Spirit." (D&C 70:13). In other words, the Spirit can be so profoundly felt that it will seem to overflow, as we realize our righteous objectives. These stay in focus because The Plan's spiritual guideposts have provided a Gospel-centered orientation and the only proven perspective in a world that is filled with many voices competing for our attention.

The Plan of Happiness is within the reach of every one of us, no matter what our cultural, social, political, or economic circumstances might be. The portals to The Plan are supported by the scriptures and buttressed by Gospel principles that testify of their strength. On our own, we can do pitifully little to influence our circumstances. It is only through the miracle of infinite, continuing, uninterrupted, unspoiled, uncorrupted, enduring, unfathomable and immeasurable grace embodied within the Atonement that we are "swallowed up in the joy of (our) God, even to the exhausting of (our) strength." (Alma 27:17).

When we reach that epiphany, our hearts will "brim with joy." (Alma 26:11). God's Perfect Plan is designed to save us in His Celestial Kingdom. His mission statement, "This is my work and my glory – to bring to pass (our) immortality and eternal life," reveals that His carefully crafted Plan is not just a hobby; it is His very real work to which He gives His undivided attention. (Moses 1:39). His Plan was not just designed so that we might live forever. Instead, it was created to teach us how to live now, how to enjoy the dominion He enjoys, how to create a heaven on earth, and how to use the tools He has provided, that we might have a hope of eternal life even as we engage mortality.

Therefore, it seems only reasonable that his perfect Plan would have the depth, breadth, majesty, and capacity to encircle all His children within His warm embrace. As the poet wrote: "He scribed a circle that drew me out. Heretic, rebel, a thing to

flout! But love and I had the will to win. We scribed a circle that drew him in." (Edwin Markham).

This may be why, after the conclusion of the War in Heaven, when God pronounced

His subsequent creations as "good" He said that His crowning achievement, man, was, in fact, "very good." (Moses 2:4, 10, 12, 18, 21, 25 & 31). The earthly environment He had fashioned for us was ideally suited to nurture not only the favored "first part" of His creations, but also the "second" part, and perhaps, for all we know, even the "third" part.

The Lord's Atonement, after all, is the keystone of The Plan that was conceived before the foundation of the world. We are taught that it is infinite and eternal in its scope, and it directly influences the vast majority of Heavenly Father's spirit children who have not known Christ. As Paul said to those gathered by Mars Hill: "As I passed by, and beheld your devotions, I found an altar with this inscription, 'To the Unknown God. Whom therefore ye ignorantly worship,' him declare I unto you." (Acts 17:23).

Not all have been as fortunate as Jacob, who "knew of Christ, and … had a hope of his glory many hundred years before his coming." (Jacob 4:4). With its breathtaking reconciliation of Justice and Mercy within the matrix of free will, the Atonement makes The Plan perfect, even for the men and women of Athens in Paul's day. It seems reasonable that it would allow the worst of us to work out our salvation and earn the privilege, as prodigal sons and daughters of God, to rejoin His household in full fellowship, with all the rights and privileges one would expect, following the reformation of errant behavior. Is this not what the principle of repentance is all about? After all, there is so much good in the worst of us, and so much bad in the best of us, that it hardly behooves any of us to talk about the rest of us.

None of us wants to miss the "Glory Train" that has been provided by The Plan. We all want to "hear the whistle sound, for those souls heaven bound." We are all eager to "climb onboard the glory ride and set our earthly bonds aside." Most assuredly,

that "old train will leave some day, boarding Christians along the way." We can see it even now in our mind's eye, "roaring down those one-way tracks, and bound for heaven; it won't be back." We can hear the urgent call: "Get your ticket while you can. If you want a ride to Glory Land, we'll meet at the Lords' station. There's no time left for hesitation." When we climb on board, there will be enough seats for all who want to experience the ride of their lives, because "this long black train has no gears. It's full throttle ahead leaving here." We'll be in good company, for "the archangel will be our engineer. We'll depart amidst angelic cheers." All Christians of conscience will soberly realize "the price of the ticket is paid for you. Jesus died on the cross for sins you do. Surrender to the Good Shepherd your all, before you miss that last boarding call." The promise is: "We'll glide on the ride to heavens' shore, where we will endure troubles no more. So shed your shackles. There's no need to pack. Board that Glory Train with one-way tracks!" (Kenneth Ellison, "Glory Train").

"The time is fulfilled, and the kingdom of God is at hand. Repent ye, and believe the gospel."
(Mark 1:15).

Chapter Twenty Two

The rapids of life.

Wo unto those who are not prepared, for the
time is at hand that they must repent,
or they cannot be saved!
(See Alma 5:31).

I hope that each of us will have, at one time or another, the opportunity to serve the youth of the Church. Positions in the Young Men and Young Women programs are especially challenging. They are exciting because of the great potential of the youth, and also because of the circumstances surrounding their weekly activities where many memorable events spontaneously occur.

On one occasion, when I was serving as Priest Quorum Advisor, we planned an activity that involved the three Aaronic Priesthood quorums. We organized a canoeing trip down the Little Spokane River, from Colbert Road to Pine River Park. Necessary preparations were made, half a dozen canoes were secured, and off we went, three to a canoe. The weather was pleasant, the water was warm, and soon we were involved in splashing each other as we struck our paddles on its surface.

Canoe races followed, with bumping and pushing at every opportunity. Soon, one canoe capsized, then another, and yet another, and we found ourselves bobbing along in the water.

Of course, every individual had a life vest, and there was little danger. Because the swamped canoes moved much more slowly than the current, the group in the water became scattered, and one young man in particular was carried swiftly downstream. We waved to him as he bobbed along in his life vest, receded from our view, rounded a bend in the river, and was gone from our sight. After righting the canoes, bailing water, and counting noses, we continued on our way. In an hour or so, we arrived at Pine River Park, where we were greeted by the young man who had earlier been carried downstream. He was lying on the bank sunning himself, and his life vest was drying at his side.

As we portaged the canoes to waiting vehicles, the young man remarked to me how much fun it had been to float down the river all by himself, secure in his life jacket, particularly because he did not know how to swim! I almost had a heart attack right on the spot.

My thoughts have since turned to another young man with whom I was well acquainted. He was on the swim team at the University of Southern California and worked during the summers as a lifeguard at the beach. He was at home in the water, and loved aquatic sports. He especially enjoyed white water rafting, and during the summer after his junior year in college he had the opportunity to go to the Rogue River in Oregon, which is well known for its challenging rapids. Such outings, full of spills and thrills, seem to be particularly thrilling for the youth, especially when they are potentially dangerous and destructive.

If common sense prevails, basic equipment when shooting rapids includes the raft, oars, a swimsuit, a helmet, and a life vest. These are generally adequate to insure a safe experience without attenuating the excitement. But for some reason, on that warm summer day in Oregon, my young friend left both his helmet and his vest on

the beach before shoving off into the river. By the time his companion in another one-man raft had noticed this breach of the safety rules, my friend had been caught by the current, and was out of sight in the rapid's foam and spray.

His companion then anxiously shot the same rapids, straining his eyes for a glimpse of his friend. When he reached calm water a mile or so downstream, all he found was an empty raft floating upside down, and two scattered oars. The cold and lifeless body of my young friend wasn't found for four days, lodged in brush several miles downstream from the scene of the tragedy.

Why had he left these most essential pieces of equipment behind? Why had he not at least taken the simple precaution of putting on his life vest, and snugly securing it in place? These unanswered questions haunted his grieving family and friends for some time.

Heavenly Father knows us quite well, and has made provisions for our welfare as we shoot the rapids of life. Our U.S.C.G. Approved P.F.D.. is the Gospel of Jesus Christ. It is the genuine article, and is authorized with priesthood support, direction, and inspiration. But we must read the instructions relating to its use, in order to know how to benefit from its careful design. We have been provided with the scriptures, with the Relief Society, with Melchizedek Priesthood Quorum Personal Study Guides, and with the Come Follow Me Sunday School program. We have Priesthood Purposes, Young Women Values, and The Proclamation on The Family. Ultimately, we have the influence of the Holy Ghost and the gift of discernment. These are true 24/7 "Help Lines."

Before embarking on perilous adventures, we take a few deep breaths of celestial air, carefully plot our course well in advance, and reconnoiter potential dangers. We pre-play before we re-play, and rehearse how we would react to perilous situations. We get to know the river; we know where the rocks and rapids are; we know how large the cataracts are, how deep the holes are, and where the shallow pools of quiet sanctuary are. We learn where we can regroup in order to clear our

heads before the next challenge presents itself.

In the Church, we are fortunate to be led by "river-rats" who are seasoned with experience. They have been blessed with the ability to see the rocks and rapids before they come into our view on the swiftly flowing river of life. As we push off from the shore and embark on our own individually tailored river-rafting experiences, the programs of the Church permit us to progress through the Primary while we are still in relatively calm water. As the current quickens, the Young Men and Young Women programs shepherd us through rougher water. Finally, the Melchizedek Priesthood and Relief Society organizations shelter us from direct frontal assaults of towering waves, paralyzing cataracts, and fearsome holes.

During the journey, we are continually blessed with the aforementioned river guides who have shot the rapids many times before. These old geezers are anxious to impart their knowledge to the novice river runners who follow in their wake. We should listen to them as if our very lives depend upon it, as in fact they do. It is important to adjust the fit of the life vest so that it is snug without chafing, binding, or inhibiting, but not so loose that our freedom of movement renders it deceptively dangerous or ineffective.

We choose to be obedient to printed and verbal instructions regarding the use of our life vest. When we do so, we realize that we have necessarily limited our options, but the trade-off is that we have also avoided the consequences of inappropriate behavior. The Gospel is the perfect law of liberty to those who have chosen to be obedient. Donning their life-vest gives them the freedom to stretch to their divine potential, uninhibited by the restraints and limitations that accompany poor choices.

Embracing the Gospel of Jesus Christ is akin to putting on the life vest, while scripture study, personal prayer, firesides, seminary, quorum and class instruction, and youth and adult activities are equivalent to wearing the properly adjusted vest. We cannot negotiate around the rapids of life, nor would we really want

to. Avoidance of risk is contrary to purpose of The Plan of Salvation that is the dynamic expression of the Gospel of Jesus Christ. The only place where we can experience the stress-free life of calm water, where we are enveloped by the suffocating reality of maximum security, is either in prison or when we are attached to the life support mechanisms of hospital intensive care units. We must stretch in order to grow. Mortality is a risky undertaking, but the availability of spiritual life-vests makes the effort worthwhile and the achievement of our goals attainable. Heavenly Father has left us with adequate means to deal with the challenges we face.

In the Ward, each of us is assisted by individuals working within organizations ideally suited to meet our needs. We are effective when we focus on our own stewardship responsibilities, and when we magnify our callings in the service of others. This creates an interdependence that is really the highest level of human interaction. The Lord has urged each of us to stand fast in our offices. (D&C 54:2). He has confidence that He will find us at our posts at all times, doing our duty.

If we see that a friend has neglected to secure his or her own life vest, Heavenly Father expects us to reach out to them, to encourage them to wear it, and to help them to do so. We must determine never to abandon them to fate, because of their inadequate preparation to negotiate the rapids of life. Discipleship demands unswerving devotion to our friends and neighbors, for we have covenanted in the name of Jesus Christ to be our brothers' keepers. The Gospel of Jesus Christ is the Lord's inspired program to shepherd us through the white water that lies ahead of us on our journey. As our life vests are securely in place, we will be prepared to deal with whatever the river might throw at us.

"Then Peter said unto them, Repent, and be baptized every one of you in the name of Jesus Christ for the remission of sins, and ye shall receive the gift of the Holy Ghost." (Acts 2:38).

Chapter Twenty Three

The Holy Ghost is an eternal optimist.

"And the Lord God called upon men by the Holy Ghost everywhere, and commanded them that they should repent." (Moses 5:14). As long as there is one soul yet to repent, the work of the Holy Ghost is unfinished. Even when we are fully committed, the Holy Ghost can bless us with repetitive moments of confirmation, when we can say, as did members of the Church in Zarahemla, that through the miracle of forgiveness by the power of the Atonement our hearts have once again been changed through faith on his name, "for <u>this</u> day (we) are born of him and have become his sons and his daughters." (Mosiah 5:7, underlining mine).

When reading the scriptures that relate to repentance, we often think of the Lord's teaching that "these words are not of men nor of man, but of me; wherefore, you shall testify they are of me and not of man; For it is my voice which speaketh them unto you; for they are given by my Spirit unto you, and by my power you can read them one to another; and save it were by my power you could not have them. Wherefore, you can testify that you have heard my voice, and know my words." (D&C 18:34-36). The commandment to speedily repent is given, He explained, "to ponder in your hearts, with

this commandment which I give unto you, that ye shall call upon me while I am near. Draw near unto me and I will draw near unto you." (D&C 88:62-63, see Alma 5:56).

Our motivation to repent is instilled within us as a fire from within. As a matter of fact, "they say that time is the fire in which we burn." (Delmore Schwartz, "Calmly We walk Through This April's Day"). This may be why Christopher Columbus intuitively recalled the driving force for his voyage of discovery by simply saying: "The Holy Spirit gave me fire for the deed." Our hearts burn within us when God gives us knowledge of the principle of repentance "by His Holy Spirit, yea, by the unspeakable gift of the Holy Ghost." (D&C 121:26 & 28). Thus, did Jeremiah describe his feelings: "His word was in mine heart as a burning fire shut up in my bones, and I was weary with forbearing, and I could not stay." (Jeremiah 20:9). When we are enveloped in the Spirit, the Lord our God is as "a consuming fire." (Deuteronomy 4:24).

The Spirit similarly worked upon Belshazzar's troubled conscience, to the extent that "the king's countenance was changed, and his thoughts troubled him, so that the joints of his loins were loosed, and his knees smote one against another." (Daniel 5:6). Joseph Smith was moved to declare of his revelatory experiences that clarified for all the world the principles of the Gospel: "Thus saith the still small voice, which whispereth through and pierceth all things, and often times it maketh my bones to quake while it maketh manifest." (D&C 85:6).

Though our "sins be as scarlet, they shall be as white as snow; though they be red like crimson, they shall be as wool." (Isaiah 1:18). As our comprehension of the power of the Atonement unfolds before our minds' eye, we recognize prophetic wisdom in the observation of Hans Christian Anderson, who said: "Our lives are as fairy tales waiting to be written by the finger of God." A number of the chapters in our story have already been set to paper, and we don't know how many yet remain to be recorded. But we do know this: God has set the standard, and we must follow the course He has established. We lack the power to start over and make a new beginning, but because of The Plan of Salvation, the Atonement, and the principles of repentance and forgiveness, we can begin now and make a new ending.

As the Sufi poet Rumi observed: "Our wounds become portals that allow light to enter us." Fortunately, because of the Atonement, those wounds will not heal imperfectly as soul-scars. Every evidence of telestial trauma disappears with the application of the healing Balm of Gilead. It was the Savior, and not us, who was wounded for our transgressions. It was He Who was bruised for our iniquities, the chastisement of our own peace was upon Him, and not upon us, and it is with His stripes that we are miraculously healed. (See Mosiah 14:5). Long ago, Jeremiah asked: "Is there no balm in Gilead? Is there no physician there?" (Jeremiah 8:22). Today, we can answer with a resounding "Yes!" The Savior of the world, our Redeemer, heals our wounds. (See Jacob 2:8).

We believe Him when He says: "If your eye be single to my glory, your whole bodies shall be filled with light, and there shall be no darkness in you; and that body which is filled with light comprehendeth all things." D&C 88:67). For "that which is of God is light; and he that receiveth light, and continueth in God, receiveth more light; and that light groweth brighter and brighter unto the perfect day." (D&C 50:24). In marvelous ways, the Holy Ghost confirms the words of Heber J. Grant, who said that as we gain spiritual maturity, "by doing our duty, faith increases until it becomes perfect knowledge." (C.R. April 1934).

As the seasons of our lives unfold, and we learn to apply the principle of repentance, we realize that "Life is a sheet of paper white, where each of us may write a line or two, and then comes night." And so, we must "greatly begin!" If we have time only for a line, we determine to make it sublime. For we have discovered that it is not failure, but low aim, that is crime. (James Russell Lowe, "For an Autograph," from "Poetical Works," 1885).

"All nations, kindreds, tongues, and people shall dwell safely in the Holy One of Israel if it so be that they will repent." (1 Nephi 22:28).

Chapter Twenty Four

Making intelligent choices.

"We believe that through the Atonement of Christ, all mankind may be saved, by obedience to the laws and ordinances of the Gospel." (3rd Article of Faith). These laws revolve around "the Gospel of Repentance." (J.S.H. 1:69).

<u>As we strive to be obedient, we determine to do the right things for the right reasons.</u>

We take heed that we do not our alms before men, to be seen of them: otherwise we have no reward of our Father which is in heaven. (See Matthew 6:1). Jesus referred to these people as hypocrites, those who pretend to have certain qualities but do not; who try to appear to be righteous but are not, or who do good things only to be seen by others. Hypocrites are wrapped up in themselves and tend to make very small packages. "They have their reward," cautioned the Savior. (Matthew 6:2). He also reminded us: "Where your treasure is, there will your heart be also." (Matthew 6:21).

William R. Bradford of the Seventy once spoke with the bishop of a ward whose youth had worked hard to earn money for an activity. The bishop asked Elder

Bradford if he would help the youth receive recognition for what they had done. To the bishop's surprise, Elder Bradford said he would not. He said that he was glad that the young people had been so diligent, but that it was not important that they receive public acknowledgement for that work. When the youth decided to donate their money to the Church's general missionary fund instead of using it for the activity, they asked if they could have their picture taken with Elder Bradford as they made the donation, and they wanted to have the photo and an article put into the newspaper. Again Elder Bradford surprised them by saying "no." He told the bishop: "You might consider helping your young people learn a higher law. Recognition from on high is silent. It is carefully and quietly recorded there. Let them feel the joy and gain the treasure in their hearts and souls that come from silent, selfless service." (C.R., 10/1987).

We can easily determine what we treasure by evaluating the resources we devote to obtaining it. Basically, we will be judged by the things for which we stand in line. On the other hand, when we do something for the right reasons, we unconsciously "lay up for (ourselves) treasures in heaven, where neither moth nor rust doth corrupt, and where thieves do not break through nor steal." (Matthew 6:20). Our spiritual bank accounts overflow with deposits that may later be withdrawn as an annuity of joy in the kingdom of heaven. (See D&C 18:14-16).

<u>We express gratitude, and follow the Savior's example of prayer.</u>

Our petitions very loosely follow this pattern: "Dear God, So far today I've done all right. I haven't gossiped. I haven't lost my temper. I haven't lied or cheated. I haven't been greedy, grumpy, nasty, selfish or overindulgent. I'm very thankful for that. But in a few minutes, I'm going to get out of bed, and from then on, I'm probably going to need a lot more help. Amen."

In fact, the Savior taught: "After this manner therefore pray ye: Our Father which art in heaven, Hallowed be thy name. Thy kingdom come. Thy will be done in earth, as it is in heaven. Give us this day our daily bread. And forgive us our debts, as we

forgive our debtors. And lead us not into temptation, but deliver us from evil. For thine is the kingdom, and the power, and the glory, for ever. Amen." (Matthew 6:9-13).

Dallin Oaks said: "We should address prayers to our Heavenly Father in words we

238

associate with love, respect, reverence, and closeness. Men and women who wish to show respect will take the time to learn the special language of prayer." (C.R., 4/1993). A favorite poem of David O. McKay reminds us: "The builder who first bridged Niagara's gorge, before he swung his cable, shore to shore, sent out across the gulf his venturing kite, bearing a slender cord for unseen hands to grasp upon the further cliff, and draw a greater cord, and then a greater yet, 'til at last across the chasm swung the cable – then the mighty bridge in air. So may we send our little timid thoughts across the void, out to God's reaching hands. Send our love and faith to thread the deep, thought after thought until the little cord has greatened to a chain no chance can break, and we are anchored to the infinite!" (Edward Markham).

We treat others kindly and fairly.

We remember that "there is so much bad in the best of us, and so much good in the worst of us, that it hardly behooves any of us to talk about the rest of us." (Anonymous). The example of Joseph Smith speaks volumes: "I am calm as a summer's morning;" he declared on his way to Carthage. "I have a conscience void of offense towards God, and towards all men." (D&C 135:4).

We exercise forgiveness of others' perceived injustices.

"Those who do not forgive others when no fault was intended are fools, and those who do not forgive others when fault was intended are usually fools." (Attributed to Brigham Young). Forgiveness is a divine attribute that exerts, as does no other quality, a nurturing and healing influence. It is also an integral part of our own repentance process. (See Matthew 18:21-22).

We obey the law.

Disciples emulate he of whom it was remembered: "He kept all Ten Commandments until he died. He walked the straight and narrow path and never lied. He never went to the theatres. He never learned to dance. He never once on shapely legs bestowed a wicked glance. He never strayed or kissed another's wife. He never took a bit of liquor in his life. He never let his temper rise. He never called his neighbor a fool, but kept strictly to the Golden Rule. Now you can be assured that he really lived on earth. But he was deaf, and dumb, and blind, and paralyzed from birth." (Anonymous).

We judge righteously.

How can we ensure that we "judge righteous judgment." (J.S.T. Matthew 7:2). Mormon was referring to the Light of Christ when he said: "Behold, my brethren, it is given unto you to judge, that ye may know good from evil; and the way to judge is as plain, that ye may know with a perfect knowledge, as the daylight is from the dark night. For behold, the Spirit of Christ is given to (us, that we) may know good from evil; wherefore, I show unto you the way to judge; for every thing which inviteth to do good, and to persuade to believe in Christ, is sent forth by the power and gift of Christ; wherefore ye may know with a perfect knowledge it is of God." (Moroni 7:15-16, see John 1:19). The Light of Christ establishes order within the universe. (See D&C 88:6-13).

Moroni continued: "But whatsoever thing persuadeth men to do evil, and believe not in Christ, and deny him, and serve not God, then ye may know with a perfect knowledge it is of the Devil; for after this manner doth the Devil work, for he persuadeth no man to do good, no, not one; neither do his angels; neither do they who subject themselves unto him. And now, my brethren, seeing that ye know the light by which ye may judge, which light is the light of Christ, see that ye do not judge wrongfully; for with that same judgment which ye judge ye shall also be judged." (Moroni 7:17-18).

"The Holy Ghost is not that which lighteth every man that comes into the world, which is the Spirit of God which proceeds through Christ to the world, that enlightens every man that comes into the world, and that strives with the children of men until it brings them to a knowledge of the truth and the possession of the greater light and testimony of the Holy Ghost." (Joseph F. Smith, "Millennial Star," 65:115). Responding to the Light of Christ leads us to the Holy Ghost, where we may receive its gift by ordinance. The Holy Ghost is only given following demonstrable obedience to Gospel principles, namely, faith and repentance which lead to the ordinance of baptism. Following baptism, shades of grey should not exist for members of the Lord's Church, because they enjoy the greater light and knowledge that is given by the Holy Ghost.

<u>We determine to serve God and do His will.</u>

"No man can serve two masters: for either he will hate the one, and love the other; or else he will hold to the one, and despise the other. (We) cannot serve God and mammon." (Matthew 6:24). We should "seek not for riches but for wisdom; and, behold, the mysteries of God shall be unfolded unto (us), and then shall (we) be made rich. Behold, he that hath eternal life is rich. (D&C 11:7).

To understand spiritual things, we must have discernment or guidance from the Holy Ghost. Those who are sincerely investigating the merits of the Gospel of Jesus Christ are taught by the Light of Christ with special assistance from the Spirit, and when they are confirmed as members of His Church they receive the gift of the Holy Ghost by ordinance. One of His purposes is to guide us from the covenant waters of baptism, along the strait and narrow path leading to the other ordinances and covenants of the priesthood that are necessary if we are to obtain eternal life. This is one reason why members of the Church are given the Holy Ghost beside the waters of baptism.

A second reason for the gift of the Holy Ghost is to persuade us to repetitively

repent, so that we may be "wrought upon and cleansed by the power of the Holy Ghost" (Moroni 6:4), which power we receive "by faith on the Son of God." (1 Nephi 10:17). It is "by the power of the Holy Ghost (that) the words of Christ will tell (us) all things what (we) should do." (2 Nephi 32:3). This includes speedy repentance. (See

Alma 30:57). "And by the power of the Holy Ghost (we) may know the truth of all things," including a testimony of the power of the Atonement and of the divine legitimacy of the principle of repentance. (Moroni 10:5). This power shall not be withheld "so long as time shall last, or the earth shall stand, or there shall be one man upon the face thereof to be saved." (Moroni 7:36).

Those who decline the offer of the riches of eternity that has been unfolded to their view by the power of the Holy Ghost are doomed to live their lives in scarcity of their basic spiritual needs. They subsist beneath the poverty level, although they may not even be aware of it. They lack a curiosity about the world around them, and are uninterested in exploring it or the people who surround them. Their potential is untested because of their self-imposed limitations. Their clothes closets may be full, but they complain that they haven't got a thing to wear. They eat so well that they are always thinking about going on a diet. They are loaded down with toys at birthdays and Christmas, and then are bored silly because there's nothing to do. They have three degrees, but feel unfulfilled in their jobs. They never take the time to stop to smell the roses.

We observe the Golden Rule.

The behavior of the disciples of Jesus Christ is framed within the parameters of the "Law of Compensation." "Therefore all things whatsoever ye would that men should do to you, do ye even so to them: for this is the law and the prophets." (Matthew 7:12).

When we consider the question: "How can I tell if I am converted to the principle of repentance?" we inevitably come to this conclusion: The best indicator that we are progressing spiritually and coming unto Christ lies in the way we treat other

people. We tell on ourselves by the way we treat others; "by the friends we seek, by the very manner in which we speak, by the way we enjoy our leisure time, and by the use we make of dollar and dime. We tell who we are by the things we wear, and in the way we wear our hair, by the kinds of things that make us laugh, and by the records we play on the phonograph. We tell who we are by the way we walk, by the things in which we delight to talk, and by the books we choose from a well-filled shelf. In these ways and more, we tell on ourselves." (Anonymous).

<u>We actively seek His kingdom.</u>

"Seek ye first the Kingdom of God, and his righteousness, and all these things shall be added unto you." (Matthew 6:33). Disciples understand that unchecked worldliness can twist our thinking, distort our perspective, cause our spirituality to shrivel, and turn our loyalty from God, while its companion greed can weaken our resolve to put our own needs aside and serve Him first. Disciples do not take expensive vacations in Idumea, nor do they incur the hidden costs of self-indulgence. They do not indebt themselves to the Devil. They do not procrastinate their enrollment in the Lord's university system, or defer the curriculum of the Gospel in favor of worldly pursuits that ask for pitifully little in terms of commitment or effort.

As Jesus neared the end of His Sermon on the Mount, He described the process of admission to the kingdom of heaven. "Enter ye in at the strait gate," He taught, "for wide is the gate, and broad is the way, that leadeth to destruction, and many there be which go in thereat; Because strait is the gate, and narrow is the way, which leadeth unto life, and few there be that find it." (Matthew 7:13-14).

If mortality could be visualized in spatial dimensions, it would take the shape of an hourglass, with the strait gate its narrow midsection. After passing through that constriction following an exercise of faith, purposeful repentance, and baptism, unparalleled vistas would open up to reveal untapped potential and unparalleled opportunity. But initially, many of us would be caught in conceptually confusing cul-de-sacs that would prevent us from comprehending the purpose of The Plan. We

would wander to and fro, dazed and disoriented, like flotsam and jetsam on the sea of life.

Some of us would be stalled in telestial traffic jams that would overheat our engines, foul our lubricants, seize our moving parts, and restrict our access to freely flowing spiritual energy. Others would lack restraint, as if their brake pads were worn, interfering with their ability to slow down and avoid the sand traps of transgression as they negotiated the minefields of mortality. Their ability to move forward with purpose would thereby be compromised. They might lose their traction even as they tried to move upward, and they might feel as if their gears were grinding and their clutch plates were slipping under the weight of sin.

A few might squander scarce resources, as if their thermostats were inoperable, allowing their cooling systems to boil over from the excitement of excessive exertion in the steam plant of sin. All these mechanical issues might combine to overwhelm them in a perfect storm of trial and temptation, forcing, as it were, lifestyle compromises that would make self-control and self-actualization all the more difficult, while making rationalization and self-justification more tempting options.

But for the few of us who might be lucky enough to pass through the constriction in the hourglass, there would come a realization that the time to stand and deliver had arrived. As Brutus observed, we would face that "tide in the affairs of men which, taken at the flood, leads on to fortune. Omitted," we would realize that the voyage of our lives would be condemned to be "bound in shallows and in miseries. On such a full sea," however, we would find ourselves "afloat, and we" would "take the current when it serves, or lose our ventures." (Shakespeare, "Julius Caesar," Act 4, Scene 3).

Those who make it through the strait and narrow way, are fortunate, indeed, to find that by following the blueprints of The Plan, enough wiggle-room exists to be able to successfully flex their spiritual muscles and exercise their moral agency

in a forum of free will that engages opposition in a vigorous tug-of-war. They realize that The Plan works best when its participants are able to make good choices in the midst of less attractive competing options. They hope to be sensitive to spiritual promptings, to be stimulated by the light of Christ, to receive the Gift of the Holy Ghost, to be thereby guided, and to be replenished with the high octane fuel of faith that ignites the fire of fortitude and propels them onward, through repentance, to their eternal reward.

Those who seize the moment, thread the eye of the needle, and negotiate the strait and narrow path, realize that what at the outset had felt like a confinement and a constraint, is in fact a birth canal, or a portal through which all must pass in order to progress eternally. They feel as if they have been literally born again. Expanding circles of opportunity that had beforehand been hidden from their view snap into sharp focus. They see beyond the limited horizon of their sight, and comprehend a vision in which the perfect law of liberty stretches out before them in a vista of incomprehensible proportion. They see that God's Plan rests on solid footings that are reinforced with the rebar of our resolve, and that it is upon the foundation of the covenants that we make with Him, and particularly upon the Gospel of Repentance, that celestial sureties are constructed, leading to eternal life in His mansions above.

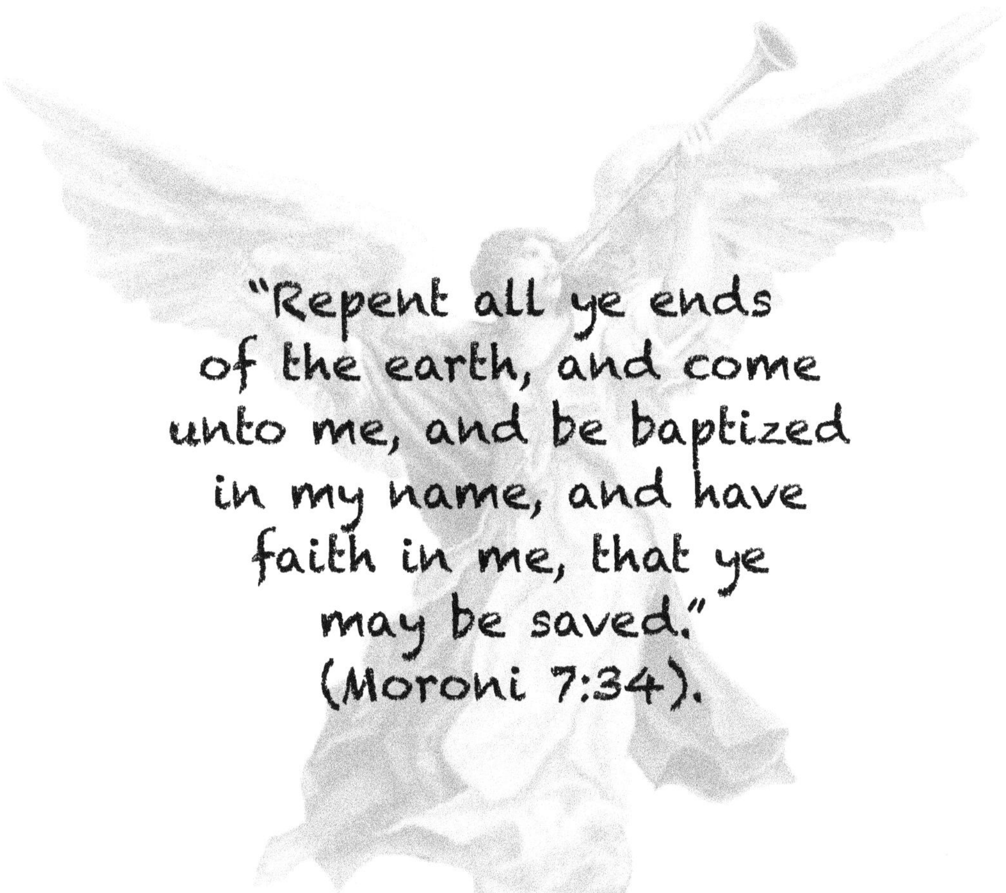

"Repent all ye ends
of the earth, and come
unto me, and be baptized
in my name, and have
faith in me, that ye
may be saved."
(Moroni 7:34).

Chapter Twenty Five

Giving vitality to life's playbook, through repentance.

When Alma met the Sons of Mosiah on the road as they were leaving the land of Gideon, fourteen years after they had bid each other farewell at the commencement of their missions, it must have seemed altogether remarkable that his highest and best hopes for their welfare had been confirmed. As he learned the details of their experiences during those eventful years, he surely recognized and appreciated the unchangeable formula for success that had guided them so unerringly. Ammon, Aaron, Omner, and Himni "had waxed strong in the knowledge of the truth; for they were men of a sound understanding and they had searched the scriptures diligently, that they might know the word of God." (Alma 17:2).

"Who shall ascend into the hill of the Lord?" David had asked. "Or who shall stand in his holy place? He that hath clean hands, and a pure heart; who hath not lifted up his soul unto vanity, nor sworn deceitfully. He shall receive the blessing from the Lord, and righteousness from the God of his salvation." (Psalm 24:3-5). The Sons of Mosiah precisely fit this description, just as do those who repent on a regular basis, in order to be right with the Lord.

The scriptures had become their message and were the tools of their trade. Their confidence, we shall see, was directly related to their knowledge of holy writ. "But," Mormon explained, "this is not all. They had given themselves to much prayer, and fasting; therefore they had the spirit of prophecy, and the spirit of revelation, and when they taught, they taught with the power and authority of God." (Alma 17:3). They were missionaries who had endured and overcome every obstacle that had been thrown in the path of their progress. They were not perfect, but we can be sure that they were perfect in their repentance. "God help all honest men," said Marion G. Romney, "to be born again, to be of sound understanding, to know the word of God, and to maintain the spirit thereof by study, fasting, prayer, and work." (C.R., 10/1941).

The challenges we face are part of life, and the example of the Sons of Mosiah gives us courage to push on with less concern about winning or losing. What is important is to carry the struggle further. In our pursuit of excellence, we know that we will face our share of trials, all tailored by a wise Father to meet our individual needs for growth. Because of the Atonement, and the powerful principle of repentance, we view these not as stumbling blocks to our progression, but as stepping-stones to greater heights of achievement. We carry the struggle as far as need be, relying upon His strength and His saving grace to sustain us when we feel we have gone as far as we can by ourselves.

We will have spiritual challenges.

But we will recognize chastisement from the Lord as an invitation to repent. Throughout the week, we will prepare ourselves to receive the Sacrament each Sunday. We will strengthen our testimonies through fasting and prayer that accompanies our repentance. To reinforce our understanding of Gospel principles, we will undertake a consistent program of scripture study. We will make the sweet spirit within the temple a regular part of our experience. We will resist temptations by recognizing and avoiding the trigger points of compromising situations, and particularly those that have been tailored by the tempter to address our weaknesses.

We will learn to act upon spiritual promptings and exercise our agency wisely.

We will have intellectual challenges.

But we will deal with them by reading uplifting literature and by exercising our minds with stimulating thoughts and meaningful conversation with others. We will speak with purpose. We will maintain a working knowledge of the current events that shape the world around us, but ignore the media when it focuses attention on negative news and trivial matters. We will constantly push ourselves to develop new interests in creative fields and become mentors to those who show interest in developing expertise in those areas in which we excel.

<u>We will face emotional challenges head-on.</u>

When we have time on our hands, we will remember to ponder and pray rather than wander and play. When things do not seem to go our way, we will fall back on our eternal perspective. We will use a cosmic yardstick to measure our progress. Our only recreational drug of choice will be endorphins. We will make extraordinary efforts to positively influence those situations over which we retain some control. We will learn to accept that which we cannot change, but at the same time create reservoirs of positive energy upon which we may draw in time of need, to change those things over which we do have some control.

We will make every effort to avoid the pitfalls of the poor soul who "worked out for years to reduce all his fat; whose muscles were firm and whose stomach was flat; who jogged day and night to keep himself trim, and still found time to play tennis and swim. He drank protein drinks, and ate health food galore, then lifted, stair-climbed, and lifted some more. He told family and friends that it gave him a 'high.' They encouraged him on as he waved them good-bye. 'If things work out,' he yelled back from afar, 'I'll be a great athlete; I'll be a big star!' But how could he miss the big truck up ahead? One thud, and his beautiful body lay dead. And then, he saw something that filled him with fright. His spiritual body was one sorry sight!

No more than a skeleton, covered with skin. He got up to heaven, but didn't get in! 'Another soul's mine!' Satan started to scream. 'Give man something nice, and he'll take the extreme!' OK, I'll admit it; I'll outright confess. For the fast way to hell, take the excess express." (Peter G. Czerny).

<u>We will have physical challenges as the years pass.</u>

In anticipation of these, we will pre-emptively establish fitness programs tailored to our individual needs and designed to help us sustain higher levels of health. We will view physical limitations positively as opportunities to develop patience and perspective. We will regularly re-evaluate our adherence to the spirit of the Word of Wisdom and commit ourselves to goals of improvement based upon greater adherence to its principles. We will view the blessing of the health in our navels and the marrow in our bones, of our ability to run and not be weary, and walk and not faint, as a gift, enabling us to engage in a vigorous reappraisal of our standing before the Lord, that we might make course corrections, as needed.

<u>There will be service challenges.</u>

Our time is always at a premium and there will always be competition between selfish and selfless endeavors. We will consistently discipline ourselves to make time to be of service to our own families, to individuals outside our families, and to the body of Christ. We will trust in the Lord's protection when we consciously and deliberately put ourselves at risk as we venture out into the world to reclaim lost sheep. We will commit to regular and sustained efforts to contribute in positive ways to the welfare of our communities, region, nation, and the world.

<u>We may face character challenges along the way.</u>

To guard against compromise, we will learn to appreciate experiences that teach us humility, we will look forward with anticipation to those that challenge our paradigm, and we will apply the principle of repentance when we make mistakes

as we move forward. We will attempt to so live our lives that we would be happy to give our parrot to the town gossip. We will try to be the kinds of persons our dogs believe us to be. We will commit the 13 Articles of Faith to life as well as to memory, and make them the tangible particles of our faith. We will be honest, true, chaste, benevolent, virtuous, and do good to others.

As our faith increases, so will our capacity to see God's influence over all aspects of our lives. We will learn to recognize and accept the suffering that is a part of life, and strive to see adversity as a necessary and beneficial aspect of our experience. We will apply the Atonement in our lives.

In times of trial, we will try to remember the Savior, Who descended beneath all things, and Who is our Exemplar. We will shun the shadows as we are drawn to His light. As we are immersed in the Spirit as a tangible element, we will exult in His glorious influence. It will become part of our nature to relate comfortably with all that is virtuous, lovely, of good report and praiseworthy. We will seek after that which creates an atmosphere conducive to improvement.

<u>Our challenges will stimulate within us our innate capacity for extraordinary responses.</u>

As Joseph Smith exhorted the Church, so we will declare: "Shall we not go on in so great a cause? Go forward and not backward. Courage … and on, on to the victory! Let your hearts rejoice and be exceedingly glad. Let the earth break forth into singing … and let all the sons (and daughters) of God shout for joy!" (D&C 128:22-23).

Because of the Atonement, we are able to visualize our reunion with our Father. We can imagine stepping on shore, and finding it heaven. We sense ourselves taking hold of a hand, and finding it God's hand. We envision breathing deeply, and discovering it is celestial air that fills our lungs. We picture in our mind's eye

feelings of invigoration, and realize that it is immortality. We create the atmosphere of passing from storm and tempest to an unbroken calm. In our dreams we pre-play the self-fulfilling prophecy of awakening, and finding it Home.

We realize that "God speaketh once, yea twice, yet (we) perceiveth it not. In a dream, in a vision of the night, when deep sleep falleth upon (us), in slumberings upon the bed, then he openeth (our) ears, and sealeth (our) instruction." (Job 33:14-16).

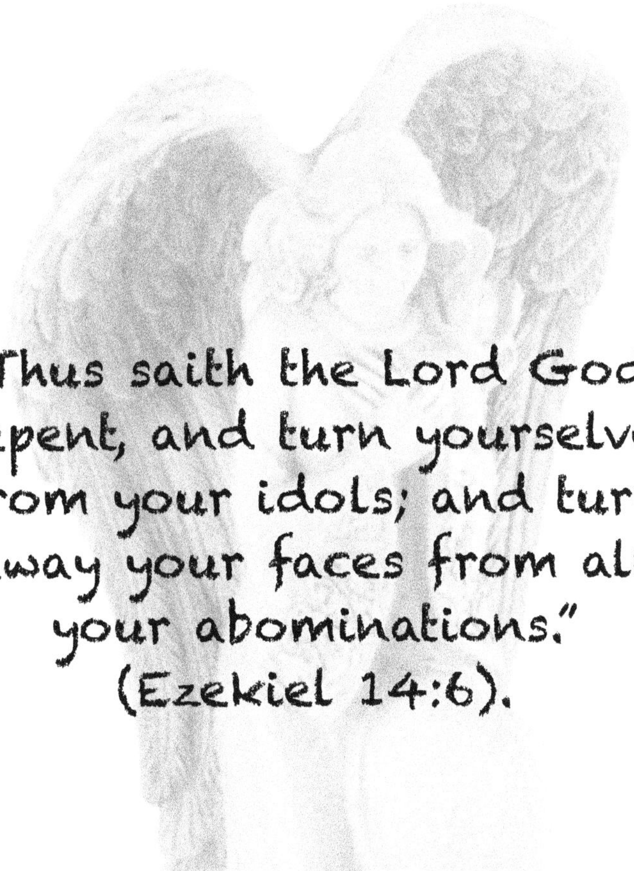

"Thus saith the Lord God;
Repent, and turn yourselves
from your idols; and turn
away your faces from all
your abominations."
(Ezekiel 14:6).

Chapter Twenty Six

Repentance and the Plan of Happiness. (Alma 34:31).

In our busy and complex world, it is very difficult to tell just what brings us happiness. Neither fame nor anonymity holds the key. Both poverty and wealth have failed miserably. Neither sickness nor health has the ability. Both principalities and the absence of worldly influence are inadequate. Neither beauty nor the beast has the advantage. In their quest for happiness, people sometimes forget that with nurturing rain they are also going to have to deal with some mud, that the road is rocky, with potholes and other hidden obstacles, and is uphill most of the way against a powerful headwind. After all, "the dark threads are as needful in the weaver's skillful hand as the threads of gold and silver, in the pattern he has planned." (Benjamin Malachi Franklin, "The Weaver"). People can never hope to find meaning if they view life superficially, and they will never find happiness without first comprehending its price and then steadfastly seeking its reward. When our quest is casual, we are as vain imposters, and our experiences can be false and misleading and without the anticipated long-term effects.

We generally do not value that which we do not deserve. In the Savior's parable, it was a wise merchant who, when he found one pearl of great price, "went and sold

all that he had" in order to possess it. (Matthew 13:46). So it is with happiness, and as we follow the path that leads to it, we make frequent stops along the way at sites that are prominently marked by signs that invite us to pause for repentance, refreshment, and recommitment to proven principles.

Satan uses telestial trivia that rely on the treasures of the earth, as counterfeit pleasures for the blessing of happiness that our Father in Heaven reserves for His repentant children. He knows how easy it is for us to fashion gods of wood and stone to satisfy our appetites, conceits, passions, and vanities, and to assuage our consciences. We have all witnessed those of weak character, who may think that they have found happiness in these pleasures, because they have not learned to recognize and have never experienced the inner peace that follows forgiveness of sin. In fact, they may even live "after the manner of happiness for a season," because both their level of understanding and their behavior harmonize with worldly standards. As long as they can shut out the Light of Christ, they may live in the deception of that fantasy world. But sooner or later, the discrepancy between their behavior and Gospel ideals will become so great that their short-lived pleasure in their worldly ways will crumble. The Lord will not always suffer the wicked "to take happiness in sin." (Mormon 2:13).

The unrepentant wicked can only conduct their lives in opposition to the laws of heaven for so long, before "critical mass" is reached. At that point, a readjustment is required, bringing errant individuals back into harmony with nature. Those who worship idols of any kind are blinded to the recognition that their faith is flawed, and that the objects of their desires have no power to deliver on their promises. Sooner or later, the master pretender will reveal his true character as the father of lies. (See 2 Nephi 9:9).

Of the confused, abandoned, and disillusioned disciples who lie strewn in his wake and who litter the broad boulevards of the twin cities of worldliness and pleasure, the Savior declared: "They seek not the Lord to establish his righteousness, but every man walketh in his own way, and after the image of his own god, whose image is in the likeness of the world, and whose substance is like that of an idol,

which waxeth old and shall perish in Babylon, even Babylon the great, which shall fall." (D&C 1:16). The blueprints of Babylon are always drawn with a stylus moved by the unsteady hand of man's own might. But we are put on notice, as we remember that even though Babylon was for a time the greatest city of the ancient world, it grew weak because it rotted from within, and it was conquered from without, left desolate, and has been forgotten.

Well did the poet write: "I met a traveler from an antique land who said: Two vast and trunkless legs of stone stand in the desert. Near them, on the sand half sunk, a shattered visage lies, whose frown and wrinkled lip and sneer of cold command tell that its sculptor well those passions read, which yet survive. Stamped on these lifeless things, the hand that mocks them and the heart that fed; and on the pedestal these words appear: 'My name is Ozymandias, King of Kings. Look on my works, ye mighty, and despair!' Nothing beside remains. Round the decay of that colossal wreck, boundless and bare, the lone and level sand stretches far away." (Percy Bysshe Shelly, "Ozymandias").

The world has always been mesmerized by an endless stream of illusions of influence, even though each is only a caricature of happiness. Because telestial treasures provide what appears to be an overflowing cornucopia of comfort, it is all too easy for those who make their homes in Babylon to put their trust in material resources, rather than in God. When a siren song seduces people with the creation of an insatiable desire for goods, it is easy for their priorities to be out of order. As their vision blurs, they confuse a vacation in Idumea with life on the strait and narrow path. When that happens, and they forget to speedily repent, they lose power, purpose, and focus. People who have grown to depend more on a secular safety net than upon spiritual preparedness and rejuvenation through repentance are more inclined in times of crisis to grasp at the world's goods, rather than to drop to their knees, hold tightly to their faith, and work their way out of their problems with the help of their Father in Heaven, the gentle nudging of the Holy Ghost, and the Atonement of the Savior.

When the world becomes distracted by pagan gods of its own invention and construction, it is led into spiritual bondage, until it is "as the heathen, as the families of the countries, to serve wood and stone." (Ezekiel 20:32). Jeremiah asked: "Shall a man make gods unto himself, and they are no gods?" (Jeremiah

16:20). If we unwisely set our hearts on the vain things of the world, which are those things that lack the power to deliver on their promises, we become infected by the desire to obtain that which we have not earned, do not deserve, cannot appreciate, and will never retain.

We become as strangers from a realm of light, who have forgotten all - the memory of our former life, and the purpose of our call. (See "Saturday's Warrior," lyrics by Doug Stewart). Repetitive repentance reinforces a religious recognition that endows us with the power to enjoy the spiritual insight and understanding that can change and perfect our lives. As Isaiah invited Israel, so may we that have not the means "buy wine and milk without money and without price." (Isaiah 55:1).

It is little wonder that God set the standard in the Decalogue, when He warned His children about the virus of covetousness. One of the seven deadly sins, it is a communicable disease that is dangerously self-serving, decidedly unproductive, doggedly virulent, and deceptively unsatisfying. The antidote is clear: "Look to God, and live" abundantly. (Alma 37:47).

In the Last Days, Nephi warned, "the lofty looks of man shall be humbled." (2 Nephi 12:11). His mentor Isaiah urged Israel not to trust in the arm of flesh, whose power is impotent, and in man's puny energies, "whose breath is in his nostrils," but rather to trust in God who has given man "the breath of life," that he might become "a living soul," capable through divine intervention of experiencing unspeakable joy. (2 Nephi 12:22). It is easy to see why the mission of The Church of Jesus Christ of Latter-day Saints is simply to teach the principles that are related to true happiness, for when people have forsaken their core values, they characteristically succumb to an obsession for things that can never satisfy their appetites.

Such shifting sands can never provide the solid foundation that is necessary to launch us on the eternally escalating course envisioned by our Fathers' Plan. With vivid imagery, the scriptures encourage the repentant faithful to "increase in beauty, and in holiness," and Zion to "arise and put on her beautiful garments" in preparation for her happy reunion with her Creator. (D&C 82:14).

The children of men never do evil so cheerfully as when they think they are doing good. To compound the deception, Satan's substitutes for joy actually dull our senses and make us even more vulnerable to his enticements. If we persist in behavior that is in opposition to the laws relating to happiness, we may even ask the Lord: "What have we spoken against thee?" Is our lifestyle really so bad? We are inclined to believe that "it is vain to serve God, and what doth it profit that we have kept his ordinances and that we have walked mournfully before the Lord of Hosts?" We haven't immediately seen the rewards that come from repentance, and since we've never really been converted, it doesn't seem profitable to keep the commandments. It is only natural, then, for us to deny the faith. From our perspective, "we call the proud happy." It seems to us that they "they that work wickedness ... yea, they that tempt God are even delivered." To us, black is white, and white is black, and so does it really matter? (Malachi 3:13-15).

The distinction is clear, however, to those who have tried the virtue of the word of God, and who can "discern between the righteous and the wicked, between him that serveth God and him that serveth him not." (Malachi 3:18). Life is all a stage, but when the bouquets are thrown at the feet of the players, and they are summoned for a curtain call after the final act, it will only be the faithful and true who will, with joy, will turn to the Master Choreographer to give Him the standing ovation that only He deserves.

As we endure to the end, we must be especially vigilant. We must avoid embracing "idea-gods" that rivet our attention, consume our energies, demand our devotion, divert our direction, obscure our objectivity, and dilute our capacity for

repentance. Sitting with our engines idling while wasting time in telestial traffic jams can damage our ability and desire to move forward. Overzealously pursuing caricatures created with smoke and mirrors, or jousting with windmills, is ultimately delusional and self-destructive.

As we embrace the principles of the Gospel, our path is clear and our destination is well-defined. We do not confuse knowledge for intelligence, nor do we think that when we are learned we are wise. We understand that to be learned is good, but only if we are humble and obedient. When we are grounded in the bedrock of the Gospel, and we regularly repent, our testimonies are protected, the work and the glory of God move forward, we approach a fulness of joy, and our souls are saved.

Samuel the Lamanite charged the people of Zarahemla: "Ye have sought all the days of your lives for that which ye could not obtain, and ye have sought for happiness in doing iniquity, which thing is contrary to the nature of that righteousness" which is in God. (Helaman 13:38). The adversary finally betrays his followers, because he cannot deliver on his promises. His enticements lead the unwary into conceptual cul-de-sacs, from which there is no exit except rationalized retreat, frantic flight from responsibility, a stammering shifting of blame, brazen back-pedaling, and confused complacency leading to senseless stupor of thought and total defeat. His cunning caresses entice the weak-willed to plunge into a perceived freedom, which is really a doctrinal dead-end that leads only to a bottomless pit of misery.

In a perverted way, "the Devil seeks that all men might be miserable like himself." (2 Nephi 2:27). Never does he dare to promise that those who follow him will be happy. Instead, he influences his disciples to engage in the twisted reasoning that allows them to rationalize their quest for the Holy Grail of power, wealth, dominion, position, and influence, that are poor substitutes for humility, meekness, modesty, restraint, and happiness.

"There are many spirits which are false spirits, which have gone forth in the earth, deceiving the world." They would entice us to persist in

wickedness, relying on the quick fix of pleasure as a mean substitute for happiness. They have "sought to deceive you," cautioned the Lord, "that (they) might overthrow you." (D&C 50:2-3). They do this with cunning and guile, and often with genuine sophistication, for as Shakespeare wrote, even "the Devil can cite scripture for his purpose." ("The Merchant of Venice," Act 1, Scene 3).

Among his many counterfeits, the adversary often uses pride as a lame excuse for our failure to repent. This is one reason why the world is in such a frenzied pursuit of material gain. As it accumulates more and more, in an endless quest for "enough," many are puffed up with inflated egos in a race that may not be well-defined, will never be over, and certainly can never be won. There is no "exit strategy" because there is no conscious recognition that a personality disorder even exists. There is no one left to shout, "Stop the insanity" because everyone who thought they were waiting for the train bound for glory has instead pushed and shoved to clamber aboard the Excess Express. (Susan Powter).

The Excess Express is a train whose fanatical passengers have lost sight of their objectives and have consequently redoubled their efforts. These over-zealous commuters ride those rails to reduce all their fat; to keep their muscles firm and their stomachs flat. They jog day and night to stay nice and trim, and still find time to play tennis and swim. They chug protein drinks, and eat health food galore. They lift weights, stair-climb, and lift even more, telling family and friends that it gives them a "high." Their friends encourage them on, as they wave them good-bye. "If things work out," they yell from afar, "we'll be great athletes, we'll be big stars!" But how could they miss the washed-out trestle on up ahead? In one short instant, their beautiful bodies lay dead! Only then, will they see something that will fill them with fright. Their spiritual bodies will be one sorry sight! No more than skeletons, covered with skin. Though they get close to heaven, they'll never get in! "Another soul's mine!" Satan will scream. "Give man something nice, and he'll take the extreme!'" OK, we'll admit it; we'll outright confess. For the fast way to hell, take the Excess Express. (Anonymous).

Those who refuse Heavenly Father's invitation to repent seek refuge in the fortress of a perceived satisfaction in their own accomplishments. But that requires the fabrication of a façade that demands inordinate attention to trivial detail and continual cosmetic reconstruction. President Ezra Taft Benson called pride "the universal sin, the great vice" and identified its central feature as "enmity toward God and enmity toward our fellowmen." The insidiously evil and destructive nature of pride "is essentially competitive in nature, arising when individuals pit their will against God's, or their intellects, opinions, works, wealth, and talents against those of other people." He warned the Latter-day Saints that "pride is a damning sin" for "it adversely affects all our relationships and limits or stops progression." (C.R., 4/1989). It effectively extinguishes our desire to repent, and is contrary to the nature of happiness.

When pride swells in our bosom, it occupies such a volume that it squeezes out our capacity for heart-felt repentance. N. Eldon Tanner observed that "the craving for praise and popularity too often controls actions, and as a people succumb, they find themselves bending their character, when they think they are only taking a bow." As a result, many become disillusioned when their misguided search for happiness and for peace of conscience rings hollow and leaves a sour aftertaste imprinted upon the spirit. Such individuals, who are driven by the desire for acquisition, accumulation, and gain, have never learned that "happiness is like a butterfly. The more you chase it, the more it eludes you. But if you turn your attention to purposeful repentance with a renewed determination to be obedient, it will come and sit softly on your shoulder." (Anonymous).

Joseph Smith declared that happiness "is the object and design of our existence, and will be the end thereof, if we pursue the path that leads to it; and this path is virtue, uprightness, faithfulness, holiness, and keeping all the commandments of God." ("Teachings," p. 255). We must consciously pursue this path, for God will always grant to His children the gift of free will, "for behold, they are their own judges, whether to do good or do evil." (Alma 41:7). Although we may pick our own poison, we cannot choose to escape the resulting consequences.

On the one hand are happiness and well-being; on the other are misery and despair. "The decrees of God are unalterable; therefore, the way is prepared that whosoever will may walk therein and be saved" from the pain and anguish that follow poor choices. (Alma 41:8). Many of our most valuable lessons come as a result of the repentance process. One of these is the firm testimony gained by experience, that "wickedness never was happiness." When we recognize that truth, its corollary snaps into focus: We cannot "be restored from sin to happiness." (Alma 41:10). As Lehi put it: "If there be no righteousness, there be no happiness." (2 Nephi 2:13).

Sometimes, with a gut-wrenching sense of hopelessness that comes "because of iniquity," we learn that despair, that is the antithesis of happiness, fills the vacuum created by sin. (Moroni 10:22). Too late, the wicked learn that every law has both blessing and punishment components. When the law is obeyed, a blessing is given that results in happiness, or joy. When that law is disobeyed, however, punishment follows that results in unhappiness, or misery. Despair is the feeling of abandonment and isolation that accompanies unresolved disobedience. Sooner or later, it will bear down heavily on every person who has adopted a lifestyle at odds with The Plan of Happiness. If we succumb to such feelings, our subsequent behavior tends to be reinforcing and contributes to our downward spiral in an accelerating free-fall from faith.

Alma explained that "all men that are in a state of nature, or I would say, in a carnal state, are in the gall of bitterness and in the bonds of iniquity; they are without God in the world, and they have gone contrary to the nature of God; therefore, they are in a state contrary to the nature of happiness." (Alma 41:11). The Savior taught that if we lack vision, and build "upon the works of men, or upon the works of the Devil," we may have joy "for a season." (Mormon 2:13). We may briefly enjoy the fruits of our labor, however ill-gotten is its gain, because eternal law obeys no man's timetable. In fact, were every act of obedience immediately rewarded, and every act of disobedience immediately punished, all would do right, but for the wrong reasons.

Faith is developed by degrees, as we take baby steps into the unknown. Some of the blessings associated with faith are literally out of this world, and are reserved for those who inherit eternal life in the resurrection. However, we can be certain that for the wicked, "by and by, the end cometh, and they are hewn down and cast into the fire, from whence there is no return." (3 Nephi 27:11).

As we begin to understand how The Plan of Happiness operates, we realize that "the meaning of the word restoration is to bring back again ... good for that which is good; righteous for that which is righteous; just for that which is just; (and) merciful for that which is merciful." (Alma 41:13). In other words, if we consistently conduct our lives in harmony with the principles of The Plan, particularly in harmony with the principle of repentance, the Law of Restoration assures us of happiness.

Meanwhile, the world has done a remarkable job of rationalizing its predictably wicked behavior and redefining in double-speak the legitimacy of its ways, in an effort to circumvent the Law of Just Compensation. In such jargon, unrepentant wickedness takes on an air of respectability in an attempt to circumvent the pain that is the natural consequence of poor choices. "Public drunkenness" is ationalized as "social drinking." "Obscenity" matures into "adult content," and "sexual deviancy" is transformed to an "alternative lifestyle." "Lying" is characterized as "hyper-exaggeration." "Pro-choice" puts a positive spin on "abortion," and the "Holy Sabbath" morphs into "the weekend."

But life has no coherence, and is in fact, a cruel joke, without the spiritual symmetry and balance that the Lord's fitness program can bring. Alma applied the principle of restoration to Corianton when he explained: "Therefore, my son, see that you are merciful unto your brethren; deal justly, judge righteously, and do good continually; and if ye do all these things then shall ye receive your reward; yea, ye shall have mercy restored unto you again; ye shall have justice restored unto you again; ye shall have a righteous judgment restored unto you again; and

ye shall have good rewarded unto you again." (Alma 41:14). In short, such conduct guarantees the restoration and perpetuation of happiness, for, as Alma taught, "that which ye do send out shall return unto you again." (Alma 41:15). Perhaps this is why Paul warned: "The wages of sin is death, but the gift of God is eternal life." (Romans 6:23).

Because our capacity for happiness is so frequently threatened, we need the power of covenants to provide the opportunity for recommitment to the behavioral lifestyle that pertains to righteousness. So that we may appropriately manage the circumstances with which we grapple, and effectively deal with the events that influence us, we need unequivocal understanding and clear definitions that can only come from the Holy Ghost. These will protect us from the worldly influences that encroach upon the fortress of our spiritual security, symmetry, and stability.

Internalizing Gospel principles creates an impenetrable shield of faith. As we gain eternal perspective, we can discern between the polarized opposites that are so prevalent in our world today. We can discriminate between happiness and its worldly counterfeits. The counsel of our Heavenly Father will strike familiar chords within us, even as Satan's fingerprints are more easily distinguished on the profane idols with which he tempts us. Little wonder that the Master said that His sheep would recognize His voice, and follow Him. (See John 10:27).

The sturdiest plants that bear the best fruit are those that have deep roots in good, rich, nurturing soil. So, to be facilitate our repentance, we must surround ourselves with the best that can be provided in music and art, conversation, example, decency, virtue, and honor. Then, our spirits will grow freely, even as we send down taproots in Gospel soil to secure a solid footing. As we do so, we recommit the 13th Article of Faith to our lifestyle, as well as to our memory. "If there is anything virtuous, lovely, or of good report or praiseworthy, we will seek after these things." (See Philippians 4:8). To the extent that we do this, we may expect to blossom enthusiastically with the "fire of God" and feel the effects of the Atonement in our lives.

If we don't, we may experience hell while yet on earth, which is the mental anguish that is the recognition of lost opportunities. It is felt as the guilt and pain of unresolved sin, which is "like an unquenchable fire" that can leave our hope for happiness in ashes. (Mosiah 2:38). Mercy has no claim upon those who refuse to take advantage of repentance, and Justice demands their never-ending torment. (See Mosiah 2:39). Those who find themselves in these circumstances are most profoundly on their own, in a state of eternal unhappiness, for their state is as if no Atonement for sin had been made. To avoid such a fate, Benjamin urged his people to awaken "to a remembrance of the awful situation of those that have fallen into transgression." (Mosiah 2:40). In contrast, he portrayed in his sermon "the blessed and happy state of those that keep the commandments." (Mosiah 2:41).

An understanding of happiness requires knowledge of the Fall of Adam. It is the doctrine of the Church that there was opposition from the beginning, but that in the Garden of Eden, Adam and Eve did not have true moral agency; therefore, they could not have been happy before the introduction of the enticements of Satan. The scriptures teach that "it must needs be that the Devil should tempt the children of men, or they could not be agents unto themselves; for if they never should have bitter, they could not know the sweet." (D&C 29:39).

We know that Satan did not deceive Eve. Rather, her intelligent and conscious decision to partake of the forbidden fruit was the result of a correct understanding of the requirements of the Gospel Plan of Happiness. Both Adam and Eve "fell that men might be" eternally happy. (2 Nephi 2:25). Little wonder then, that "the morning stars sang together, and all the sons of God shouted for joy" when the selfsame Plan was introduced to them before the foundation of the world. (Job 38:7).

Not knowing the mind of God, that there must needs be opposition in all things, the serpent sought what he thought would be the end of happiness, or the misery of all mankind. With his congenital shortsightedness and his typical stratagem of promoting half-truths, the forbidden fruit was offered to Eve. "Ye shall be as God, knowing good and evil," he promised. (2 Nephi 2:18). He knew that we would then

have the capacity for happiness, but he was confident that he could influence us to be miserable.

Our Father knew that life in Eden before the Fall was not ideal, hence His counsel to Adam and Eve: "Nevertheless, thou mayest choose for thyself, for it is given unto thee." (Moses 3:17). But with the temptation of Eve came our first parents' only opportunity to find eternal happiness. As Lehi clearly taught, had Adam and Eve not transgressed the Law in the Garden, they would have vegetated there forever in a morally static environment. Our Father knew that His children must fall as a critically operative part of The Plan of Happiness.

One of the basic messages of the Restoration, then, is that Adam and Eve fell so that, through repentance, activated by faith in the power of the Atonement, they and their posterity might live in a state of happiness on earth and inherit eternal joy in heaven. When the Fall is considered in conjunction with the Atonement of Christ, it is powerfully clear that both are critical to success of The Plan of Happiness, for we can only attain a fulness of joy in a personal, tangible, perfected resurrection in the Celestial Kingdom, made possible by the Savior of the world Who suffered for our sins. "For man is spirit, the elements are eternal, and spirit and element, inseparably connected (by the power of the Atonement) receive a fulness of joy." (D&C 93:33).

It is Christ's way for us to act for ourselves. (See 2 Nephi 2:26). It is Satan's way for us to be acted upon. The perfect law of liberty requires that we be free according to the flesh. (See 2 Nephi 2:27, & James 1:25). The choice is between liberty, eternal life, and happiness, or captivity, spiritual death, and misery. But to earn these blessings, we must repent, and abide by the other laws of the Gospel, otherwise, unbridled freedom makes us travel along a slippery slope above a personality precipice that leads to oppression and tyranny. We are free to choose the direction we will take, but we cannot choose to escape the consequences of our poor choices.

Satan's tactics rely on compulsion, deny agency, and require obedience. If we

voluntarily give up our freedom to act independently, we are trapped in the gaping jaws of bad habits, and snared by Satan. We are bound by his strong chains. His heavy cords around our necks restrict the righteous exercise of our agency, making it easier for him to drag us down to hell. It is very hard to break free of the grip of bad habits, because we have given up our freedom to act independently in order to acquire them.

Satan and all who follow him are miserable because, entrenched in sin, they no longer enjoy the freedom to choose, rendering them powerless to change their circumstances. They know all too well where the exercise of their agency has taken them. Because they are past repentance, and happiness is beyond their reach, their torment is excruciating. But misery loves company, and Satan desires that the children of God might be as he is. (See 2 Nephi 2:27). If we give up our birthright of happiness for the mess of pottage characterized by the fleeting pleasures of the world, we will be left with an empty, sick feeling in the pit of our stomach, when we realize that we have been duped by the siren song of that master snake oil salesman named Satan.

Heavenly Father does not operate this way. He sees the eternal principle of agency differently. The exercise of free will does entail risk, because the element of failure is real, but it is the only way that we may justify our claim to unspeakable joy in our Father's kingdom. Rather than enslaving us in good habits, He repeatedly gives us the opportunity to recommit ourselves to the tried and true practice of repentance. At the same time, He promises to introduce us to the laws that pertain to happiness, so that we might qualify to receive its blessing. This is one of the most important reasons why repentance is vital to our spiritual well-being, inner peace, and continual progression.

Brigham Young taught that "the Spirit is pure, and (is) under the special control and influence of the Lord, but the body is of the earth, and is subject to the power of the Devil, and is under the mighty influence of that fallen nature that is of the earth. If the Spirit yields to the body, the Devil then has power to overcome the

body and Spirit of that man, and he loses both." ("Discourses of Brigham Young," p. 69-70).

If we sink into the quicksand of carnality and lose our wide-eyed innocence, purity, and holiness, we forfeit the happiness that accompanies untroubled souls. As we choose the better part, however, we yield our hearts to the Savior. We ponder the great and terrible consequences of Gethsemane, travel with Him to Calvary, and enjoy the sweetness of the redeeming power of the Atonement, which is the keystone of The Plan of Happiness. "All things which pertain to our religion are only appendages to it," declared the Prophet Joseph Smith. The particles of our faith support and sustain the mission statement of the Savior, Who said that His work and glory (through His Atonement) is to bring about our immortality and eternal life in a state of perpetual and unmitigated happiness. ("Teachings," p. 127, see Moses 1:38).

If we value our spiritual welfare, love the Lord, and observe His commandment to repent, we will find happiness. Heber J. Grant once said: "I bear witness to you as an Apostle of the Lord Jesus Christ, that material and spiritual prosperity is predicated upon the fulfillment of the duties and responsibilities that rest upon us as Latter-day Saints." (C.R. 10/1889). When we keep the laws of God, we will experience "that happiness which is prepared for the Saints." (2 Nephi 9:43). Such happiness can transcend temporal security and worldly comforts.

These teachings give us insights into the spiritual roots of human relationships, expressed in happiness based on the common bonds of spiritual interdependency. They helps us to live in the world without being tainted by it. They emphasize the power of the Atonement to transform life on this telestial world into a celestial experience. As the Savior revealed: "Abundance is multiplied unto (the Saints) through the manifestations of the Spirit." (D&C 70:13). Only when we pay attention to the commandments of our Heavenly Father, do our righteous objectives stay in focus, and may we enjoy the sustaining influence of His sweet Spirit.

It is most remarkable that our opportunity for happiness is a gracious gift from

God that harmonizes perfectly with the principle of repentance. It is by His infinite, continuing, uninterrupted, and uncorrupted grace that we enjoy our mortal experience, after all we can do on our own. (See 2 Nephi 25:23). Brigham Young rightly observed: "There is no man who ever made a sacrifice on this earth for the kingdom of heaven except the Savior. I would not give the ashes of a rye straw for that man who feels he is making sacrifices for God. We are doing this for our own happiness." (J.D., 16:114).

Alma's plea to the Saints in Zarahemla to "try the virtue of the word of God" was an invitation to enjoy the fruit of the Tree of Life and to open their senses to the matchless realm of joy available only through obedience to the principle of repentance. (See Alma 5:34). We repent that our eyes might ever be before the Lord (see Psalms 25:15), that our skin might shine with exceeding luster (see Mosiah 13:5), and that we might righteously seek after everything that is virtuous, lovely, of good report and praiseworthy (see the 13th Article of Faith & Philippians 4:8). We do so because these divine characteristics are the very things that will make us happy.

Repentance and the Atonement neutralize the negative aspects of the opposition in all things that is a foundation principle of The Plan. They harmonize the incomprehensible blessings of the eternal world with the challenges of our every day experiences, and make heaven seem worth working for. They define the divine nature of God, and bring His attributes within our grasp. They are the very things that will make us happy.

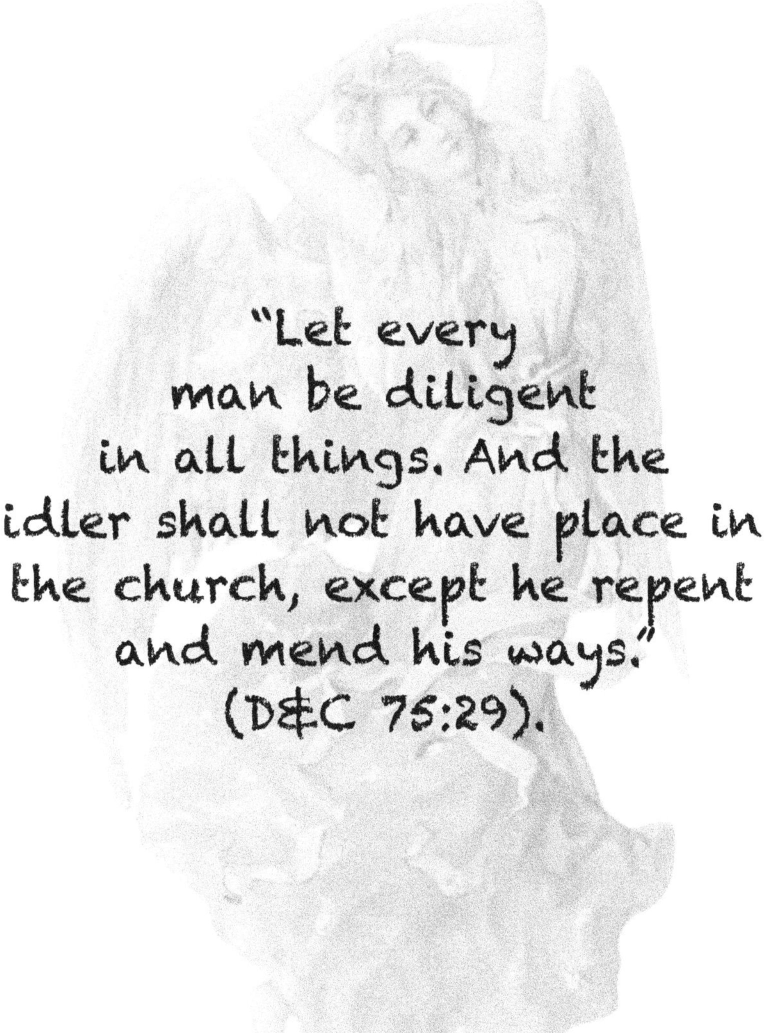

"Let every
man be diligent
in all things. And the
idler shall not have place in
the church, except he repent
and mend his ways."
(D&C 75:29).

Chapter Twenty Seven

The success strategy of repentance.

Because they had already proven themselves in the crucible of adversity and temptation, the Master called His disciples to an even higher plane of spirituality and to a commitment by covenant to selfless consecration of effort. He advised them to "lay up for (themselves) treasures in heaven, where neither moth nor rust doth corrupt, and where thieves do not break through nor steal." (3 Nephi 13:19-20). To help them accomplish this task, He identified a number of strategies, the implementation of which would be key to overcoming telestial tendencies and maintaining spiritual stability in an uncertain world.

Because everyone needs to repent (see Moses 6:23), He inspired his disciples to recommit themselves to service by focusing their attention on their less fortunate brethren. In doing so, He knew that they would align themselves in harmony with divine attributes. Patterning their lives after His would transform their nature as they assumed both the image and likeness of God. (See 2 Peter 3:18). "And ye shall be even as I am, and I am even as the Father, and the Father and I are one," said the Savior. (3 Nephi 28:10).

Secondly, He asked His disciples to exercise saving faith in Him and in His Gospel. The standard of the world is: "Seeing is believing." But as Harold B. Lee taught: "You must learn to walk to the edge of the light, and then a few steps into the darkness.

Then the light will appear and show the way before you." ("B.Y.U. Today," 3/1991, p. 22-23). This is the way faith is developed and strengthened.

The Savior asked His disciples to take that step or two into the darkness, to allow faith, the spiritual strong searchlight, to illuminate the way before them. A classic definition of faith in the scriptures is that it "is not to have a perfect knowledge of things; therefore if ye have faith ye hope for things which are not seen, which are true." (Alma 32:21). This is correct in the ultimate sense. In Alma's usage, however, the verse might more clearly read: "Faith is not to have a perfect knowledge of things gained through our own experience." Trust in only the physical senses is the rational approach that is the enemy of faith. If we are to rely upon the power of the Atonement in our purposeful repentance, we must exercise faith in Jesus Christ.

The Savior knows that our repentance follows a natural progression, and that the success of the Atonement to save us from our sins hinges upon a deeper and more abiding faith, "the substance of things hoped for, the evidence of things not seen." (Hebrews 11:1). This is true during the genesis of faith, as our desire to believe in the power of Christ propels us out of darkness into the light. Then, under the right circumstances, when the stage has been set by our preayerful preparation, when the necessary groundwork has been laid, "by doing our duty, faith increases until it becomes perfect knowledge." (Heber J. Grant, C.R., 4/1934). We can know, without the shadow of a doubt, that the Savior has rescued us from the consequences of our sins.

Initially, faith is to believe what we do not see, and the reward of faith is to see what we believe, with clear understanding and perfect familiarity. Flawless faith implies ownership of the principle toward which our efforts have carried us. This is especially true of repentance. Our claim on mercy does not have a monetary cost

and it cannot be purchased at any price. Instead it carries a performance cost. It must be earned and then paid for by that which is of greatest worth, our broken heart and contrite spirit. (See D&C 59:8). Those who desire to obtain it must not hold anything back. They must invest everything they have, including their trust, confidence, conviction, assurance, anticipation, and expectation in its ability to deliver on its promise.

Ultimately, the success of mercy to redeem us is determined in the crucible of adversity, for we "receive no witness until after the trial of (our) faith." (Ether 12:6). It is important to remember that in the matter of our faith in the power of the Atonement, the Lord is not on trial. At the Bar of Justice, our previous acceptance or rejection of the evidence presented to the Judge will determine our reward or punishment. The trial of our faith is eminently fair, but heavily weighted in our favor is our comprehensive repentance.

Faith is an essential element of our success strategy because it is the foundation of our hope in Christ, with the assurance of peace and the comfort of our convictions that the momentum in our lives will carry us, through repentance, on a trajectory that arches heavenward. As Mormon taught, hope is born of faith. He said that we should "have hope through the Atonement of Christ and the power of His resurrection, to be raised up unto life eternal, and this because of (our) faith in Him according to the promise." (Moroni 7:41).

Hope is more than wishful thinking or a misguided trust in promises that cannot be fulfilled. It is not a high stakes gamble based on statistical improbabilities. Hopeful people do not write checks they cannot cash. Their hope is the reasonable expectation of promised blessings that flow from obedience. Hope is the inevitable reward of well-founded faith, and is the interest earned on an investment made in their undeviating trust in God, in the principles of the Gospel, and in His promise of His power to save.

Our success strategies that are related to repentance and forgiveness ultimately

carry us to a new dimension, that of charity, which is the supreme characteristic of faithful disciples. Mormon taught: "If a man be meek and lowly in heart, and confess by the power of the Holy Ghost that Jesus is the Christ," with a sure hope born of faith, "he must needs have charity." (Moroni 7:44).

Charity is found in abundance in those who have received a forgiveness of their sins through repentance. It is patient, and nurtures sensitivity toward others. It is empathic and is less concerned with telestial trinkets and is more focused on celestial sureties. It is humble and selfless, and it reflects poise under provocation. It has no secret agenda to follow. Repulsed by sin, it is drawn toward the light, and is continually open and receptive to that which is good. Without it, we cannot progress and our lives are empty shells of wasted efforts. As Paul confessed: "Though I speak with the tongues of men and of angels, and have not charity, I am become as sounding brass, or a tinkling cymbal." (1 Corinthians 13:1).

Charity is a bellwether of our repentance. Mormon confirmed: "If ye have not charity, ye are nothing, for charity never faileth. Wherefore, cleave unto charity, which is the greatest of all (the spiritual gifts of God), for all things (and especially the completion of our repentance process) must fail" without it. (Moroni 7:46).

Because "charity is the pure love of Christ ... it endureth forever, and whoso is found possessed of it at the last day, it shall be well with him." (Moroni 7:47). Because it is so intimately linked to repentance, charity prepares us to be like God. It is a gift and a manifestation of His grace, designed to reconfigure our carnality into celestial certainty and elevate us to exaltation.

The Lord admonished us to be full of faith, to be bright with hope, to abound in charity, and to develop other noble character traits, such as "virtue, knowledge, temperance, patience, brotherly kindness, godliness, humility, (and) diligence." (D&C 4:6). We do this, Peter wrote: "That we might be partakers of the divine nature." (2 Peter 1:4). It is only because of the mighty principle of repentance that the Lord's admonition to be perfect, as He and His Father in Heaven are perfect, makes any sense. (See Matthew 5:48).

When God said: "Let us make man in our image, after our likeness," He meant not only that we should have the same physical qualities as our Parents, but the same spiritual characteristics as well. (Moses 2:26). When we are like-minded, we seek each other out, are drawn to each other, have a natural affinity for each other, stand by each other, comfort and encourage each other, and bring out the best in each other. "For this end was the law (of repentance) given," to prepare us to be Christ-like. When the Law illuminates these personality traits, "we are made alive in Christ." (2 Nephi 25:25).

We cannot successfully repent without the nourishment of the Holy Scriptures, whose purpose is to testify of the Savior. Alma recognized the virtue of the word, or in other words, the incredible power of Christ to touch our hearts. (See Alma 31:5). Many examples from the life of the Savior teach this principle. On one particular occasion, the multitudes were drawn to Him as they often were, to satisfy their innermost yearnings. Jesus, in turn, being a wellspring of the Spirit, sensed each moment when need drew upon that source: "And a certain woman, which had an issue of blood twelve years ... when she had heard of Jesus, came in the press behind, and touched his garment. For she said, If I may touch but his clothes, I shall be whole. And straightway she felt in her body that she was healed. And Jesus, immediately knowing in himself that virtue had gone out of him, turned him about and said, Who touched my clothes?" (Mark 5:25-30).

This episode assures us that, in a wonderfully whole and complete manner, God is sensitive to our needs and to our prayers, however small or insignificant they may seem in the grand scheme. He does hear us, because in conformity to law, we draw upon the source of virtue that is the Spirit of God. Every time we call upon God, we are, in effect, touching His garment. How it is accomplished no-one can describe, for it must be directly experienced by those who have known the exhilaration of forgiveness of sin.

"The wind bloweth where it listeth, and thou hearest the sound thereof, but canst not tell whence it cometh, and whither it goeth. So is everyone that is born of the

Spirit." (John 3:8). Redemption is facilitated by a familiarity with the way, the truth, and the life, that leads to direct experience with God. As the Lord explained in the Doctrine & Covenants: "These words are not of men, nor of man, but of me; wherefore, you shall testify they are of me and not of man. For it is my voice which speaketh them unto you; for they are given by my Spirit unto you, and by my power you can read them one to another; and save it were by my power you could not have them. Wherefore, you can testify that you have heard my voice, and know my words." (D&C 18:34-36).

As Jacob put it: "No man knoweth of (God's) ways, save it be revealed unto him." (Jacob 4:8). "No matter what ability and talent we may possess, all must come under this rule if we wish to know the Father and the Son. If knowledge of them is not obtained through revelation (that comes by the Holy Ghost) it cannot be obtained at all." (John Taylor, "The Gospel Kingdom," p. 112). Our redemption is given by personal revelation when truth from all three members of the Godhead speak directly to our soul.

Particularly destructive, however, are the habit patterns of those who are enslaved by drunkenness, selfish indulgence, or intemperance. "O God, that men should put an enemy in their mouths to steal away their brains! That we should ... transform ourselves into beasts!" (Shakespeare, "Othello," Act 2, Scene 3). "Wo unto them that rise up early in the morning, that they may follow strong drink, that continue until night, and wine inflame them!" (2 Nephi 15:11). Such people are blinded to the power of redemption that is before them. "They regard not the work of the Lord, neither consider the operation of his hands." (2 Nephi 15:12).

They are captive because their character is flawed. Their intemperance can never slake their spiritual thirst, or their desire to be clean in the sight of God. On the contrary, both willful and ignorant misbehavior lead to inevitable consequences. As Isaiah prophesied, in the Last Days, even "honorable men (will be) famished, and their multitude dried up with thirst." (2 Nephi 15:13). When men decline the invitation to repent, "hell hath enlarged herself, and opened her mouth without

measure; and their glory, and their multitude, and their pomp, and he that rejoiceth, shall descend into it. And the mean (or common) man shall be brought down, and the mighty man shall be humbled, and the eyes of the lofty shall be humbled. But the Lord of Hosts will be exalted in judgment, and God that is holy shall be sanctified in righteousness." (2 Nephi 15:14-16).

The Lord is patient and long-suffering. He is an eternal optimist with unflappable faith in His power to save. He extends His arm of mercy long after the faint-hearted would have given up hope. When Elijah complained to the Lord: "The children of Israel have forsaken thy covenant, thrown down thine altars, and slain thy prophets with the sword; and I, even I only, am left; and they seek my life to take it away," the Lord responded: "Yet I have left me seven thousand in Israel, all the knees which have not bowed unto Baal, and every mouth which hath not kissed him." (1 Kings 19:14 & 18). There are always souls to be saved in Israel.

Satan's alternative to repentance is a recipe for disaster. His formula is the worst form of virulent infectious disease. When individuals venture onto his turf they are truly in the "Hot Zone." In fact, "the greatest crime in all this world is to lead men and women away from … true principles" by recruiting them into the legions of the Adversary. (Joseph Fielding Smith, Jr., C.R., 4/1951). The bar must not be lowered by compromise or complacency to accommodate his rationalizations. There is a standard of human decency, concern, and brotherly kindness that is expected of each of us. It is part of the severance package we accepted when we sustained The Plan of Salvation and committed to leave our home in heaven and come to earth.

Before Fiorello La Guardia became mayor of New York City, he was a magistrate. One day there appeared before him a man accused of stealing a loaf of bread. Upon questioning, the man explained that he'd committed the crime to feed his family, for they were starving. Whereupon, La Guardia dismissed the case, and sentenced all present in the courtroom to pay a fine for living in a city where a man must steal to feed his family. The Lord illustrated the Gospel principle of

forgiveness of sin when He said: "I am the bread of life: He that cometh to me shall never hunger; and he that believeth on me shall never thirst." (John 6:35). There will be for each of us an Eternal Court of Justice, where a penalty will be executed for our failure to provide others with the Bread of Life, or for feeding them only stale, or moldy, or otherwise unwholesome bread.

When we have internalized and personalized the principle of repentance taught by the Master, we have a responsibility to fortify others with the same hope in Christ. Thomas Carlyle said: "The mystic bond of brotherhood makes all men one." The family of man is, after all, "but one great city, full of beloved ones, divine and human, by nature endeared to each other." (Epictetus). We are an interdependent family, irrevocably committed and connected to each other. Our familial bonds are "an integral part of Christianity no less than the Fatherhood of God; and to deny the one is no less infidel than to deny the other." (Lyman Abbott). Little wonder that we are enjoined to "speak with the trump of God, with a voice to shake the earth, and cry repentance unto every people!" (Alma 29:1).

Our repentance forges an unbreakable relationship with God that is intimately tied to the Atonement of His Son. The covenants we make with God are founded on the sacrifice of Jesus Christ. They define the bounds and conditions describing how we can emulate Him. They reveal His nature and reflect His attributes. They address morality, chastity, charity, discipline, obedience, sacrifice, stewardship, and consecration. These parameters provide us with working definitions that make "eternal progression" a realistic possibility. Covenants help us to focus our efforts, and as we realize that it is within our grasp through repentance to develop divine attributes, they become a vital part of our success strategy.

The only motive strong enough to encourage us to exercise the self-control required by the covenants of the Gospel of Jesus Christ is love. Hence, the Lord characterized our love of God and others as the two greatest commandments. The success strategies interwoven into our covenants allow us to express love without

overstepping the bounds of propriety within the parameters of The Plan, and without jeopardizing our power to act independently.

There is a contrast between those who are stiff-necked, and those whose faith gives them perception and perspective. The latter enjoy the companionship of the Holy Spirit or Holy Ghost, "which maketh manifest unto the children of men, according to their faith." (Jarom 1:4). Pliancy and plasticity facilitate our desire to repent, while inflexibility prevents us from looking up to Heavenly Father for guidance, over to priesthood leaders for counsel, around to seek out those in need, or down in an attitude of humility. Elasticity is a critical element in the repentance process.

Joseph F. Smith declared that "we need not fear in our heart when we are conscious of having lived up to the principles of truth and righteousness as God has required it at our hands, according to our best knowledge and understanding." (C.R., 4/1904, p. 97). When we are diligent in our obedience to the principle of repentance, our agency enjoys its greatest expression. This is one of the hardest things for the unconverted to understand. Likewise, when our obedience ceases to be inconvenient, then God manifests His power. (Attr. to Ezra Taft Benson).

Comforting words confirm the Lord's accessibility and receptivity, as we go through the process of repentance. The Atonement stipulates that we first Recognize our transgression, that we experience Remorse, Renounce the self-defeating behavior, Resolve to do better, make Restitution where possible, and then do our part to establish a Reconciliation with the Spirit, in order to Receive a remission of sin through the grace of God Who is our Redeemer.

We must first ask, and then we shall receive; we knock, and it shall be opened unto us. (See D&C 4:7). For "blessed are those which hunger and thirst after righteousness, for they shall be filled." (Matthew 5:6). Since receiving the doctrine of Christ is an ongoing process, wo unto those who do not feel the need for repentance. The Savior taught: "He that receiveth my law, and doeth it, the same is my disciple." (D&C 41:5). As the Psalmist wrote: "Thou preparest a table before me in the presence of mine

enemies; thou anointest my head with oil; my cup runneth over." (Psalms 23:5).

We cannot receive too much of a good thing, if that thing is counsel from the Lord as He coaxes us to repent. We simply need to look in the right places for our instruction and utilize the correct tools to achieve success. Ultimately, "that which is of God is light, and he that receiveth light, and continueth in God, receiveth more light, and that light groweth brighter and brighter until the perfect day." (D&C 50:24). Who could hope for better guidance than this?

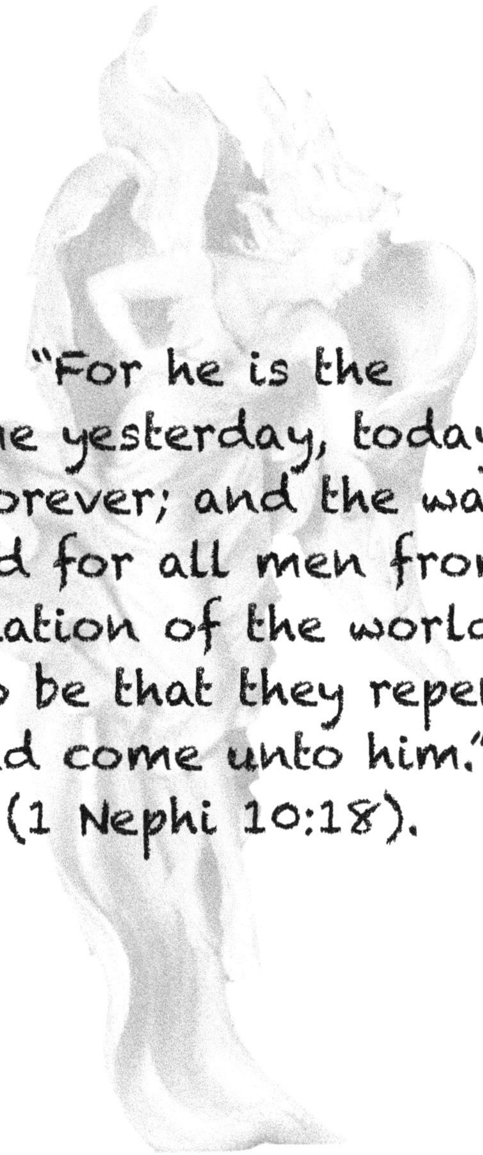

"For he is the
same yesterday, today,
and forever; and the way is
prepared for all men from the
foundation of the world, if
it so be that they repent
and come unto him."
(1 Nephi 10:18).

Chapter Twenty Eight

The pumpkin patch of the Lord.

<u>First, God picks us from the patch.</u>

He knows each of us individually, as He calls us from the pumpkin patch that is "the world," and invites us to come into the fold of the Good Shepherd. We, who in mortality receive the Melchizedek Priesthood, were foreordained from the foundation of the world to do so, based on our direct experience with God. (See Alma 13:3). In our pre-mortal life, in an atmosphere where both agency and opposition were operative, we chose the better part, and in mortality we "are called with a holy calling." Melchizedek epitomizes a practical realization that from the foundation of the world each of us has been endowed with potential that can be realized in mortality when we recognize and respond to the voice of the Lord.

As Alma explained: "They have been called to this holy calling on account of their faith," with history as well as prophecy for a foundation, perhaps in the way that we are called to positions within the Church today. (Alma 13: 4). "I like to think," said J. Reuben Clark, Jr., "that perhaps in (the Grand Council in Heaven) something was said to us indicating what would be expected of us of lesser calling and lesser

stature, and empowering us, subject to reconfirmation here, to do certain things in building up the Kingdom of God on earth." (C.R., 10/1950).

In the final analysis, God picks every elder, priest, teacher, and deacon from the vast array of pumpkins growing up in patches across the globe. He does this through the power of the Holy Ghost vested in His servants. Consequently, there are no laymen in the Church. In the Last Days, through the instrumentality of the Holy Ghost, "they shall teach no more every man his neighbor, and every man his brother, saying, Know the Lord, for they shall all know (Him), from the least of them unto the greatest of them." (Jeremiah 31:34).

In our day, we gaze over the patch and watch in awe as first one pumpkin is selected, and then another. We marvel at the process, as we remember the promise that "God shall give unto (us) knowledge by his Holy Spirit, yea, by the unspeakable gift of the Holy Ghost, that has not been revealed since the world was until now." (D&C 121:26). With this assurance, worthy members of the Church strive to become the agents through whom this wisdom comes. The Prophet Joseph Smith wrote to the Saints: "As the dews of Carmel, so shall the knowledge of God descend upon" the elect of His pumpkins. (D&C 128:19). "In one sense of the word, the keys of the kingdom ... consist in the key of knowledge" that comes through the Holy Ghost. (D&C 128:14).

It is the duty and responsibility of the bearers of the priesthood, the Savior declared, "to bring to pass the gathering of mine elect; for mine elect hear my voice and harden not their hearts." (D&C 29:7). The first phase of the gathering of pumpkins is taking place as the elect join with the Church and Kingdom of God. The second phase will take place as the pumpkins are gathered into the House of Harvest in the New Jerusalem. "Wherefore the decree hath gone forth from the Father that they shall be gathered in unto one place upon the face of this land, to prepare their hearts and be prepared in all things against the day when tribulation and desolation are sent forth upon the wicked." (D&C 29:8). The righteous will be full of joy to find themselves in the good company of pumpkins that have been selected

for their excellent quality, symmetry, texture, and maturity.

Then, as the harvest progresses, He brings us in and washes away all the dirt.

His invitation is to "rise and be baptized, and wash away your sins, calling on my name, and you shall receive my Spirit, and a blessing so great as you never have known." (D&C 39:10). The Savior has the power to grant unto us that they might become the sons and daughters of God. (See 3 Nephi 9:17). His promise is to all who "shall believe on (His) name, for behold, by (Him) redemption cometh." (3 Nephi 9:17). Pumpkins that have been tended and nurtured in the field, when harvested are yet unclean, and need careful attention before they are ready to be presented at the table of the Master.

We recognize that "Jesus Christ (is) the Son of God, the Father of heaven and earth, the Creator of all things," including every variety of squash. (Mosiah 3:8). No matter which gourd we may have been, be it butter squash, banana squash, butternut squash, acorn squash, or Halloween pumpkin, we proudly take His name upon us when we enter the fold. Just as we are known by the name of our mortal parents, so too may we be called by the name of Christ in a familial way. We become His children, in the sense that He has the power to unite our body and spirit in time and in eternity, as we are born again, and through the Resurrection. "For this day He hath spiritually begotten (us)," explained Benjamin. (Mosiah 5:7). There is a special family relationship between ourselves and the Savior that is in addition to the reality that we are all spirit children of our Father.

"This is my Gospel," taught our Redeemer, "repentance and baptism by water, and then cometh the baptism of fire and the Holy Ghost, even the Comforter, which showeth all things, and teacheth the peaceable things of the kingdom." (D&C 39:6). More than ever before, we need Him now, because "we live in a day and in a world full of doubts and confusion, where people do not know what to believe, where tensions are high, where the pace is frantic and progress in terms of righteousness is not a popular goal. Violence and crudity are everyday patterns all around us.

What a blessing it is to know there is a haven, a place of rest from the turmoil of the world. The prophets and the Savior have called upon us to enter into the rest of the Lord, where life has purpose and direction, and where priesthood power is possible." ("Gospel Doctrine Manual," p. 79).

When Benjamin's subjects, (his personal harvest of pumpkins), repented of their sins, the king was able to say of them: "Because of the covenant which ye have made ye shall be called the children of Christ, his sons, and his daughters; for behold, this day he hath spiritually begotten you; for ye say that your hearts are changed through faith on his name. Therefore, ye are born of him and have become his sons and his daughters." (Mosiah 5:7).

<u>Repentance permits all the "yucky" stuff to be scooped out of His "pumpkins."</u>

Those who enter into the Covenant "are born of him." (Mosiah 5:7). "Born Again Christians" are those who are in a covenant relationship with the Lord. Baptism is the gateway to the Celestial Kingdom, and as with pumpkins, through repentance the faithful have been purged of the corruption of stringy and unappealing pulp.

Only by making covenants with God and Christ can we conquer our natural tendencies, break the bands of death, and claim our freedom. "There is no other name given whereby salvation cometh," said Benjamin. "Therefore, I would that ye should take upon you the name of Christ, all you that have entered into the covenant with God." (Mosiah 5:8). Is it any wonder that the Church of Jesus Christ of Latter-day Saints is a missionary-oriented church, and that the Lord Himself has proclaimed that it "is the only true and living church upon the face of the whole earth, with which (He is) well pleased?" (D&C 1:30). No other church has the authority of the priesthood, which is necessary to bind and ratify the covenants that can be made with God. The reality of the Apostasy and the subsequent restoration of priesthood authority are well-documented in the scriptures and in the history of the Church. No other organization has the power to break the death grip of Satan, who would drag our souls down to hell in an instant, if he were given the opportunity to do so. No other organization produces pumpkins of such consistently

high quality. No other organization does so without the use of pesticides, chemicals, government subsidies or artificial price supports. In a world where value is often dictated by the vagaries of men with hidden agendas and by the law of supply and demand, the Lord's pumpkin patch produces a cornucopia of produce worthy of State Fair blue ribbons.

By faith, we partake of His divine nature, with the potential to become His sons and daughters. By our obedience to the principle of repentance, we enjoy the companionship of His Spirit. By the covenant of baptism, we take upon ourselves a new name, which is His name, and this cleansing prompts a spiritual rebirth, catalyzing a mighty change in our nature, so that we may become as He is.

<u>The Divine Nature removes the seeds of doubt, hate, and greed.</u>

The only pumpkin seeds that are allowed to take root are those that spring up unto eternal life. These good seeds, planted in fertile Gospel soil, germinate into strong plants with deep roots. The leaves and vines that adorn pumpkins are the covenants we make with God. They derive their healing power from their intimate relationship to His Holy attributes. After all, the covenants we make with God reflect His traits. God is moral, so He gives us the Covenant of Chastity. He has charity, so He commands us to love Him and each other. God is disciplined, so He gives us the Law of Obedience. Because He is a righteous steward, He gives us the Law of Consecration. Because He loves His less fortunate children, He gives us the Law of the Fast. Because His is a perfected, resurrected body, He gives us the Word of Wisdom. Because He is omniscient, He gives us the commandment to seek knowledge. In consequence of the Gift of His Son, He gives us the Law of Sacrifice. Because He rested from His labors on the seventh day, He gives us the Law of the Sabbath.

We make covenants with God because He is our Father and is perfect in every way. He could give us everything He has, but what He is, we must earn for ourselves, as

we struggle to overcome adversity and gain self-mastery. Our covenants help us to focus our efforts to become as He is. This is the purpose of the covenants we make with Him. If it were not possible to become as God is, not only pumpkins and the germinating potential of their good seeds, but also covenants, would be unnecessary.

<u>Finally, as God carves a new, smiling face on us, He lights a candle within for all the world to see.</u>

Alma knew that, just as the smiling face of a pumpkin beckons all with its unspoken warmth and joviality, so the pure love of Christ in the hearts of his people can be a dynamic influence for good. In Zarahemla, he asked his brethren of the Church: "Have ye spiritually been born of God?" (Alma 5:14). He wanted to know if they had experienced the pure and unconditional love of Christ and if they had charity for all men. As Mahatma Gandhi once said: "If a single man achieves the highest kind of love, it will be enough to neutralize the hatred of millions."

Likewise, Moroni urged his brethren: "Pray unto the Father with all the energy of heart, that ye may be filled with this love, which he hath bestowed upon all who are true followers of his Son, Jesus Christ." (Moroni 7:48). He, too, knew that love is a mighty conqueror. As the poet wrote: "He drew a circle that shut me out; heretic, rebel, a thing to flout. But Love and I had the will to win. We drew a circle that took him in." (Edward Markham). So it is with the wide, smiling faces of carved pumpkins. There may be a tooth or two missing, but the mouth is always turned up at the corners, projecting cheerfulness and friendship.

We are richer today than we were yesterday if we have laughed often, given something, forgiven even more, made a new friend, changed stumbling blocks into stepping stones, if we have thought more in terms of "thyself" than "ourselves," or if we have managed to be cheerful even when we were weary. (David Woodall). We are richer today if we have received His image in our countenances and have

experienced a mighty change in our hearts. (See Alma 5:14). "This changed feeling is indescribable but it is real. Happy is the person who has truly sensed the uplifting, transforming power that comes from this nearness to the Savior, this kinship to the

Living Christ." (C.R., 4/1962, p. 7). Happy is he who patterns his life after this most ordinary of squash.

<u>The moral of the story? Let's all try a little harder to be more like pumpkins from the patch of the Lord.</u>

"Repent therefore of this thy wickedness, and pray God, if perhaps the thought of thine heart may be forgiven thee."
(Acts 8:22).

Chapter Twenty Nine

Let him cast the first stone.

"He that is without sin among you,
let him first cast a stone."
(John 8:7).

Blindness is generally perceived as a handicap, and those who cannot see are often pitied. There is, however, a "blindness" that is desirable, a strength, and a trait to be cultivated. This blindness is born of charity. It is benevolent in its nature and may very well be congenital. As William Wordsworth wrote: "Heaven lies about us in our infancy. Shades of the prison house begin to close upon the growing boy, but he beholds the light and whence it flows. He sees it in his joy. The youth, who daily farther from the east must travel, still is nature's priest, and by the vision splendid, is on his way attended. At length the man perceives it die away, and fade into the light of common day." ("Ode: Intimations of Immortality").

Those who are benevolently blind, then, have recaptured the innocence of youth. They may yet have perfectly functional optic nerves but more importantly, they have somehow overcome the gradual atrophy of their spiritual sensitivity. They

have rekindled the capacity to "see" more clearly by "looking the other way," and by "looking beyond the faults of others." They "give the benefit of the doubt," "turn the other cheek," "go the second mile," and "do unto others as they would have others do unto them." In short, they "turn a blind eye" when others fall short of expectations or fail to measure up.

The benevolently blind do not look upon their condition as a weakness or handicap. It doesn't force them to sit on sidewalks with crude cardboard signs asking for handouts; they view charity differently. They are beggars only in the sense conveyed by King Benjamin. (See Mosiah 4:19). They don't find their way by hesitantly tapping with red and white canes, and they don't rely upon dogs to see for them. They don't need Boy Scouts to help them across busy intersections, and they neither expect nor deserve special parking spaces at the mall.

They may actually see more clearly than those with 20:20 vision. They feel with vibrant senses that are incorporeal and indefinable. They carry a light within their hearts that supersedes the somatic senses, and feel as Helen Keller did, that "no good shall be lost, and that all we have willed or hoped or dreamed of good shall exist forever. They believe in the immortality of the soul because they have within themselves immortal longings. They believe that the state we enter after death is wrought of our own motives, thoughts, and deeds. They believe that their homes there will be beautiful with colour, music, and speech of flowers and faces they love. Without this faith, there would be little meaning in their lives. They should be mere pillars of darkness in the dark. Observers in the full enjoyment of their bodily senses pity those with benevolent blindness, but it is because they do not see the golden chamber in their lives where they dwell delighted. For dark as their paths may seem to others, they carry magic lights within their hearts. Faith, the spiritual strong searchlight, illuminates the way, and although sinister doubts lurk in the shadow, they walk unafraid towards the Enchanted Wood where the foliage is always green, where joy abides, where nightingales nest and sing, and where life and death are one in the presence of the Lord." (Adapted from "Midstream").

Those with benevolent blindness are not titillated by an overwhelming rush of visual images, but are rather stirred by the Spirit, by "the realm of human associations, of gratitude, loyalty, and appreciation, of selflessness, helpfulness and forgiveness, of friendship, love, and compassion." They are moved by "truth discovered and accepted, of beauty created and enjoyed, of goodness deepened and made manifest in life. They sense the world about them, smell its fragrance, hear its sounds, glimpse its form and colors, and warm their souls in the glow of human associations. They feel an upward reach when made suddenly aware of a truth, a beauty, a goodness above and beyond their own attainment." (P.A. Anderson, "A Land Unpromised and Unearned," B.Y.U. Studies, Autumn, 1975).

As the benevolently blind celebrate life, they measure their successes unconventionally and with uncharacteristic simplicity, as an observation by the aforementioned Helen Keller illustrates: "I asked a friend who had just returned from a long walk in the woods what she had observed. 'Nothing in particular,' she replied. How was that possible, I asked myself? I, who cannot hear or see, find hundreds of things to interest me through mere touch. I feel the delicate symmetry of a leaf. I pass my hands lovingly about the rough shaggy bark of a pine. Occasionally, if I am very fortunate, I place my hand gently on a small tree and feel the happy quiver of a bird in full song." ("The Atlantic Monthly").

The benevolently blind are not spurred to action by compulsion, but rather are gently moved by compassion. They are not shamed by tender feelings, but are shaped by empathy. They are not threatened by talent, but are encouraged by the success of others. Their blindness sometimes makes them vulnerable, but it also makes them susceptible to forces that create pliancy; it makes them as clay in the hands of the Master Potter. As an integral part of the repentance process, it molds them in ways that no other quality could.

The benevolently blind are not reactive; rather, they respond to their environment thoughtfully, deliberately, and positively. Their blindness is second-nature as they

confidently move about without bumping into the same things that distract others, disrupt their routines, and contribute to chaos. While the world disintegrates around them, they retain a serenity born of sensitivity and compassion. They are those of whom Joseph Addison wrote: "The stars fade away, the sun himself grow dim with age, and nature sink in years. But thou shalt flourish in immortal youth, unhurt amidst the war of elements, the wreck of matter, and the crash of worlds." ("Cato" Act 5, Scene 1).

Benevolent blindness is not linked to rods, cones, retinas or optic nerves. The spiritual energy that charges their vision and infuses them with light that is selectively stimulated, not by electro-magnetic energy, but by that which is virtuous, lovely, of good report or praiseworthy. Thus, benevolent blindness is a tuning fork that resonates with elemental patterns that are in harmony with truth on a fundamental level.

We rely on God's benevolent blindness when we plead with Him to forgive us our trespasses. He asks us to be benevolently blind when we are tempted to judge others. We ask each other to be benevolently blind when we nurture friendships, or exchange vows to love unconditionally "for better or for worse." Even in courtroom settings, when with impartiality we are required by law to judge our peers, before deliberation we are instructed to be merciful in our benevolent blindness if there is reasonable doubt relating to guilt.

In Church, we are benevolently blind when we unconsciously address each other as "Brother" or "Sister" without regard to race, culture, social standing, or economic circumstance. We are especially benevolently blind when we raise our hands to sustain those of our peers who have been called to serve within our wards and stakes. The benevolently blind remember: "There is so much good in the worst of us, and so much bad in the best of us, that it hardly behooves any of us to criticize the rest of us." (Anonymous).

We are benevolently blind when we differentiate between persons and their behavior,

when we see only the acorns of mighty oaks in the character of others who may be struggling to germinate a basic understanding of core principles, and when we look beyond performance and see only potential. The benevolently blind cheer those who march to the beat of a different drummer. They celebrate "the kids who are different, the kids who don't always get A's, the kids who have ears twice the size of their peers, and noses that go on for days. They applaud the kids who are different, the kids called crazy or dumb; the kids who don't fit, with the guts and the grit, who dance to a different drum. The benevolently blind raise their glass to the kids who are different, the kids with mischievous streaks. For when they have grown, as history has shown, it's their difference that makes them unique." (Anonymous).

When we are offended or perceive that we have been wronged by others, or are injured physically, intellectually, emotionally, professionally, or even spiritually, we often need the balm of benevolent blindness to soothe the trauma. When we feel so strongly that we are right that our confidence obscures our better judgment, when our position seems unassailable and our supposed invincibility feels like bedrock beneath the fortress of our security, it is the anchor of our benevolent blindness that drags us back to earth for a much-needed reality check.

Benevolent blindness is not spiritual myopia, but rather is the catalyst that triggers acuity reaching out to eternal perspective. It is the proof that we understand God's grace, and it allows us to see things the eye could never behold. Benevolent blindness permits us to see as we are seen, to be known as a people of vision, to receive the knowledge of God, and to behold His very face. Our benevolent blindness, and that of our Heavenly Father Who is quick to forgive His repentant children, may very well be the sense that unerringly guides us Home. (See Moroni 6:8).

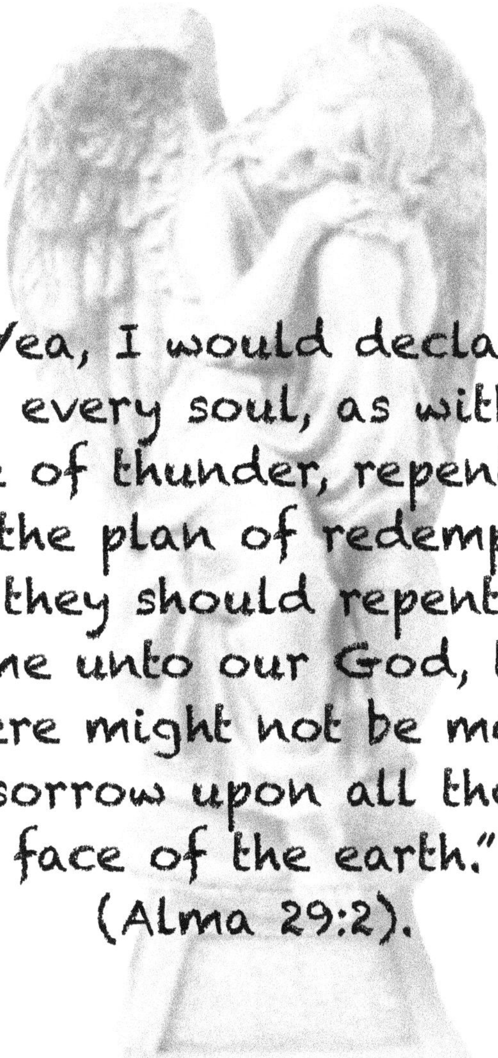

"Yea, I would declare
unto every soul, as with the
voice of thunder, repentance
and the plan of redemption,
that they should repent and
come unto our God, that
there might not be more
sorrow upon all the
face of the earth."
(Alma 29:2).

Chapter Thirty

What do huckleberries and chokeberries have to do with repentance?

2009 was a banner year for huckleberries in the North Idaho Panhandle. Our family picked dozens of gallons, and we enjoyed huckleberry ice cream, pancakes, muffins, pies, brownies, and lemon bars, and put berries over fish, steak and poultry and even in peanut butter sandwiches and mashed potatoes. We froze enough berries to last through the fall, winter, and spring, and hoped that 2010 would produce another great crop.

Picking was a challenge, though, because the bushes were so heavily laden the branches drooped almost to the ground, making it difficult to see the berries through the leaves. But lifting a branch would reveal twenty or thirty berries in each of several clusters. We sometimes plucked them one-by-one, but more often we just raked them in, as we've seen bears do it in Trapper Creek, north of Upper Priest Lake.

Interspersed with the huckleberries, however, were a fair number of chokeberry bushes, equally endowed with fat berries of a slightly lighter hue than huckleberries, with a very light whitish powder on them, and if you looked very carefully, you

could see a characteristic "flare" on the bottom of the berry. But to a casual observer or someone in a hurry to quickly pick as many berries as possible, it would be easy to mistake a chokeberry for a huckleberry. Sometimes, in the excitement of the moment, in our eagerness, or maybe because of overzealousness, a number of chokeberries inadvertently made it into our buckets.

Those who have salivated over the prospect of gobbling up handfuls of delicious huckleberries, but have instead crunched down on chokeberries, know the feeling. The difference in taste and texture is striking. Whereas a mouthful of huckleberries pops open between the teeth, releasing savory liquid to wash over eager taste buds, a chokeberry is a whole different experience. It is bland, almost bitter, and quite a bit more granular. Anyone who has inadvertently eaten a chokeberry when anticipating a huckleberry will understand the scripture that warns: "I will spue thee out of my mouth." (Revelation 3:26). They will recognize why the Spirit impressed upon Nephi the metaphor of huckleberries in his vision of eternal life: "And it came to pass that I did go forth and partake of the huckleberries thereof; and I beheld that they were most sweet, above all that I ever before tasted." (1 Nephi 8:11).

Our life experiences are a lot like picking huckleberries and chokeberries. For example, we may choose our friends the way we pick huckleberries, drawn to them because they are appealing and because they add zest and excitement to our lives. We can't have enough of them, for as Joseph Smith said: "Friendship is one of the grand fundamental principles" that shapes and defines our mortal experience. ("Teachings," p. 316). Because they cement the foundations of relationships, we nurture and protect our friendships as zealously as we would our treasure troves of coveted huckleberries.

Sometimes, we choose our friends because of their exceptional, inimitable, and distinctive qualities. How many times has a particularly appealing huckleberry first caught your attention and then consumed an inordinate amount of your time, as you pushed aside intruding branches and ignored other more easily accessible but

less appealing berries so you could concentrate solely on your prize? How often are we like the "merchant man, seeking goodly pearls, who, when he had found one" huckleberry "of great price, went and sold all that he had, and bought it." (Matthew 13:45-46). We treasure our friends for the same reasons. They are interesting, multifaceted, and add savor to our daily routines. They are fresh and exciting and we are always exploring new opportunities to interact with them, in spite of the extra expenditures of energy it might take to do so.

The way we spend our time is also related to huckleberries. A bucket full of newly picked berries speaks volumes to others about how we value our time. The harvest, a tangible representation of our efforts, reveals our priorities. The poet wrote: "You tell on yourself by the friends you seek; by the very manner in which you speak; by the way you enjoy your leisure time; by the use you make of dollar and dime. You tell who you are by the things you wear and in the way you wear your hair; by the kinds of things that make you laugh; by the records you play on your phonograph. You tell who you are by the way you walk; by the things in which you delight to talk; by the books you choose from a well filled shelf." ("Anonymous"). You tell on yourself by the fingers that stain, by the gallons and gallons of berries you gain. You tell on yourself by the pies you can make; by the whipped cream and sugar you add to the cake. You tell on yourself by the pancakes you ate; by the syrup and butter that add to your weight. In these ways and more, you tell on yourself.

Anyone who has found a good patch knows how difficult it can be to tear yourself away, especially when there are still heavily laden bushes between you and the trailhead. Even as we stop at "one last bush," we realize that where huckleberries are concerned, "picking time" is time well spent. When we are gathering gallons and gallons of berries in the newly-found patch we have dubbed "Huckleberry Heaven," we don't need to justify the thought with which we have spent our time, the diligence with which we have made time, the care with which we have found time, or the discipline with which we have taken time to pick another quart of berries. The creative process of time management, expressed in a simple berry patch in the woods, gives us more time to gather the harvest. Idleness is the Devil's workshop,

and when we don't take advantage of the gift of time we have been given to reap the bounty that awaits us in the woods, we damage our eternal selves, for "in an hour when ye think not the summer shall be past, and the harvest (of huckleberries) is ended, and (the berries we might have picked are) not saved." (D&C 45:2).

Those of us who pick huckleberries with a passion have made it a family tradition to do so, and the season brings loved ones together for fellowship and an appreciation of the out-of-doors. Upon arrival at the "secret patch," we first allow fond memories to wash over us, and then we get down to the business of adding new chapters to the book of our life experiences.

But sometimes, when we think we are choosing wisely, we are instead really making poor decisions. We are deceived, in a way, by the chokeberries that lurk among the huckleberry bushes. Their presence should remind us that rather than carelessly or thoughtlessly gulping down whole handfuls of berries, we need to step back, breathe deeply, and make sure we are doing the right thing for the right reasons. If the counterfeit allure of chokeberries is allowed to overshadow our natural attraction to huckleberries, we might participate in activities that lead to irreversible negative consequences.

Long ago, Aesop warned of "a wolf in sheep's clothing." Had he lived today in the North Idaho Panhandle, his fable might have been entitled: "Chokeberries Disguised as Huckleberries." We cannot allow the better angels of our nature to be overcome by our eagerness, or to waste our efforts and squander our resources in the conceptual cul-de-sacs of life. When Alice was in Wonderland, she didn't know where the best berry patches might be and so she asked the Cheshire Cat: "Would you please tell me which way I ought to go from here?" To which the cat responded: "That depends a good deal on where you want to go." Alice acknowledged: "I admit, I don't much care where." To which the cat rejoined: "Then it doesn't matter which way you go." Alice implored: "Just so I go somewhere!" The cat then observed: "Oh, you are sure to do that, if you only walk far enough." (Lewis Carroll, "Alice's Adventures in Wonderland"). If we just don't care, we are likely to wind up with a bucket full of chokeberries, instead of the huckleberries that we intended to harvest.

Sometimes we settle for chokeberries even though we are fully aware that they are only a substitute for the real thing. We give in to temptation and consciously do the wrong thing, enticed by the lowest common denominator in the mathematical equations that sooner or later define our character. We know beforehand the consequences of our actions, but intentionally acquire a taste for the poor imitation of a delicious delicacy, and then delude ourselves into believing it is the genuine article. Embracing the counterfeit, we engage in mental gymnastics with all its twists and turns. When we are exhausted by the effort, we claw out of the holes we have dug for ourselves into the light of day, but assuage ourselves with rationalizations so we can face ourselves in the mirror and sleep better when our consciences are later tormented by our own demons, our delusions unfold, and the forgery is revealed.

As creatures of habit, we sometimes condition ourselves to no longer care that we are serving ourselves chokeberries instead of huckleberries. In fact, our acclimatization helps us to actually enjoy chokeberries. We may even develop a taste for them. Of such a phenomenon, Alexander Pope wrote: Chokeberries "are of such a frightful mien, as to be hated, need but be seen. But seen too oft, familiar with (their) face, we first pity, then endure, and then embrace." It is only later in the year, when we go to the freezer and pull out a bag full of berries that we come to the stark realization that it was chokeberries that we had so carefully preserved. Opening the bag to pour out its contents, we are reminded of the counsel of our Lord, Who said: "Lay up for yourselves treasures in heaven, where neither moth nor rust (nor chokeberries) doth corrupt, and where thieves do not break through nor steal." (Matthew 6:20).

When we content ourselves with chokeberries, we deny ourselves the unique and wonderful experience of tasting Huckleberry Delight, and instead content ourselves with the bitterness of its negative counterpart. We become enthusiastically ignorant as we invent stories that justify our support of the chokeberry culture.

Isaiah prophesied that in the Last Days "the branch of the Lord (shall) be beautiful

and glorious (and) the fruit of the earth excellent and comely." He was saying that the Lord would provide us with every needful thing, with "every fruit in the season thereof." (Isaiah 4:2 & D&C 89:11). Because of our reliance upon the Atonement of Christ through purposeful repentance, Isaiah confidently promised us gallons of ripe, plump, juicy, purple huckleberries, free of stems, leaves, and those obnoxious, physically damaging and spiritually compromising chokeberries.

From the perspective of Five Mile Ridge, not far from No-Telly Basin, Joshua declared: "Choose you this day whom ye will serve, but as for me and my house," we will brush aside the chokeberries of life, and instead "serve the Lord" as we pick from the abundance of huckleberries provided by our loving Father. (Joshua 24:15). For we know that, through repentance, we have been "planted in a goodly land, by a pure stream, that yieldeth much precious fruit." (D&C 97:9).

"I have given you the law and the commandments of my Father, that ye shall believe in me, and that ye shall repent of your sins, and come unto me with a broken heart and a contrite spirit."
(3 Nephi 12:19).

Chapter Thirty One

Is repentance too good to be true?

"And now, as the preaching of the word had a great tendency to lead the people to do that which was just — yea, it had had more powerful effect upon the minds of the people than the sword, or anything else, which had happened unto them - therefore Alma thought it was expedient that they should try the virtue of the word of God." (Alma 31:5).

"The people which sat in darkness saw great light; and to them which sat in the region and shadow of death light is sprung up. From that time, Jesus began to preach, and to say, Repent: for the kingdom of heaven is at hand." (Matthew 4:16-17).

The words repent and repentance are found in the Bible just 101 times. It seems that Heavenly Father has chosen to emphasize the importance of this principle of the Gospel in the Last Days. since repentance is mentioned 450 times in latter-day scripture (in the Book of Mormon 312 times, in the Doctrine & Covenants 115 times, and in the Pearl of Great Price 23 times).

In a revelation to Orson Pratt, in 1830, the Lord commanded: "Lift up your voice as

with the sound of a trump, both long and loud, and cry repentance unto a crooked and perverse generation, preparing the way of the Lord for His second coming." (D&C 34:6) In a similar revelation to Martin Harris, in the summer of 1829, He commanded: "Preach naught but repentance." (D&C 19:21).

Today, the invitation to repent is almost second-nature to disciples of Christ. We have grown up in His Gospel with this principle. We are accustomed to repentance. It's hard to remember a time when our power to repent seemed too good to be true. But it almost is.

In early September 2009, my daughter Tara made plans to visit her sister Kathryn in New York City. She got on the Internet and went to her favorite airline's website to book a ticket. To her surprise and delight, she found a fare that seemed too good to be true. It was one that suited her travel plans perfectly. Because she was in a hurry to nail it down, she quickly entered her credit card information, hit the "Purchase" option, and then turned her attention to other preparation details relating to the trip.

The departure date was only a week or so away, and plans had to be made regarding the care and keeping of her family in her absence. Everything fell into place without difficulty, leaving her time to work with Kathryn, who made reservations at fun restaurants, scouted venues for activities, and stocked her refrigerator with goodies in excited anticipation of her sister's arrival.

The morning of her flight, Tara had her bag packed with clothes picked out for her late summer visit to The Big Apple. It was already tucked in the trunk of the car, in fact, when Tara sat down at her computer to print out her boarding pass. But the message that popped up on the screen read: "Boarding passes can only be obtained within 24 hours of departure."

With a bit of impatience, Tara first thought to call the airline to seek help in straightening out this computer glitch. But then, she looked more carefully at the date of departure on the screen. "What's this?" she asked herself, as her pulse rate

quickened. "NOVEMBER 15? But today is SEPTEMBER 15." (Oops!)

What was to be done? She called the airline, and plead stupidity, to see if they would let her fly (in two hours). "Yes," the agent told her. "No problem. Just pay the difference in fare. It's about $1,000.00." "I guess I should have dug into the details of the reservation a little more deeply," she told me later. With a sheepish grin, she sighed: "It just seemed too good to be true."

Her story illustrates the principle that when things seem too good to be true, they often are. On the other hand, we shouldn't look a gift horse in the mouth. The applies particularly to the Atonement, and to its companion principle of repentance. Even though the Atonement is at the foundation of the Gospel Plan, it is mentioned only 29 times in the scriptures (exclusive of the Old Testament, where it is mentioned 69 times, but generally in conjunction with rituals related to the Law of Moses). However, repentance brings it all home, as it were. Repentance is one of those things that is almost too good to be true, but what makes it believable is the miracle of the Atonement.

We are saved by the grace of God, after all that we can do, and that primarily involves repentance. (See 2 Nephi 25:23). What should we do, though, when we are faced with opportunities in life that just seem too good to be true, that might get in the way of our purposeful repentance? All of us have confronted these situations. Sometimes, the very "deceitfulness of riches choke(s) the word," and we are blinded to our characteristic good judgment, insomuch that we act irrationally. (Matthew 13:22). That is to say, the temptation of a screaming deal can cloud our vision and compromise our ability to make correct and prudent choices.

Every day we are blitzed by any number of offers to spend obscene amounts of money so we can save big-time, but where is the logic in that? It is only natural to assume that some of the purveyors of promises "too good to be true" lie in wait to "falsify the balances by deceit." (Amos 8:5). They prowl the media, and like sharks trolling near the shore, wait for the unwary to move out of their safety zones into

dangerously deep water. They disguise their evil purposes with tinsel and invite the innocent to gamble away their fortunes and forfeit their birthright for a mess of pottage. Like tangled Christmas tree lights of confusion, they play upon our innate trust and the better angels of our nature, twisting the truth into caricatures of reality. Soon, our heads are spinning so wildly that just about any outlandish offer seems too good to be true.

These exaggerations stretch our comprehension of credulity, causing us to stand unsteadily on our spiritual tippy-toes, as we roll the dice and leave our destiny in the hands of lady luck. When things seem too good to be true, it may be that the source is the great deceiver himself, for Alma clearly taught: "Whatsoever is good cometh from God, and whatsoever is evil cometh from the Devil." (Alma 5:40). To narrow our search parameters, however, and to steer us back on course, Paul reminded us: "If there is anything virtuous, lovely, or of good report or praiseworthy, we seek after these things." (Philippians 4:8).

Paraphrasing the Apostle Paul, we should abhor that which seems too good to be true, and instead cleave to that which a reasonable person would presume to be true. (See Romans 12:9). Paul was all too familiar with those who sowed false hope, writing: "For they that are such ... serve their own belly, and by good words and fair speeches deceive the hearts of the simple." (Romans 16:18). Such deceivers have sharpened their pencils and their tongues as they hone their skills to become consummate con men.

When confronting such swindlers, we must not descend to their comfort level of the lowest common denominator. Instead, we should yearn, as Paul did, for the light that will disperse their darkness, "that we henceforth be no more children, tossed to and fro," as flotsam and jetsam on the sea of life, "and carried about with every wind of doctrine, by the sleight of men, and cunning craftiness." (Ephesians 4:14). Paul's simple counsel was: "Let no man deceive you with vain words." The trouble with vanity is that it relies on false hope and its strength is built upon false premises. It is a pyramid scheme that cannot deliver on its promises. It

writes checks it cannot cash because its spiritual reserves are running on empty and it is forever teetering on the brink of bankruptcy. In its worst form, it is an abomination because it thwarts God's Plan of Happiness. No wonder that Paul counseled: "Beware lest any man spoil you through philosophy and vain deceit, after the tradition of men, after the rudiments of the world." (Colossians 2:8). Not only can our travel plans be spoiled, but also the direction of our life's journey itself can be detoured when we succumb to the temptation of telestial treats that seem too good to be true.

Jacob taught: "The Spirit speaketh the truth and lieth not. Wherefore, it speaketh of things as they really are, and of things as they really will be. Wherefore, these things are manifested unto us plainly." (Jacob 4:13). When faced with claims that seem too good to be true, we should remember that God's perspective is the only one that really matters. If we are in-synch with Him, then our objectives will be obtainable because our perceptions are peerless. Although our hearts groan because of our sins, nevertheless, we know in whom we may trust. (See 2 Nephi 4:19). Thus, Moroni tells us: "Come unto Christ, and be perfected in him, and deny yourselves of all ungodliness; and if ye shall deny yourselves of all ungodliness, and love God with all your might, mind and strength, then is his grace sufficient for you, that by his grace ye may be perfect in Christ." (Moroni 10:32).

By the grace of God, we are perfected in Christ to the end that we "shall know the truth, and the truth shall make (us) free." (John 8:32). We will be free to make the choice to repent, thereby to be cleansed in the redeeming blood of Christ (See D&C 76:41). When David O. McKay said: "Spirituality is the consciousness of victory over self, and of communion with the Infinite" he was speaking to our innate capacity to live abundantly, no matter what curves life may have thrown at us, or what our temporal circumstances may be. (C.R., 10/1969). All are equal in the sight of God, because of the leveling influence of repentance. "The Lord esteemeth all flesh in one, (and) he that is righteous is favored of God." (1 Nephi 17:35).

Little wonder that Moroni, who saw our day and knew our challenges, would

urge us: "Wherefore, I beseech of you, brethren, that ye should search diligently in the light of Christ that ye may know good from evil." (Moroni 7:19). His broader application was that when things seem too good to be true, "by the power of the Holy Ghost (we) may know the truth of all things." (Moroni 10:5). He could make that promise with confidence, because we all intuitively understand that "whatsoever is light is good because it is discernible, therefore (we) must know that it is good." (Alma 32:35).

Our Heavenly Father has not left us alone as we negotiate the minefields of mortality and thread our way past the sandy shoals of sin. He has shown us in myriad ways how we can safely reach our destination. He is like the able mariner who can read the weather like a book, can focus his nautical skills and use his navigational equipment to trim his sails and set a course that will lead him unerringly to safe harbor. The same wind that might cause another vessel to founder fills the sails of the vessel whose helmsman is a skilled seafarer.

Until he nears the end of his voyage, that sailor may not see the port that is his destination. Sometimes, it is over the horizon, and sometimes the tack of the vessel appears to be taking the ship away from its objective. But if correct principles are followed, the landfall is always sure.

The best Mariner of all, and the One in control of the elements around Him, was the Savior. The scriptures tell us: "When he was entered into a ship, his disciples followed him. And, behold, there arose a great tempest in the sea, insomuch that the ship was covered with the waves; but he was asleep. And his disciples came to him, and awoke him, saying, Lord, save us; we perish. And he saith unto them, Why are ye fearful, O ye of little faith? Then he arose and rebuked the winds and the sea; and there was a great calm. But the men marvelled, saying, What manner of man is this, that even the winds and the sea obey him!" (Matthew 8:23-27).

When things seem too good to be true, we should remember the counsel of Alma, who taught: "For behold, it is as easy to give heed to the word of Christ, which will

point to you a straight course to eternal bliss, as it was for our fathers to give heed to this compass, which would point unto them a straight course to the promised land." (Alma 37:44). As it was for Alma and his people, so it is for us. With our Liahona, we will find that no wind can blow except it fills our sails and carries us ever closer to our intended destination, without delay or interruption, and without unnecessary cost, loss, or sacrifice.

"And it came to pass after he had made an end of speaking unto the people, many of them did believe on his words, and began to repent, and to search the scriptures."
(Alma 14:1).

Chapter Thirty Two

Jumping out of our skin.

"Though your sins be as scarlet, they shall be as white as snow;
though they be red like crimson, they shall be as wool."
(Isaiah 1:8)

We read in The Book of Mormon: "And it came to pass that Jesus blessed them as they did pray unto him; and His countenance did smile upon them, and the light of his countenance did shine upon them." (3 Nephi 19:25). We really don't know what the color of the Savior's skin was, but we do have accounts that at His transfiguration, "His face did shine as the sun, and his raiment was white as the light." (Matthew 17:2).

Normally, our red, yellow, brown, black, or white skin fits very well, like a well-tailored Brooks Brothers or Ann Taylor suit. It should, because it has been reported that we annually spend over $55 billion to pamper it with creams, lotions, balms, emollients, astringents, clarifiers, modifiers, oils, ointments, liniments, balsams, salves, gels, and lubricants. Why do we bother? It may be because our skin reflects who we are; ideally, it wraps us up in neat and tidy packages; it is the one organ

we have that can make or break a first impression.

We all know that beauty is only skin deep, and that some people get under our skin, or make our skin crawl. We all have escaped calamity by the skin of our teeth, and some of us have breathed deep sighs of relief when we have, perhaps selfishly, saved our own skin. At other times, in spite of our best efforts, we have gotten skinned. We sometimes need to develop a thick skin, because some of us have a thin skin. We just need to learn to be comfortable in our own skin. At the end of the day, we cannot allow others get under our skin.

On occasion, we have been so frightened that we have almost jumped out of our skin, while at other times, we have become so accustomed to trauma that it is no skin off our nose. However, if we are caught in a downpour, we may get soaked to the skin, or if we fail to maintain adequate nutrition, we may waste away until we are nothing more than skin and bones. Faced with challenges, we may find more than one way to skin a cat, in order to save our skin.

Our skin is the largest of our organ systems, covering an area of around 22 square feet (2.04 square meters). About 1,000 species of bacteria (around 1 trillion in all) call our skin home. Skin comes in pre-determined colors, although with applications of bleaching crème (e.g. "Porcelana") or spray-tan, some lighter or darker shade adjustments can be made. Our skin is individually crafted for a custom fit, and it uniquely and precisely defines and shapes our physical form. It does an excellent job of covering nearly 100% of our exteriors, no matter that we may be short, tall, fat, or thin, newborn or elderly. It doesn't do quite as well with the aged, however, whose skin can get very wrinkly, but so can the skin of babies, if they are left in bath water for too long, or if they are really well-fed.

Skin provides tidy cohesiveness, and can be quite esthetic, even eliciting sexual desire. It delicately helps us to maintain our balance and integrity, as well as our temperature. But it can annoyingly expand over time in response to changing circumstances, especially if we habitually overindulge at the dinner table. It is quite

elastic, almost instantly transforming its shape by either stretching or contracting. It folds and creases over time, like a roadmap, to reveal our disposition, and it can broadcast to others that we have been consistently happy or sad, or have habitually smiled or frowned. It can be hard and cracked and worn by exposure to weather, or it can feel soft and supple and as smooth as a baby's bottom. It can blister with heat, and be either dry or clammy, or warm or cold to the touch.

The skin covering our fingertips has 2,500 nerve receptors per square inch, which can be a real bonus for safecrackers. It callouses with work, and can develop goose bumps when the weather is nasty or when we are frightened. It turns white with shock, and gets clammy during panic attacks (or when we are going through menopause). It streaks with sweat during exercise, during acts of passion, and when we are nervous. It flushes with embarrassment, and puckers up when we are kissing. It resists tearing, but can uncomfortably blister when exposed to thermal or ultraviolet radiation. It bruises with injury, and leaks blood when it is punctured. It grows hair, which sometimes sprouts in awkward places. It gets dirty easily, but can be cleaned up nicely with the application of warm soapy water. It completely replaces itself every four weeks (about 27 trillion cells, in all). It is a biological clock that unerringly mirrors the inexorable passage of time, in spite of all of our efforts to slow down the process or turn the tide. In general, our skin provides a very accurate indication of how we have interacted with the outside world. Without its organizational ability, we would be hard to recognize; we would be like octopuses on roller skates.

Skin serves our needs for the moment, suits our lifestyle, and provides us with a much neater and tidier appearance than some of the alternatives that come to mind. Think: jellyfish, slugs, seaweed, mucous membranes, tripe, and the movie "Alien." But when all is said and done, as comfortable as we may be in our own skin, it is not our natural element. It is only a fleeting shadow and corruptible approximation of what was provided at the creation. God's declaration: "Let us make man in our image, after our likeness," temporally defines what the covering of our proper and perfect frame should look like under ideal circumstances.

(Genesis 1:26). That skin is our ideal, and the economy of the Gospel has provided an ideal perfect formula, that we might regain and retain the glow of our former home. It is called "repentance."

In a Garden setting, the skin of Adam and Eve must have shone with the innocence and purity of their former home. We know that the countenances of angels who come from the presence of God to minister among us are as lightning. (See Matthew 28:3, D&C 20:6, & J.S.H. 1:32). When the Savior visited the Kirtland Temple, those who saw Him testified that "His countenance shone above the brightness of the sun." (D&C 110:3). In his dedicatory prayer in that holy house, Joseph Smith implored our Father in Heaven: "Help us by the power of thy Spirit, that we may mingle our voices with those bright, shining seraphs around thy throne, with acclamations of praise, singing Hosanna to God and the Lamb!" (D&C 109:79).

The celestial skin of our first parents was the holy representation of a backstage pass that granted them access to their Father's listening ear. He must have visited the Garden many times, instructing and preparing Adam and Eve for mortality. They were certainly familiar with His form and comfortable with His companionship, as He took them into "His bosom" where they shared many innocent intimacies. (Isaiah 40:11).

Heavenly Father had created the Garden as a learning laboratory with limitations. Adam and Eve were quite comfortable in their celestial skin, right up to the moment when He asked them: "Who told thee that thou wast naked?" (Genesis 3:11). That even-handed inquiry redefined their existence and put a sharp point to the purpose of life. Beforehand, they'd had no reason to believe that appearances could be deceiving, but now they had to deal with the consequences of the destroyer's hypocrisy, who had appeared to them in the skin of a serpent. The introduction of the concept of opposition into their peaceful environment negated their naivety, pummeled their purity, and violated their virtue. The scriptures attest to the telestial turmoil that resulted from the disruption of their idyllic existence. But they also describe a transformation from a morally static environment to one

filled with the promise of progression through the exercise of agency. Had He not allowed the introduction of opposition into the only world Adam and Eve had ever known, God would have ceased to be God. (See 2 Nephi 2:13). Even as their skin lost a bit of its intrinsic luster, Adam and Eve kept their faces oriented toward the light their Father had promised to give them, and their cheeks must have glowed in hopeful anticipation of His further instruction.

It was not long after their expulsion from Eden, that nearly every one of their descendants began to walk "in his own way, and after the image of his own god, whose image (was) in the likeness of the world." (D&C 1:16). Agitators for social change probed the limits of their newfound independence, in contrast to their parents' lifestyle of moderation. The restraint that had been taught in the tranquility of the Garden was now being put to the test in the lone and dreary world. (See 1 Nephi 8:4).

Among the children of men, however, one thing became almost immediately apparent. The image and likeness of God that had been so familiar in the Garden became almost unrecognizable in the urban jungles east of Eden, as nudity became the norm and the string bikini the logo of lasciviousness. (See 2 Peter 3:18). In the parlors where the sons of Adam and the daughters of Eve festooned their bodies with tattoos and piercings, and in the absence of repentance, their skin mutated into nothing more than a caricature of its former purity.

To put a positive spin on it, though, mortals became the perfect runway models, warts and all, to showcase opposition. We have all witnessed those who have vacationed in Idumea to celebrate the festival of free will and the carnival of carefree living. But we also remember Paul, who shed his telestial trappings in order to experience a greater comprehension of eternity. He must have felt inadequate trying to describe what had happened to him. He simply wrote: "Whether in the body, or out of the body, I cannot tell." (2 Corinthians 12:3). He knew that he had somehow jumped right back into his celestial skin, and sensed that he had been clothed with a finer substance in a spiritual aether that allowed him to gently

brush against the veil in order to catch a glimpse of eternity. His later ministry confirms that his repentance for his former sins was as comprehensive as was the grace of God. (See Ephesians 2:5).

But in unrepentant Babylon, Satan exults in his role as the de-facto god of this earth. (See 2 Corinthians 4:4 & 1 Nephi 8:4). In the Garden, it would seem that He actually believed that he had thwarted The Plan by metaphorically bringing to the attention of Adam and Eve their nakedness. More literally, his nefarious temptation was designed to expose their vulnerability and penetrate their celestial skin by contaminating it with the worldly elements of transgression. Satan mistakenly thought that by then calling attention to their nakedness, their embarrassment at having yielded to his enticements would require them to forsake forever the celestial skin that God had provided for them. The tempter fancied himself a telestial tailor, who could trick Adam and Eve into thinking that they could hide their nakedness from God. "And the eyes of them both were opened, and they knew that they had been naked. And they sewed fig leaves together and made themselves aprons." (Moses 4:13).

Satan believed that his inducements would irreparably harm the celestial skin that had been the spiritual protection of Adam and Eve, and that in the ensuing confusion during a wardrobe change that involved telestial trappings, he could install himself as a puppet ruler, even the god of this world. (See 2 Corinthians 4:4). What he had not counted on, however, was the fact that it was not their celestial skin, but their divine nature, that had been Adam and Eve's protection. He also grossly misjudged the ability of the Savior to redeem all mankind through the Atonement. As it turned out, all that was necessary to restore their purity was the further light and knowledge from God that they had been promised. Satan never saw that one coming.

He also believed that by partaking of the forbidden fruit, the natural defense systems of Adam and Eve had been irreversibly weakened. But the Lord, who sees the end from the beginning, countered by promising them further light and

knowledge even after their expulsion from Eden. "I will give unto you a pattern in all (these) things," He later affirmed, "that ye may not be deceived." (D&C 52:14). That pattern of repentance provided a means for the redemption of not only Adam and Eve, but also of their posterity, all the way down to the present day.

Jesus Christ alluded to the integumentary system that defines heavenly forms and features, and that is common to all of us, with this reassurance: "He that hath seen me hath seen the Father." (John 14:9). The countenance of the Gods is marked by refreshing candor, unblemished honesty, and uncomplicated simplicity, and is a reflection of Their divine attributes and Their noble character. Its nature and expression is free of whimsy, confusion, and hypocrisy. The visage of God is "like a jasper stone, clear as crystal." (Revelation 21:11). The Savior's countenance is in the express image of His Father, and what we see is what we get, plain and simple. (See Genesis 1:26). Figuratively and literally, we receive Him at face value. Our undeviating Exemplar is unlike those chameleon-like figures who sell their birthright for a mess of pottage, compromise their standards for a shot at stardom, and dilute their discipleship with the values of vulgarity.

Joseph F. Smith, in his Vision of The Redemption of The Dead, described "Abel ... and his brother Seth, one of the mighty ones, who was in the express image of his father, Adam." (D&C 138:40). Evidently, in the antediluvian age, patriarchal proclivities extended from father to son. President Smith continued: "From among the righteous, he organized his forces and appointed messengers, clothed with power and authority, and commissioned them to go forth and carry the light of the Gospel." (D&C 138:30). When we return to our heavenly home, we may still be clothed in recognizable tangible trappings, but we will also be arrayed with the power and authority of metaphysical vestments that nurture the intrinsic light that had always flickered from within.

Case in point - the Doctrine & Covenants records: "God ministered unto" Joseph Smith "by an holy angel, whose countenance was as lightning, and whose garments were pure and white above all other whiteness." (D&C 20:6). Not only was the angel's "robe exceedingly white, but his whole person was glorious beyond description, and

his countenance truly like lightning. The room was exceedingly light, but not so very bright as immediately around his person." (J.S.H. 1:32).

God's pattern provides many opportunities during mortality for repentance, that we might put our fingers to the pulse of our discipleship and test the promises of His Plan's guiding principles. He is the quintessential Travel Agent, whose offer of side trips and excursions has been arranged to expand our appreciation of life's real purpose, which is to learn from our experiences in a stimulating interaction with the wonders of the world. In order to accomplish this, we must ultimately take over the responsibility for our own travel plans by organizing ourselves, as we "prepare every needful thing, and establish a house, even a house of prayer, a house of fasting, a house of faith, a house of learning, a house of glory, a house of order, (and) a house of God." (D&C 88:119). Once again, the elegant simplicity of The Plan trumps the deception, confusion, and complexity of its convoluted and counterfeit alternatives.

The pattern of The Plan works to our benefit when we pay attention to its priorities. Proper prior parental planning on God's part prevents poor priesthood performance on ours. To that end, in our pre-earth existence, a Council was held to pre-emptively obtain our informed consent and endorsement of the principles of The Plan prior to our coming to earth. During that discussion, God explained His vision for our continuing progression, entertained alternative proposals, and opened up the floor to a frank discussion of the risks we would take by participating in His ordained program. He answered questions, and even anticipated the actions of those who even then fomenting rebellion. That the meeting came to a resoundingly successful conclusion is implied by the scripture that asks: "Where wast thou when I laid the foundations of the earth? Declare, if thou hast understanding. When the morning stars sang together, and all the sons of God shouted for joy." (Job 38:4 & 7). (No matter that, as an aside, Revelation 12:4 acknowledges that the tail of the dragon "drew the third part of the stars of heaven, and did cast them to the earth").

After addressing the rebellion of Lucifer, our Elder Brother, "the Good Shepherd,"

addressed our concerns. (John 10:11). His nurturing influence during our pre-mortal sojourn helped to settle our minds regarding the uncertainties that lay ahead, and convinced us that He is "not the author of confusion, but of peace." (1 Corinthians 14:33). That peace hinged upon His role as our Redeemer, "the Lamb

Slain From the Foundation of the World," upon our eagerness to try the virtue of the word of God, and upon our willingness to exercise, for the first time in our lives, the principle of repentance. (Revelation 13:8).

What happened to us later was akin to "going down a rabbit hole." (See "Alice's Adventures in Wonderland," Chapter 1, by Lewis Carroll). The journey from our first estate was measured not so much in distance as it was in proportion. As we squeezed through the birth canal into the breathtaking expanse of the wide, wide world, the memory of our former life was erased, but new vistas soon opened up to fill in the void. To reinforce our understanding of the principles we had aforetime internalized, religious recognition came into play. It triggered a re-cognition, a re-knowing, or an intuitive remembrance of our former glory. The Light of Christ cast a steady glow over the nursery that we now called home. Carefully articulated Articles of Faith had been formulated that would be sent as love-letters from Home, to "ring a bell" and stir our memories. To describe the process, the expression "Deja-vu" was coined.

These ingenious devices were provided to show us how to jump right back into the celestial skin that had defined our familiar heavenly home from the beginning. For those who would be lucky enough to follow the Savior to the waters of baptism and be "born again," that shield would be akin to the barrier protection afforded to health care providers that protects them from the relentless assault of pathogens during critical patient care. With equivalent "barrier protection" shielding our divine center, the likelihood of a return to the full form and stature of our spirit could be maximized.

The Plan has been tested in the crucible of countless classrooms across the cosmos. (See Moses 1:33). It is "fair as the moon, clear as the sun, and terrible as an army

with banners." (D&C 109:73). Its worth defies argument. Its dedication to proven principles is incontrovertible. Its learning opportunities minimize the risk of succumbing to the wiles of a counterfeit and corruptible curriculum that is only a caricature of canon.

The Devil is the original "Wile E. Coyote" who "is the author of all sin," and the architect of the aforementioned cowardly curriculum. (Helaman 6:30). Even as he gloated in the "nakedness" of Adam and Eve in the Garden, he "knew not the mind of God." (Moses 4:6). The high-fives Satan and his henchmen must have exchanged turned out to be a bit premature. God parlayed his trickery right into the execution of The Plan. "Wo unto them that are deceivers and hypocrites," warned the Savior, for their deceptions will come to naught. (D&C 50:6).

Anciently, a "hypocrite" was the mask worn by the actors of classical Greece in the plays written by Aeschylus, Euripedes, Aristophanes, and others. The term has come to derisively characterize those who make false appearances with the intent to deceive. It describes those who pretend to be something they are not. If we are not careful, hypocrites can get under our skin; they can worm their way right into our hearts, minds, and souls after our barrier protection has been compromised. Unless we are quick to repent, they can then distort our celestial features into the caricatures of a hypocrite's mask.

In the novel "The Picture of Dorian Grey," by Oscar Wilde, a particularly handsome young man's enchanting portrait degenerates over time in response to his moral depravity and self-indulgence, while at the same time his own face retains its alabaster innocence. He embraces the philosophy that the only way to eliminate a temptation is to yield to it. After many years of decadence have taken a mighty toll on his character, he loses his mind, grabs a knife and attacks the picture that with such stark realism and accuracy has reflected his mounting depravity. The servants of the house awaken to a cry from the locked room of the anguished debaucherer, and break down the door. Before them lies the body of an unrecognizable old man, stabbed in the heart, his face withered and decrepit. Only by the ring on his finger can they identify the disfigured corpse as their master. (The Ring of Gyges comes

to mind. See below). Beside the emaciated figure is the picture of Dorian Gray that has reverted to its original loveliness.

In Book 2 of Plato's "The Republic," Glaucon and Adeimantus present the myth of the Ring of Gyges, by means of which Gyges is able to make himself invisible. They then ask Socrates: "If one came into possession of such a ring, why should he act justly?" Socrates replies that although no one could see their body, the soul would be horribly disfigured by the evils that had been committed behind the illusory shield of invisibility.

Thankfully, God has turned the tables on Satan by providing the principle of repentance, that we might jump out of our skin whenever it has become corrupted and contaminated by sin. We need not fear that our spiritual portraits will lose their luster. We need not be like that unfortunate soul who took the Excess Express, and who, when he got to heaven, "saw something that filled him with fright, for his spiritual body was one sorry sight! No more than a skeleton, covered with corruptible skin. He got up to heaven, but didn't get in!" (Anonymous).

God's Plan of Repentance and Mercy smooths out the bumps on our ride through mortality, and gives our experiences a profoundly positive twist, energizing them with vitality and us with the ability to re-write the last chapters of our life-story; even to alter eternity. We cannot go back and start a new beginning, but we can start today and make a new ending. We can re-boot the system, get rid of bad code, and restore damaged files. We can create enough RAM and additional disk space to write a bedtime story in which we all live happily ever after. Hans Christian Anderson said it best: "Our lives are fairy tales waiting to be written by the finger of God."

He has made it possible for us to be dermatologically transformed, to physically manipulate the makeup of our bodies, to figuratively influence our integumentary systems, and to defeat spiritual death without the need for expensive creams, lotions, balms, emollients, astringents, clarifiers, modifiers, oils, ointments, liniments,

balsams, salves, gels, and lubricants. He has provided a discerning prequel to the resurrection, by allowing us to have the experience of jumping out of our corruptible skin. This may be a collective experience, but it is always intensely personal. It was our Exemplar, after all, Who stood beside an empty tomb, and cautioned Mary: "Touch me not, for I am not yet ascended to my Father." (John 20:17). She then went and told the other disciples that she had witnessed a miracle. (John 20:18).

When we present ourselves before God, we too will be uncompromised by corruption. (See Alma 5:14). As the people of Zarahemla exclaimed, so must we: "The Spirit of the Lord Omnipotent ... has wrought a mighty change in us, or in our hearts, that we have no more disposition to do evil, but to do good continually." (Mosiah 5:3). Given these transformative circumstances, the last thing we would want to do would be to compromise our spiritual solidarity by denying ourselves the opportunity to repetitively throw ourselves upon the mercy seat of God. Repentance allows us to grasp the horns of sanctuary that are provided by The Great and Eternal Plan of Deliverance from Death (2 Nephi 11:5).

The Plan has the inherent power to accomplish the transformation of 27 trillion skin cells, not after four weeks' time, but in an instant, after being wrapped in the "clean linen cloth" of the Gospel. (Matthew 27:59). If the clothes in which we have gone out to play on terra firma have been soiled by sin, we can forsake our filthiness in favor of clean heavenly vestments. Unlike the clothing made for the Emperor in the tale by Hans Christian Anderson, ours celestial garments are tangible; they are real. We need not fear the cries of children in the streets: "But they aren't wearing anything at all!" ("The Emperor's New Clothes").

The scriptures prepare our minds with additional contrasting examples. When Belshazzar of old saw the prophetic writing upon the wall, his "countenance was changed, and his thoughts troubled him, so that the joints of his loins were loosed, and his knees smote one against another." (Daniel 5:6). A fundamental transmutation with intensely personal negative consequences was in the works.

Soon thereafter, he was "weighed in the balances, and found wanting." (Daniel 5:27). The celestial skin provided by God to Belshazzar had mutated through apostasy, and without repentance, the resultant 20 pounds or so of dermal and epidermal cells (comprising not only the largest, but also the heaviest organ system in the human body) no longer afforded him spiritual protection from the elements of his cankered and cancerous environment.

Things turned out better for leprous Naaman, the captain of the hosts of the king of Syria, who was told by the messenger of Elisha: "Go and wash in Jordan seven times, and thy flesh shall come again to thee, and thou shalt be clean. Then went he down, and dipped himself seven times in Jordan, according to the saying of the man of God: and his flesh came again like unto the flesh of a little child, and he was clean." (2 Kings 5:10 & 14).

The skin of other lepers benefitted from the application of celestial salve, as well. The scriptures record that as Jesus "entered into a certain village, there met him ten men that were lepers, which stood afar off: And they lifted up their voices, and said, Jesus, Master, have mercy on us. And when he saw them, he said unto them, Go shew yourselves unto the priests. And it came to pass, that, as they went, they were cleansed." (Luke 17:12 & 14). But let us not forget that, while Jesus has power to Atone for our sins, in every instance following our repentance, we hear Him say: "Neither do I condemn thee. Go, and sin no more." (John 8:11).

Joseph Smith recorded his impressions after many encounters with the Spirit: "Often times it maketh my bones to quake while it maketh manifest." (D&C 85:6). Faithful members of the Church have had similar feelings in preparation to receive "health in their navel and marrow to their bones," as they experience the miracle of forgiveness and jump out of telestial trappings into celestial garments. (D&C 89:18). More than a nutritional nuance or a medical marvel, this priesthood transformation insures a metaphorical manipulation through rhetorical analogy: "Though (their) sins be as scarlet, they shall be as white as snow; though they be red like crimson, they shall be as wool." (Isaiah 1:18).

King Benjamin suggested: "The natural man is an enemy to God, and always has been from the beginning," even from that time so long ago when Adam and Eve initially jumped out of carefully crafted and meticulously maintained celestial skin. (Mosiah 3:19). It is clear that each of us must, as Paul suggested, be fitted by the Master Tailor to receive a heavenly vestment and become "a new creature" in Christ. (2 Corinthians 5:17). "Have ye spiritually been born of God?" Alma asked. "Have ye received his image in your countenances? (Alma 5:14).

When the Spirit has stretched and molded us, its expression will be manifested in an unblemished and alabaster skin-tone. (See Mosiah 13:5 & D&C 20:6). We will have "the look." Like it or not, by the time we are middle-aged, the record of the conduct of our lives will have been indelibly etched into the unalterable expressions of our countenances. If we have mouthed the lyrics of the celestial melodies that move us to "sing the song of redeeming love," our countenances will shine with a radiance that reveals the presence of the Lord that rests upon us. (Mosiah 5:26, see D&C 138:24).

After his parents' expulsion from the Garden, "Cain was very wroth," and he found himself shedding his celestial skin. (We do not know for sure, but this may have occurred during those difficult teenage years). In any event, he was in a flat spin from which he could not recover. His "countenance fell." (Genesis 4:5). He could neither overcome his fallen nature nor endure the molting process we all must face when we make 'the leap.' But it is only at that moment that we are able to slough off the telestial trash of dead skin cells, (all 27 trillion of them), so that our "sleeping dust (may be) restored unto its perfect frame." (D&C 138:17). It is only then that "the sinews and the flesh upon them, the spirit and the body (will be) united, never again to be divided." (D&C 138:17). It is only then that "old things shall pass away," (D&C 29:24), "and there shall be a new heaven and a new earth." (Ether 13:9). Only then, will we discard the trappings of our former life, and "every limb and joint shall be restored to its body; yea, even a hair of the head shall not be lost; but all things shall be restored to their proper and perfect frame." (Alma 40:23).

In the meantime, God gives us repetitive opportunities to practice jumping out of our telestial skin, off of complacency plateaus, into the more comfortable and form-fitting celestial silhouette that enables us to leap tall buildings at a single bound. We must repent with measured consideration, testing its claim of protection from the scorching sun in the heat of the day. Sometimes, we must jump from the frying pan right into the fire. With practice, when we jump we will land on springboards to action that propel us upward to safety; that we might confidently balance on pinnacles of perfection. We should always look before we leap, but leap we must. Sometimes, we are prompted, or are so intensely invested, so spiritually charged, or so inspired, that we only need to heed the admonition: "Who hath faith to leap shall leap." (D&C 42:51). We must repent, and we must do it now.

At a critical juncture in their trek through the far reaches of the galaxy, Captain Jean Luc Picard of the Star Ship Enterprise urged his crew: "Now, this will put us at risk. Quite frankly, we may not survive. But I want you to believe that I am doing this for a greater purpose, and that what is at stake here is more than any of you can possibly imagine. I know you have your doubts about me, about each other, about this ship. All I can say is that although we have only been together for a short time, I know that you are the finest crew in the fleet. And I would trust each of you with my life. So, I am asking you for a leap of faith, and to trust me." ("All Good Things," 5/23/1994).

If we happen to be startled by the corruptible reflection we see in the windows of a great and spacious building, we need to jump out of our skin without hesitation, remembering that "the Lord seeth not as man seeth; for man looketh on the outward appearance, but the Lord looketh on the heart." (1 Samuel 16:7). We need to jump without even thinking about it, emulating those Saints who have rejoiced in their resurrection. Of these, Joseph F. Smith observed: "Their countenances shone, and the radiance from the presence of the Lord rested upon them." (D&C 138:24). We need to jump so that our afterglow is so compelling that its lingering effects overshadow any latent images of our reflection in the windows of even the tallest telestial towers.

When Joseph Smith and Oliver Cowdery attended the dedication of the Kirtland Temple, they shed their telestial trappings to enjoy an unprecedented vision of the Savior. "His eyes were as a flame of fire," Joseph recorded, and "the hair of his head was white like the pure snow; his countenance shone above the brightness of the sun." (D&C 110:3). The Lord's appearance was untainted by familiar telestial trauma. He was "Alpha and Omega, the beginning and the ending, the Lord, who is, and who was, and who is to come, the Almighty." (J.S.T. Revelation 1:8). Joseph and Oliver were provided with a preview of the extreme makeover, punctuated by a spiritual change of wardrobe, that awaited them in the Celestial Kingdom.

Joseph's observations went beyond garments and compelled him to consider the spiritual center of resurrected beings. Of the Angel Moroni, he had recorded: "His hands were naked, and his arms also, a little above the wrist. So, also, were his feet naked, as were his legs, a little above the ankles. His head and neck were also bare. I could discover that he had no other clothing on but this robe, as it was open, so that I could see into his bosom. Not only was his robe exceedingly white, but (also) his whole person was glorious beyond description, and his countenance truly like lightning. The room was exceedingly light, but not so very bright as immediately around his person." (J.S.H. 1:31-32).

But what about those of us who are less sure of ourselves? What happens if we look in the mirror and see the face of a stranger staring back at us? What if our knees wobble at the prospect of a leap of faith that requires an "identity transplant?" This has happened enough times in the scriptures that the "face" is referenced 684 times, "new" 206 times, "image" 166 times, "change" 104 times, and "countenance" 70 times. "Image of God" is mentioned a dozen or so times, and "visage" 4 times. The scriptures provide a lot of information regarding the purposes behind our packaging.

Since the first partial face transplant was performed on a woman in France in 2006, psychologists have been asking if such a procedure carries the risk of psychological impairment, or if it might, on the other hand, offer the possibility of

enriching the narrative of one's life by giving identity a new look. The jury is still out on that question, but it begs another: What happens under ideal circumstances, when the Lord's witness protection program functions optimally, and Satan can no longer find us, because we have been "born again; yea, born of God," and changed from our "carnal and fallen state, to a state of righteousness, being redeemed of God, becoming his sons and daughters?" (Mosiah 27:25). What happens when we are no longer recognizable as our former selves, when all ties to our past lives have been severed? What positive changes occur when we really take advantage of the Atonement, and jump out of our skin, when our repentance is perfect, "old things are passed away, (and) all things are become new?" (2 Corinthians 5:17).

The simplest answer to these questions might be found in the recorded experiences of those who have had a "heart transplant" when they accepted the Gospel. Alma spoke of his own father's conversion: "According to his faith, there was a mighty change wrought in his heart." (Alma 5:12). Paul may have been thinking along the same lines, when he described the new Gospel-oriented identity that is found in the "fleshy tables of the heart." (2 Corinthians 3:3). Converts often emerge from the refiner's fire having had spiritual open-heart surgical procedures, wherein the dross of their former lives has been burned out of their systems by the white-hot fire of God.

The identity crisis of such individuals is mitigated because of God's care and concern relating to these extreme makeover procedures. It turns out that the grass really is greener on the other side of the fence, where a pleasant pastoral environment promises a new perspective. The prophet may have been alluding to the repentant, when he wrote: "Say to the prisoners, go forth. To them that are in darkness, shew yourselves. They shall feed in the ways, and their pastures shall be in all high places." (Isaiah 49:9).

In any event, there is a visibly different new look to those who have repented, taken their vows, and moved upward to new plateaus that are springboards for affirmative action. Their features are flushed with confidence. They stand out from

the crowd. They are enthusiastic, passionate, fervent, eager, animated, excited by life, and get a high from the natural release of endorphins in their systems.

These dedicated disciples remind us of Abinadi, of whom the scriptures record: "The

Spirit of the Lord was upon him and his face shone with exceeding luster." (Mosiah 13:5). They stand in sharp contrast or opposition to those whose yoke is a heavy burden because they are mired in sin and bound in iniquity. Of them, Jeremiah wrote: "Their visage is blacker than a coal they are not known in the streets their skin cleaveth to their bones it is withered." (Lamentations 4:8).

Those who have brushed against physical death often describe an "out of body" experience akin to "jumping out of their skin." Today, members of the Lord's Church feel the same when they have been redeemed from spiritual death; when they "walk in newness of life." (Romans 6:4).

Latter-day Saints come full circle, and end where they began, albeit with a wider perspective from a higher vantage point. It is strangely familiar to read about how "the Gods went down to organize (them) in their own image, in the image of the Gods to form (them), male and female to form they them." (Abraham 4:27).

To really take advantage of their temporal travels and put a positive spin on their telestial trials, Latter-day Saints learn to repent, that they might jump out of their skin, to be restored to their "proper and perfect frame," and ultimately to face their destiny, clothed in glory, immortality, and eternal life. (Alma 40:23). They constantly remind themselves that they are "strangers from a realm of light, who have (nearly) forgotten all - the memory of their former life and the purpose of their call. And so, they are eager learn why they're here, and who they really are." (See "Saturday's Warrior," lyrics by Doug Stewart).

"Repent, therefore, and bring forth
fruits meet for repentance."
(J.S.T. Matthew 3:35).

Chapter Thirty Three

Redeemed by the grace of God.

Nephi clearly taught that "it is by grace that we are saved, after all we can do." (2 Nephi 25:23). Latter-day Saints, however, tend to emphasize works to the point that it may seem to others that the grace of God takes a back seat to their own efforts to earn salvation. In spite of our focus on accountability, agency, industry, and labor, as we are exhorted to greater dedication, diligence, and duty, the truth is that nothing we can do will ever qualify us to enjoy eternal life. Paul echoed Nephi, writing that it is "by grace ye are saved, through faith, and that not of yourselves. It is the gift of God." (Ephesians 2:8). And in his epistle to Titus, Paul affirmed that it is "the grace of God that bringeth salvation." (Titus 2:11). Luke similarly taught, "We believe that through the grace of the Lord Jesus Christ, we shall be saved." (Acts 15:11).

Grace is one of God's attributes, consisting of the love, mercy, and power by which He may bring us to His stature. Because of His grace, we may enjoy not only what He has, but also what He is. On earth, our lives are days of probation, of testing, or of putting to the proof our declared values. Therefore, as we learn to conform to His lifestyle, we may more fully enjoy His grace.

This process allows us to be raised from physical death by the power of the Resurrection, and from spiritual death by the power of the Atonement. We receive grace proportionately as we conform to the standard of personal righteousness that is required by the Gospel Plan. Thus, we are commanded to "grow in grace" until we are sanctified and justified "thru the grace of our Lord and Savior Jesus Christ." (D&C 50:40 & D&C 20:30-32). It is in this sense that Nephi declared that we are saved by grace only "after all we can do," which is primarily to repent of our sins. Because the two are inextricably linked, when the day of repentance is past, so is the day of grace. (See Mormon 2:15).

In the scriptures, works are generally associated with obedience to the commandments. Thus, the Savior denounced the Jews, declaring unto them: "If ye were Abraham's children, ye would do the works of Abraham." (John 8:39). In this sense, Paul taught the Romans that "not the hearers of the law are just before God, but the doers of the law shall be justified." (Romans 2:13). Martin Luther correctly understood that faith is "no merely intellectual assent to a proposition, but is vital, personal self-committal to a practical belief. He heartily approved of good works; what he denied was their efficacy for salvation. 'Good works,' he said, 'do not make a good man, but a good man does good works.' And what makes a man good? Faith in God, and Christ." (Will Durant, "The Reformation," p. 374-375).

The scriptures clearly teach: "They which have believed in God (should) be careful to maintain good works. These things are good and profitable unto men." (Titus 3:8). There is always the possibility, however, that we "may fall from grace and depart from the living God." (D&C 20:32). Therefore, James admonished his brethren, as did Paul, to be "doers of the word, and not hearers only, deceiving your own selves." (James 1:22). Without works, it is all too easy to "fall into temptation." (D&C 20:33). When this happens, we lose our focus, slacken our pace on the path of discipleship, and wander off in "mists of darkness." (1 Nephi 12:17). In this sense, James taught: "Faith without works is dead." (James 2:26).

The grace of God cannot save those who are determined to ignore His entreaties

to commit themselves by covenant to an undeviating standard of personal righteousness. To believe that He would do so, that He would extend His grace to those who only "professed" His name, is delusional. Saving faith is the catalyst that propels us to embrace the principles and ordinances of the Gospel. If our hearts are right, "then we have confidence toward God. And whatsoever we ask, we receive of him, <u>because we keep his commandments, and do those things that are pleasing in his sight.</u>" (1 John 3:21-22, underlining mine). Of course, "we should believe on the name of his Son Jesus Christ, and love one another." (1 James 3:23). But this is not all we must do. We must correctly apply the scriptures to our own behavior, without wresting them, for it is "Satan (who) doth stir up the hearts of the people to contention concerning the points of (His) doctrine. (D&C 10:63).

It is our responsibility to teach the true points of His doctrine, in order that the Gospel might be established among the nations and that contention might be eliminated. Twisting the scriptures that admonish us to good works from their true or proper signification perverts them from their correct application. Such is the case when individuals alter their meaning to justify the damnable doctrine that we are saved by works.

Brigham Young clearly understood and was comfortable with his relationship to God. He was totally and utterly dependent upon Him for his personal salvation. He once declared: "There is no man who ever made a sacrifice on the earth for the Kingdom of Heaven, except the Savior. I would not give the ashes of a rye straw for that man who feels that he is making sacrifices for God." (J.D., 16:114). He knew that it is through His grace alone, through the sacrifice of His Son, that we are saved.

Mormon related his inadequacy to his debt to God. Thus, he wrote: "O how great is the nothingness of the children of men; yea, even they are less than the dust of the earth." (Helaman 12:7). In this vein, King Benjamin had urged his people to thank God, and not him, for their peace and prosperity. He said that if they praised Him, and served Him "with all (their) whole souls, yet (they) would be unprofitable

servants." (Mosiah 2:20-21). That is because we can do nothing that puts God in our debt. His grace is completely beyond our ability to pay. But God does not ask us to settle our account with Him; He only asks that we keep His commandments. The marvel of His love is that the more we try to serve Him, the more He blesses us.

Therefore, we become even more deeply indebted to Him, and remain so forever. When we are redeemed by the precious blood of Christ, it is by grace alone that we enjoy salvation.

We risk falling into transgression in consequence of a shallow understanding of principles and doctrines. As Alma declared to the inhabitants of Ammonihah, "Behold, the scriptures are before you. If ye will wrest them it shall be to your own destruction." (Alma 13:20). Picking apart the scriptures can distort dogma into meaningless fragments without any coherent connection, or it can redefine doctrine into bizarre and nonsensical definitions.

In 1820, the Lord characterized such individuals as those who "draw near to me with their lips, but (whose) hearts are far from me. They teach for doctrines the commandments of men, having a form of godliness, but they deny the power thereof." (J.S.H. 2:19). To rely upon our own puny efforts instead of the boundless grace of God reduces The Plan of Salvation to a crude caricature without meaning or substance.

The children of men do not easily hearken to counsel. Instead, when things are going reasonably well, they say: "Behold, we are the sons of God. Have we not taken unto ourselves the daughters of men? And are we not eating and drinking, and marrying and giving in marriage? And our wives bear unto us children, and the same are mighty men, which are like unto men of old, men of great renown." (Moses 8:21). However, the actions of such self-righteous and self-indulgent individuals are all form and no substance. They are the sizzle without the steak. True character is revealed when "every man (is) lifted up in the imagination of the thoughts of his heart, being only evil continually." (Moses 8:22).

In contrast, the doctrine of Christ has been clearly revealed. (See 2 Nephi 31:21). Anything less than this is evil, because it keeps us from reaching our potential by denying us the opportunity to be obedient to the laws of The Great Plan of

Salvation. (Alma 42:5). The keystone of this doctrine is His grace, that is extended to all who claim salvation through faith on His name.

The expected performance requirement of His accountable disciples focuses solely on the principles and ordinances of His Gospel. "Whosoever repenteth and cometh unto me," said the Lord, "the same is my Church. Whosoever declareth more or less than this, the same is not of me, but is against me. Therefore, he is not of my Church." (D&C 10:67-68).

Since the organization of the Church on April 6, 1830, this doctrine has not changed. It has been taught without modification since that time. Simply stated, this doctrine is that when we have faith in Jesus Christ, truly repent of our sins, and enter into a baptismal covenant with Him, we will receive the Holy Ghost, Who will then direct our development, revealing to us the things we must do to merit salvation. "For the gate by which ye should enter is repentance and baptism by water; and then," in a mystical and incomprehensible way, comes "a remission of your sins by fire and by the Holy Ghost." (2 Nephi 31:17). This puts us on the "strait and narrow path which leads to eternal life" through the grace of God. (2 Nephi 31:18).

As the gates of baptism swing open to reveal a strait and narrow way before us stretching away to a glow of light on the eastern horizon, our real journey to Christ has only begun. Having been born again, we must continue to press forward with complete dedication and steadfastness, with confidence and a firm determination in Christ, having a perfect brightness of hope, or perfect faith, and a love of God and of all men, which is charity. If we do this, feasting upon the word of Christ, receiving strength and nourishment from the scriptures, and endure to the end in righteousness, all the while repenting of our sins and relying upon the Saviors' Atonement, we shall receive the grace of God and have eternal life, which is the

greatest of all gifts. (See 2 Nephi 31:20).

This is our on-going responsibility, when we have personally accepted Jesus Christ as our Savior and Redeemer. Through the Gospel plan, we are intertwined in a partnership with God. (See Moses 1:39). In our fallen state, however, it is our nature to be influenced by Satan. If we have no prior experience with God, and we allow ourselves to be tainted by unresolved sin, we are necessarily alienated from Him by spiritual death. This is why, from the Fall of Adam, He has provided us with The Plan of Salvation, The Plan of Redemption, or The Plan of Happiness, that mortality might become a preparatory state, permitting us to develop the behavioral lifestyle and qualities required for redemption from spiritual death. (See Alma 42:10).

It is for our benefit that we become acquainted with evil as well as with good, with darkness as well as with light, with error as well as with truth, and with punishment for the infraction of eternal laws, as well as with the blessings that follow obedience. (See Moses 5:10). Mortality is really our only opportunity to have these experiences. But without the overshadowing grace of God, our mortal education would be for naught. It would not lead to an honorary degree in provident living. As Ralph Waldo Emerson once asked: "What is the use of immortality to one who cannot wisely use half an hour?"

Alma reminded Corianton: "If it were not for The Plan of Redemption, as soon as (we) were dead, (our) souls were miserable, being cut off from the presence of the Lord." (Alma 42:11). Justice would demand that we eternally suffer the consequences of our own careless actions. We would be "in the grasp of justice, yea, the justice of God, which (would consign us) forever to be cut off from his presence." According to Justice, "the Plan of Redemption could not be brought about" and "Mercy could not take effect except it should destroy the work of Justice." (Alma 42:12-13).

The beauty of The Plan, then, is that it meets the demands of perfect Justice through the infinite Mercy of our Heavenly Father. The Plan allows Him to be

both just and merciful at the same time, and to extend His grace to all who approach Him with broken hearts and contrite spirits. (See D&C 20:37). The Plan of Redemption requires that "an Atonement should be made. Therefore, God Himself atoneth for the sins of the world, to bring about The Plan of Mercy, to appease the demands of justice, that God might be a perfect, just God, and a merciful God also." (Alma 42:15).

The Atonement allows Him to satisfy Justice and still mercifully reclaim us from spiritual death. By conquering death the Savior becomes the Master of the situation. In His sacrifice, the debt is paid, redemption made, Mercy is extended, Justice is satisfied, the Covenant is fulfilled, and God's will is done, all made possible by an extension of His grace. Through all, the power to save souls remains with the Savior Jesus Christ. "Even though we may scribe a circle that draws Him out, and consider the Savior a thing to flout, His love has a will to win. He scribes a circle that draws us in." (Paraphrased from Edwin Markham, "Outwitted").

"Each of us lives on a kind of spiritual credit," wrote Boyd K. Packer. "One day the account will be closed, and a settlement demanded. However casually we view it, when that day comes and the foreclosure is imminent, we will look around in restless agony for someone, anyone, to help us. And by eternal law, Mercy cannot be extended save there be one who is both willing and able to assume our debt, and pay the price, and arrange the terms of our redemption." ("Ensign," 4/1977).

As Alma reminded Corianton, the only payment required for the gift of grace is "the heart and a willing mind." (D&C 64:34). The only things that we must give up are our sins. The father of King Lamoni clearly understood this when he was taught the Gospel by Ammon. He said, "If there is a God ... wilt Thou make Thyself known unto me, and I will give away all my sins to know Thee, and that I may be raised from the dead, and be saved at the last day." (Alma 22:18). This is reminiscent of Almas' counsel to his son: "Only let your sins trouble you, with that trouble which shall bring you down unto repentance." (Alma 42:29).

The first step in that process is the turning point at which the guilty party consciously recognizes his sin. The second step in the process of repentance is a clear understanding of Justice, Mercy, and the grace of God, and of the relationship between them because of The Plan of Redemption and its harmonizing power of repentance.

Thus, Alma warned Corianton to cease excusing himself in sin. "O my son, I desire that ye should deny the justice of God no more. Do not endeavor to excuse yourself in the least point because of your sins, by denying the justice of God; but do let the justice of God, and his mercy, and his long-suffering have full sway in your heart; and let it bring you down to the dust in humility." (Alma 42:30). He was asking his son to allow repentance and forgiveness through the grace of God to profoundly transform him, as if he were pliant clay in the hands of the Master Potter.

Alma knew by his own experience how the children of men can be fashioned by grace into the sons and daughters of God. Nephi said: "This is the way, and there is none other way nor name given under heaven whereby man can be saved in the kingdom of God. And now, behold, this is the doctrine of Christ, and the only and true doctrine of the Father, and of the Son, and of the Holy Ghost, which is one God, without end." (2 Nephi 31:21). This scripture reveals that all three members of the Godhead are involved in the extension of grace through the doctrine of Christ.

Saving faith, then, is at the foundation of the doctrine of Christ, and is tied in the scriptures to a specific kind of works that is, in a sense, independent of grace. Perhaps the verse most commonly quoted in support of this supposition by members of the Lord's Church is James 2:17: "Faith, if it hath not works, is dead, being alone." The J.S.T., however, renders this verse: "Faith, if it hath not works, is dead, and cannot save you." This interpretation is both clear and unmistakable. There is no salvation in faith alone. There is no more power in faith without works than there is in food that is not eaten, or in warm clothing that is not worn. Nevertheless, "by

works (is) faith made perfect." (James 2:22). The Savior taught: "Every tree is known by his own fruit. For of thorns men do not gather figs, nor of a bramble bush gather they grapes. A good man out of the good treasure of his heart bringeth forth that which is good ... for of the abundance of the heart, his mouth speaketh." (Luke 6:44-45).

Ultimately, we are accountable for our own actions, which will either damn us or lift us into the embrace of angels. "Be not deceived," cautioned Paul. "God is not mocked. For whatsoever a man soweth, that shall he also reap." (Galatians 6:7). "For we must all appear before the judgment seat of Christ, that every one may receive the things done in his body, according to that he hath done, whether it be good or bad." (2 Corinthians 5:10). Ultimately, "he which soweth sparingly shall reap also sparingly; and he which soweth bountifully shall reap also bountifully." (2 Corinthians 9:6).

The path of eternal progression leading to the Celestial Kingdom is strait and narrow. The Gospel standard is undeviating, and there is no wiggle room for rationalization or compromise, for we are all sinners. God put us on the earth with the full knowledge that we would yield to temptation, and sin by violating His commandments. Nevertheless, there is no latitude in His declaration, when He said: "I the Lord cannot look upon sin with the least degree of allowance." (D&C 1:31). We must all face the music, and somehow deal with that harsh, yet incontrovertible, reality.

Fortunately, there is a way out of the moral dilemma created by our inability to comply with all of the requirements of God's law. Faith and repentance lead us to the covenants of the Gospel where we receive its ordinances and pass through the strait gate of baptism to obtain a remission of sins, gain membership in the Church, and find ourselves on the path leading to personal sanctification through the receipt of the Holy Ghost. It is this prescribed process that urges us on to repetitive repentance in response to recurring transgression. The grace of God exists to

lighten our burdens when we find them too heavy to bear alone, and then it will pluck us out of the gaping jaws of hell, and whisk us out of harms' way.

Through it all, the Lord has promised: "My grace is sufficient for thee: for my strength is made perfect in weakness." (2 Corinthians 12:9). As Stephen Robinson has written: "The scriptures clearly teach that God cannot tolerate sin or sinfulness in any degree. He can't wink at it, or ignore it, or turn and look the other way. He won't sweep it under the rug or say, 'Well, it's just a little sin. It'll be all right.' God's standard, the celestial standard, is absolute, and it allows no exceptions. Many people seem to have the idea that the Judgment will somehow involve weighing or balancing, with their good deeds on one side of the scales and their bad deeds on the other. If their good deeds outweigh their bad, or if their hearts are basically good and outweigh their sins, then they can be admitted into the presence of God. This notion is false. God cannot and will not allow moral or ethical imperfection in any degree whatsoever to dwell in His presence. He cannot tolerate sin 'with the least degree of allowance.' It is not a question of whether our good deeds outweigh our sins. If there is even one sin on our record, we are finished. The celestial standard is complete innocence, pure and simple, and nothing less than that will be tolerated in the Kingdom of God." ("Believing Christ," p. 1-7).

Precisely because of its unyielding standard, however, the Gospel is "The Good News" to all those who embrace it. Fortunately for us, it encompasses all the principles, covenants, and ordinances that enable us to become sanctified so that we may be worthy to live once again in a state of holiness in the presence of our Heavenly Father. Because of the grace of God, we may "come unto Christ, and lay hold upon every good gift ... and be perfected in him," as we deny ourselves "all ungodliness." (Moroni 10:30 & 32). As Alma did, so should we all "continue in the supplicating of his grace" so that we may stand blameless before Him at His Pleasing Bar. (Alma 7:3).

Sanctification, then, is the process by which we are cleansed from the effects of sin.

Thus spiritually renewed, we stand prepared to enter the presence of the Lord. We must submit our will to His, yield our hearts to Him, sustain His servants, preach His Gospel, and be obedient to all of the teachings of His Church. "Therefore," promised the Lord, "if ye do these things, blessed are ye, for ye shall be lifted up at the last day." (3 Nephi 27:22). His grace will be sufficient for all those who humble themselves before Him. (See Ether 12:27).

As the Savior taught the Nephites: "This is the Gospel which I have given unto you – that I came into the world to do the will of my Father, because my Father sent me. And my Father sent me that I might be lifted up upon the cross; and after that I had been lifted up upon the cross, that I might draw all men unto me … And it shall come to pass, that whoso repenteth and is baptized in my name shall be filled." (3 Nephi 27:13-20).

Thus, Mormon taught that "the first fruits of repentance is baptism; and baptism cometh by faith unto the fulfilling the commandments; and the fulfilling the commandments bringeth remission of sins (through repentance); and the remission of sins bringeth meekness, and lowliness of heart; and because of meekness and lowliness of heart cometh the visitation of the Holy Ghost, which Comforter filleth with hope and perfect love, which love endureth by diligence unto prayer, until the end shall come, when all the saints shall dwell with God." (Moroni 8:25-26). His people shall "receive of His fulness, and be glorified in Him (and) shall receive grace for grace." (D&C 93:20).

As we grow in grace, we become more and more like our Heavenly Father. (See 2 Peter 3:18). As we grow in spiritual stature, we are empowered to follow the counsel of the Savior, Who commanded: "I would that ye should be perfect, even as I, or your Father who is in heaven is perfect." (3 Nephi 12:48, see Matthew 5:48). God glories in the possibility that we might become like Him, which may be the ultimate expression of His matchless grace. "If ye by the grace of God are perfect in Christ, and deny not his power, then are ye sanctified in Christ by the grace of God, through the shedding of the blood of Christ, which is in the covenant of the Father

unto the remission of your sins, that ye become holy, without spot." (Moroni 10:33).

It would be difficult to state more succinctly, and yet more powerfully, the essence of the Gospel of Jesus Christ. All the teachings of the Savior and His prophets build to this climax. If we will open our hearts to the Gospel, we can become holy, and untainted by the stain of sin. Those who are thus prepared, declared Vaughn Featherstone, "will know Him. They will cry out: Blessed be the name of Him that cometh in the name of the Lord. "Thou art my God and I will praise Thee; Thou art my God and I will exalt Thee." (Psalms 118:28). Our children will bow down at His feet and worship Him as the Lord of Lords, the King of Kings. They will bathe His feet with their tears and He will weep and bless them ... His bowels will be filled with compassion and His heart will swell wide as eternity and He will love them. He will bring peace that will last a thousand years and they will receive their reward to dwell with Him." (Utah South Stake, 4/1987).

"If your brethren desire to escape their enemies, let them repent of all their sins, and become truly humble before me and contrite." (D&C 54:3).

Chapter Thirty Four

The road to repentance.

"Half this game is 90% mental."
(Yogi Berra)

In our preparation for repentance, we employ a number of success strategies. Among them, are the following two dozen.

<u>We pre-play before we re-play.</u>

We follow an established plan. "Ask for the old paths, where is the good way, and walk therein, and ye shall find rest for your souls." (Jeremiah 6:16).

<u>We learn to quickly recognize and deal with negative thoughts.</u>

We seek the Lord while He may be found, and we call upon Him while he is near. (See Isaiah 55:6). We avoid negative self-talk because it becomes a self-fulfilling prophecy. We remember that when "there is no vision, the people perish." (Proverbs 29:18).

We believe the Lord when He says: "Even as you desire of me so it shall be done unto you." (D&C 6:8, 11:8). We avoid participating in pity-parties. We remember the admonition: "How beautiful upon the mountains are the feet of those that (publish)

peace." (Mosiah 15:16). We promote the cause of Zion and proclaim peace of mind in a world gone mad.

"If I regarded my life from the point of view of the pessimist," wrote Helen Keller, "I should be undone. I should seek in vain for the light that does not visit my eyes and the music that does not ring in my ears. I should beg night and day and never be satisfied. I should sit apart in awful solitude, a prey to fear and despair. But since I consider it a duty to myself and to others to be happy, I escape a misery worse than any physical deprivation." ("Optimism").

<u>We find a sacred grove, and visit it often.</u>

We all need time to "get away," in order to maintain our sanity. The Psalmist's excellent advice was: "Be still and know that I am God." (Psalms 46:10). By physically or emotionally retreating to the quiet sanctuary of our "happy place," we are simply following the counsel of the Lord to "stand … in holy places, and be not moved." (D&C 87:8).

<u>We prepare ourselves spiritually, by listening to uplifting music that reminds of the harmony of heaven.</u>

Music inspires us, motivates us, invites the Spirit, and comforts, strengths, and calms our unruly spirits. The intrinsic harmony of music is inseparably related to our inner peace and contentment.

<u>We are eternal optimists.</u>

We remember Joseph Smith, who encouraged the Saints: "Courage, brethren, and on,

on to the victory! Let your hearts rejoice, and be exceedingly glad." (D&C 128:22). We know that reverses are a part of life, but our optimism carries us past these minor inconveniences and impediments to our progress. We realize that "to every thing there is a season, and a time to every purpose under the heaven." (Ecclesiastes 3:1).

We count our blessings.

In everything we give thanks, for God has made promises to us "with an immutable covenant that they shall be fulfilled, and all things wherewith (we) have been afflicted shall work together for our good." (D&C 98:3). We recognize the blessings in all the things that touch our lives. We remember that the Savior is our "light in the wilderness" and "His arm of mercy is extended towards (us) in the light of the day." (1 Nephi 17:13 & Jacob 6:5). We are like the one who said: "I have a hobby! I have the world's largest seashell collection. I keep it scattered on beaches all over the planet." The fact is, we never know what the next tide is going to bring in.

We concentrate on who and what we may become, in spite of past performance. We realize that life is a learning curve, and that the trajectory of our achievement will carry us to new heights. We don't define ourselves by external criteria, but instead take our cues from the inside. We look at values that are determined by dreams, ideals, and core operating principles that are not easily subject to modification and are not easily influenced by external circumstances. We dismiss ambitions that are culturally determined and defined by ever-changing circumstances, the shifting sands of social custom, and political expediency and correctness. Our vision of what we may become, that is unclouded by the cataracts of convention, the presbyopia of procedure, or the myopia of manner, allows us to be self-directed, self-managed, self-motivated, self-propelled, and self-actualized while building our self-esteem and sense of self-worth.

We forget about events and instead focus on outcomes.

Just because things are going well, we are not fooled into thinking that it is we who have controlled the circumstances, since most are beyond our control anyway. We realize that what we do have power over is our creative response to the unpredictable, fickle, and even chaotic events that are a part of our normal daily lives. We see stepping stones instead of stumbling blocks. If we are given lemons, we make lemonade. Thus, even negative experiences and crises can be transformed into opportunities that have favorable outcomes.

<u>We forget about what is absent and instead focus on what is available.</u>

We multiply our talents, instead of hiding them under rocks. We do not allow what is missing to paralyze and defeat us. Instead, we focus on accessible resources, harness them with what power we have, and mold them into forces for positive, substantial, and significant change.

<u>Instead of being grouchy, we focus on gratitude.</u>

We are aware that chronic complainers attract negative energy. We draw positive energy and channel it into a force that expands the sphere of our influence. We pray for rain, but don't forget to carry an umbrella. We realize that we can't do everything but we can do something. We are determined to express gratitude for what is right, rather than to grumble about what is wrong. When we see a pile of manure, we are quick to grab a shovel, thinking to ourselves: "There's got to be a pony in there somewhere!"

<u>We seek out trusted priesthood leaders when the Spirit tells us we need to receive a blessing.</u>

Moroni was speaking to us, when he wrote: "I am mindful of you always in my prayers, continually praying unto God the Father in the name of His Holy Child, Jesus, that He, through His infinite goodness and grace, will keep you through

the endurance of faith on His name to the end." (Moroni 8:3). We remember how Solomon was in the thoughts and prayers of "Zadok the priest, (who) took an horn of oil out of the tabernacle, (and) anointed Solomon. And they blew the trumpet; and all the people said, God save king Solomon." (1 Kings 1:39).

<u>We re-read our patriarchal blessings.</u>

We view their promises as catalysts to release the powers of Heaven in our behalf. The spirit of God expressed in our blessings is the spirit of hope and not the spirit of gloom. As we ponder our blessings, the Spirit invites to us read between the lines that we might take encouragement and be inspired.

<u>We try to comprehend the Atonement.</u>

We realize that we must feel it through suffering. As Paul wrote: "For unto you it is given in the behalf of Christ, not only to believe on him, but also to suffer for his sake." (1 Philippians 1:29).

<u>We pray earnestly.</u>

We try to remember the wise counsel of James, who said that we must "confess (our) faults one to another, and pray one for another, that (we) may be healed. (For) the effectual fervent prayer of a righteous man availeth much." (James 5:16).

<u>We read the scriptures to gain an eternal perspective.</u>

Jacob revealed his formula for success: "We search the prophets," he wrote, "and we have many revelations and the spirit of prophecy; and having all these witnesses we obtain a hope, and our faith becometh unshaken." (Jacob 4:6).

<u>We remember that The Book of Mormon is another testament of Jesus Christ.</u>

1,449 of its verses state a life-preserving truth: "It came to pass." It did not come

to stay! Life unfolds before our eyes, often in surprisingly delightful ways.

<u>We take the time to honestly evaluate our lives.</u>

We try to look within ourselves, that we might see how the stain of unresolved sin might be creating negative energy. We remember what Alma taught his son: "If there were "no space for repentance ... the word of God would have been void, and the great plan of salvation would have been frustrated." (Alma 42:5). We realize that actively relying on the power of the Atonement is a strong generator of our positive mental energy.

<u>We deal with, learn from, and let go of the past.</u>

The future lies ahead, not behind! We can't go back and start a new beginning, but we can start today and make a new ending. The apostle Paul's formula for ridding ourselves of excess baggage was "forgetting those things which are behind, and reaching forth unto those things which are before." (Philippians 3:13-14).

As we repent, we need to "finish each day and be done with it. We have done what we could. Although some blunders and absurdities no doubt crept in, we must forget them as soon as we can" after having felt sweet forgiveness through the Atonement of Christ. "Tomorrow is a new day. We shall begin it well and serenely and with too high a spirit to be encumbered with our old nonsense." (Ralph Waldo Emerson).

<u>We get to know ourselves.</u>

We recognize when we are starting to feed on negative energy. It may require spending some practice time with ourselves. But we never forget that to be forewarned is to be forearmed. When we find ourselves on an emotional roller coaster, we realize that it is driven, in part, "in consequence of evils and designs which do and will exist in the hearts of conspiring men in the last days." (D&C 89:4).

When the Spirit thins out through transgression, and we find ourselves losing our self-confidence and our positive outlook on life, we recommit ourselves to walk "in obedience to the commandments," in particular including the commandment to speedily repent. It is then that we "shall receive health in (our) navel and marrow to (our) bones, and shall find wisdom and great treasures of knowledge, even hidden treasures, and shall run and not be weary, and shall walk and not faint." Unto such are given "a promise, that the destroying angel shall pass by them, as the children of Israel, and not slay them." (D&C 89:18-21).

We tackle one problem at a time.

We don't try to fix everything all at once. The next life is required to achieve perfection. For now, we learn "precept upon precept; line upon line; here a little, and there a little." (Isaiah 28:10). Doing so, we are given "consolation by holding forth that which is to come, confirming our hope!" (D&C 128:21). Joseph Smith was comforted with the promise that his trials would give him experience and should be for his good. (D&C 122:7). Even Jesus, who led a sinless life, "still grew up with his brethren, and waxed strong, and waited upon the Lord for the time of his ministry to come." (J.S.T. Matthew 3:24).

Traveling the road of repentance in the direction of forgiveness may take ime, and in the short term, there may be reverses. But over the long haul, we will steadily move to higher plateaus. God's Plan will pull us up. In times of discouragement, we remember the observation of the Apostle James: "We count them happy which endure." (James 5:11). We also acknowledge any and all progress, and that "miracles (are) worked by small means." (Alma 37:41).

We think in terms of courage and perseverance, and not gloom and doom.

We acknowledge "opposition in all things. If not so," Lehi explained to his son, "righteousness could not be brought to pass, neither wickedness, neither holiness

nor misery, neither good nor bad." (2 Nephi 2:11). Job encouraged us to "forget (our) misery, and remember it as waters that pass away." (Job 11:16). Difficulty in times past is water under the bridge.

We use physical exercise to neutralize and dissipate depression-causing toxins.

We heed the Lord's counsel: "Cease to be idle; cease to be unclean; cease to find fault one with another; cease to sleep longer than is needful; retire to thy bed early, that ye may not be weary; arise early, that your bodies and your minds may be invigorated" with a healthy dose of endorphins. (D&C 88:124).

We hang on.

We outlast and counteract negative influences by doing everything we can to be positive and uplifted. Unless we "endure to the end (by) following the example of the Son of the living God, (we) cannot be saved" from self-defeating behaviors that eat away at our foundation. (2 Nephi 31:16). As we endure, we take consolation in "the patience of Job." (James 5:11).

We follow the advice of the prophets.

"Mine heart within me is broken because of the prophets," wrote Jeremiah. "All my bones shake. I am like a drunken man, and like a man whom wine hath overcome, because of the Lord, and because of the words of his holiness." (Jeremiah 23:9). We understand how his frame must have been reduced to quivering jelly. Jacob explained, however, that the process can lead to renewal, and to a solid footing within the fortress of faith. "We search the prophets," he revealed, "and we have many revelations and the spirit of prophecy; and having all these witnesses, we obtain a hope, and our faith becometh unshaken." (Jacob 4:6).

We seek help from priesthood leaders (including husbands, fathers, sons, and brothers).

Speaking of his relationship to his brethren, Nephi wrote: "And I know that the Lord God will consecrate my prayers for the gain of my people. And the words which I have written in weakness will be made strong unto them, for it persuadeth them to do good. It maketh known unto them of their fathers, and it speaketh of Jesus, and persuadeth them to believe in him, and to endure to the end, which is life eternal." (2 Nephi 33:4).

We continue to renew our baptismal covenants by participating in the ordinance of the Sacrament.

The key to our deliverance is come, said the Savior, if we will hearken to His voice, and call on His name. As we do so, we shall receive His Spirit, and a blessing so great as we never have known. (See D&C 39:10).

In order to keep ourselves "unspotted from the world," we have been commanded to "go to the house of prayer and offer up (our) sacraments." (D&C 59:9). We maintain an unshakeable conviction that we are sons and daughters of God with promises to keep and miles to go before we sleep.

We follow the example of Father Abraham.

We remember the Covenant, recorded in his account in The Pearl of Great Price: "Finding there was greater happiness and peace and rest for me, I sought for the blessings of the fathers, and the right whereunto I should be ordained to administer the same; having been myself a follower of righteousness, desiring also to be one who possessed great knowledge, and to be a greater follower of righteousness, and to possess a greater knowledge, and to be a father of many nations, a prince of peace, and desiring to receive instructions, and to keep the commandments of God, I became a rightful heir, a High Priest, holding the right belonging to the fathers." (Abraham 1:2).

We turn our focus outward in service.

We step outside our comfort zones and serve others. Benjamin's words to the people of Zarahemla may be among the most oft' quoted passages in The Book of Mormon:

"When ye are in the service of your fellow beings ye are only in the service of your God." (Mosiah 2:17). In this verse, the question of how to serve God is unambiguously answered. As we minister to our fellow travelers, we come to realize that there is "a time to get, and a time to lose; a time to keep, and a time to cast away." (Ecclesiastes 3:6). We recognize the profound wisdom in the Savior's statement that "whosoever will save his life shall lose it: but whosoever will lose his life for my sake, the same shall save it." (Luke 9:24).

Sometimes the answers to our own problems are revealed within the counsel we give to others. Helen Keller mused: "Once, I knew the depths where no hope was, and darkness lay on the face of all things. Then, love came and set my soul free. Once, I knew only darkness and stillness. Now, I know hope and joy. Once, I fretted and beat myself against the wall that shut me in. Now, I rejoice in the consciousness that I can think, act and attain heaven. My life was without past or future. Death, the pessimist would say, was a consummation devoutly to be wished. But words of encouragement from another fell into my hand that clutched at emptiness, and my heart leaped to the rapture of living. Night fled before the day of thought, and love and joy and hope came up in a passion of obedience to knowledge. Can anyone who escaped such captivity, who has felt the thrill and glory of freedom, still be a pessimist?" ("Optimism").

<u>We remember the promise of the Prophet Joseph Smith.</u>

"Happiness is the object and design of our existence, and will be the end thereof if we follow the path that leads to it." ("Teachings," p. 255). We walk the walk, and talk the talk. We not only believe in Christ, but we also believe Christ, when He gently reassures us that we are celestial material.

"Ye cannot hide your crimes from God; and except ye repent, they will stand as a testimony against you at the last day." (Alma 39:8).

Chapter Thirty Five

The Plan is to save our souls.

In the New Testament, there are tantalizingly few verses that speak of The Plan of Salvation. In Titus 1:2, Paul spoke of the promise of "eternal life, which God, that cannot lie, promised before the world began." (Titus 1:2). Peter wrote that Jesus Christ was "foreordained before the foundation of the world," to be the Redeemer. (1 Peter 1:20). In his letter to the Hebrews, he wrote that the Savior "became the author of eternal salvation" (Hebrews 5:9).

In the Pearl of Great Price, Abraham wrote of the creative process, and of the reasoning of the God when creating the earth: "And we will prove them herewith, to see if they will do all things whatsoever the Lord their God shall command them; and they who keep their first estate shall be added upon; and they who keep not their first estate shall not have glory in the same kingdom with those who keep their first estate; and they who keep their second estate shall have glory added upon their heads for ever and ever." (Abraham 3:25-26). Moses spoke of "the Plan of Salvation unto all men." (Moses 6:62).

But it is in The Book of Mormon that we really get a feel for The Plan. In several

verses, (1 Nephi 13:26, 29, 32, 35, 35, & 40, & 1 Nephi 14:23 & 19:3), Nephi explained that in the Last Days, the Gentiles would "stumble exceedingly, because of the most plain and precious parts of the Gospel of the Lamb" which had been distorted within or deleted from the scriptures. (1 Nephi 13:34).

But there would be a light provided at the end of the tunnel, for those whose minds had been "blinded by the subtle craftiness of men." (D&C 123:12). Today, "we have also a more sure word of prophecy ... as unto a light that shineth in a dark place, until the day dawn, and the day star arise in (our) hearts." (2 Peter 1:19).

Through His prophet, the Lord promised: "I will proceed to do a marvellous work among this people, even a marvellous work and a wonder: for the wisdom of their wise men shall perish, and the understanding of their prudent men shall be hid." (Isaiah 29:14).

The Merciful Plan of the Great Creator. (2 Nephi 9:6).

"Mercy claimeth the penitent, and mercy cometh because of the Atonement; and the Atonement bringeth to pass the resurrection of the dead; and the resurrection of the dead bringeth back men into the presence of God. For behold, Justice exerciseth all his demands, and also Mercy claimeth all which is her own; and thus, none but the truly penitent are saved." (Alma 42:23-24, underlining mine). Our conscience is a celestial spark that God has put into each of us. It is part of the Merciful Plan of the Great Creator, Whose purpose is the saving of our souls.

The Plan of our God. (2 Nephi 9:13).

The "great and eternal purposes" of The Plan of our God, "were prepared from the foundation of the world." (Alma 42:26). John Taylor taught: "To the Son is given the power of the resurrection, the power of the redemption, the power of salvation, the power to enact laws for the carrying out and accomplishment of the design. Hence, life and immortality are brought to light, the Gospel is introduced, and He becomes

the Author of eternal life and exaltation." ("Mediation and Atonement," p. 171-172).

The Great and Eternal Plan of Deliverance from Death. (2 Nephi 11:5).

One of the foundation teachings of the Gospel is that we came into this world to die. "And now behold, I say unto you that if it had been possible for Adam to have partaken of the fruit of the Tree of Life at that time, there would have been no death, and the word would have been void, making God a liar, for he said: If thou eat thou shalt surely die." (Alma 12:23). Before we came here, it was clearly understood that our experience would be part of the Great and Eternal Plan of Deliverance from Death. When Adam and Eve were sent into the Garden of Eden, it was with the understanding that they would violate or transgress a law in order to bring to pass mortality for the human family.

The Plan of Salvation. (Alma 24:14).

The Plan of Salvation is The Plan of Redemption, The Plan of Mercy, and The Plan of Happiness, because it makes possible the resurrection of otherwise imperfect mortals to an eternal life of glory. "Now, if it had not been for The Plan of Redemption, which was laid from the foundation of the world, there could have been no resurrection of the dead. But there was a Plan of Redemption laid, which shall bring to pass the resurrection of the dead." (Alma 12:25).

The Plan of Redemption. (Alma 29:2).

"According to justice, The Plan of Redemption could not be brought about" and "Mercy could not take effect except it should destroy the work of Justice." (Alma 42:13). The beauty of The Plan of Redemption, then, is that it meets the demands of Justice through the infinite mercy of a loving Heavenly Father. The Plan allows God to be both just and merciful at the same time.

The Great Plan of the Eternal God. (Alma 34:9).

None of us can hope to find meaning in our lives if we treat the integral elements of The Plan superficially or carelessly. A conscious appreciation of its value must be earned. If we take it for granted or if we abandon its core principles, its power to bless our lives may slip away and be lost forever. While The Great Plan of the Eternal God guarantees free will, it also gives us wide latitude to use our agency as we wish, with the ever-present risk that we will do so inappropriately to make poor choices. It provides us with currency sufficient for our needs, but it also allows us to substitute for legal tender wads of counterfeit cash with which late payments may be made with interest tacked on for bad behavior. If we attempt to subvert The Plan in futile efforts to obtain and retain blessings we do not deserve, our destabilizing efforts will reward us with a pyrrhic victory at best.

The Great and Eternal Plan of Redemption. (Alma 34:16).

Nephi clearly taught that "it is by grace that we are saved, after all we can do." (2 Nephi 25:23). Latter-day Saints, however, tend to emphasize works to the point that it may seem to others that the grace of God takes a back seat to their own efforts to earn salvation. In spite of their focus on accountability, agency, industry, and labor, as they are exhorted to greater dedication, diligence, and duty, the truth is that nothing we can do will ever qualify us for the blessing of eternal life. It is only because of The Great and Eternal Plan of Redemption that we are saved. Paul and Luke echoed Nephi, writing that it is "by grace (we) are saved, through faith, and that not of (ourselves). It is the gift of God." (Ephesians 2:8). "We believe that through the grace of the Lord Jesus Christ we shall be saved." (Acts 15:11). It is "the grace of God that bringeth salvation." (Titus 2:11).

The Great Plan of Redemption. (Alma 34:31).

The Great Plan of Redemption required that "an Atonement should be made. Therefore, God Himself atoneth for the sins of the world, to bring about The Plan of Mercy, to appease the demands of Justice, that God might be a perfect, just

God, and a merciful God also." (Alma 42:15). The Atonement allowed God to satisfy Justice and still mercifully reclaim us from physical and spiritual death. The Savior thus became the Master of the situation. In His sacrifice, the debt would

be paid, the redemption made, the covenant fulfilled, Justice satisfied, the will of God done, and all power, including the keys of resurrection, now given to the Son.

The Plan of Restoration. (Alma 41:2).

The Book of Mormon clearly teaches that the purpose of the Fall was to give us the opportunity to come to the earth in order to prepare for a resurrection. "And we see that death comes upon mankind, yea, the death which has been spoken of by Amulek, which is the temporal death; nevertheless there was a space granted unto man in which he might repent; therefore this life became a probationary state; a time to prepare to meet God; a time to prepare for that endless state which has been spoken of by us, which is after the resurrection of the dead." (Alma 12:24). The Atonement is the keystone of The Plan of Restoration, that allows us to be raised in the resurrection clothed in exactly the kinds of bodies for which we have prepared ourselves through repentance.

The Great Plan of Salvation. (Alma 42:5).

Without the light of The Great Plan of Salvation, we are doomed to suffer in the shadows where we experience only illusions and caricatures of reality. The discrepancy between our marginalized behavior and the ideals of The Plan will become so great that our short-lived pleasure in worldly ways will surely evaporate as the morning dew in the full light of day. Sooner or later, when this disparity has become so great that it reaches "critical mass," a requisite readjustment will tear down the façade of corruption and hypocrisy to allow the cultivation of a more nurturing lifestyle made possible by obedience to the principles of the Plan.

The Great Plan of Happiness. (Alma 42:8).

Alma taught that in the absence of repentance for our sins, and without the benefit of the Plans' saving principles, we must ultimately be in a wretched state, living forever in our sins. "And now behold, if it were possible that our first parents could have gone forth and partaken of the Tree of Life they would have been forever miserable, having no preparatory state, and thus The Plan of Redemption would have been frustrated, and the word of God would have been void, taking none effect." (Alma 12:26). Without redemption from sin, if Adam and Eve had partaken of the fruit of the Tree of Life, without first having received a remission of their sins through the Atonement of Christ, it would not have been possible for them to sustain a celestial existence, inasmuch as in their fallen condition they would have been incapable of obedience to celestial principles. Thus, The Great Plan of Happiness would have been forever frustrated.

The Plan of Mercy. (Alma 42:15).

When Adam and Eve were driven from the Garden, they were "punished" with the very things that would later prove to bring them the greatest happiness. As the Sufi poet Rumi observed: "Our wounds become portals that allow light to enter us." A Savior would be provided for them, but in the meantime, cherubim and a flaming sword would be placed to keep the way of the Tree of Life, to preserve the principle of repentance that had just been explained to Adam and Eve. (See Genesis 3:24). Both Justice and Mercy would allow them and their posterity to experience all of the wonders of mortality, without harming their eternal identity or hampering The Plan of Mercy.

The Plan of Happiness. (Alma 42:16).

The cherubim guaranteed that The Plan of Happiness would not be frustrated. "For behold, if Adam had put forth his hand immediately, and partaken of the Tree of Life, he would have lived forever, according to the word of God, having no space for repentance." (Alma 42:5). This would have posed an immediate problem that

begged a solution. Because of the transgression of Adam and Eve in the Garden, justice demanded that they "became lost forever … And now, ye see by this that our first parents were cut off both temporally and spiritually from the presence of the Lord." (Alma 42:6-7). So it was, that "they became subject to follow after their own will." The crowning principle of agency was to be honored, even if it meant that Justice must be served. Therefore, "it was appointed unto man to die" (Alma 42:6), rather than to reclaim him "from this temporal death, for that would destroy The Great Plan of Happiness." (Alma 42:8).

The Great Plan of Mercy. (Alma 42:31).

The Great Plan of Mercy gives us the opportunity to live our lives, push the envelope, and dare to take risks. When we fail to measure up to its laws, Jesus Christ intervenes in our behalf. When we Recognize our mistakes, when we experience Remorse for having made them, when we attempt to make Restitution if our behavior has wronged others, when we learn from the mistake and Reform our ways through Repentance, and Resolve to Refrain from Repeating it, we will be free to continue the path of progress, with a complete Resolution through the Atonement of what would have otherwise been incapacitating short-comings and irreconcilable inadequacy. By following this process, our powers will expand as we experience the glittering facets of the life of the Spirit wherein we are receptive to flashes of insight. We will be cast off into streams of revelation and carried along in the quickening currents of direct experience with God.

"I have repented
of my sins, and have been
redeemed of the Lord; behold, I
am born of the Spirit."
(Mosiah 27:24).

Chapter Thirty Six

Five keys to successful repentance.

Gather the people together,
men, and women, and children,
and thy stranger that is within thy
gates, that they may hear, and that
they may learn, and fear the Lord
your God, and observe to do
all the words of this law."
(Deuteronomy 31:12).

<u>If we want to observe to do all the words of the law, we first seek inspiration.</u>

We seek divine direction, and learn how to focus the powers of heaven in our behalf. We take advantage of the opportunity to be cast off into a stream of revelation as we are carried along in the quickening currents of direct experience with God. We recognize and act upon moments when the Spirit leads us, remembering that President Kimball said: "Seeking the spectacular, we often miss the constant flow of revealed communication that comes." (Munich Area Conference, 1973).

<u>We are confident in the power of the Atonement.</u>

We let virtue garnish our thoughts unceasingly. As our confidence builds, the doctrine of the priesthood distils upon our heads as the dews from heaven, the Holy Ghost is our constant companion, and guidance to complete the repentance process flows unto us without compulsory means. (See D&C 121:45-46). With unwavering confidence in the power of the Savior's Atonement, we experience success similar to that enjoyed by The Sons of Mosiah, who "waxed strong in the knowledge of the truth; for they were men of a sound understanding and they had searched the scriptures diligently, that they might know the word of God. But this is not all; they had given themselves to much prayer, and fasting; therefore they had the spirit of prophecy, and the spirit of revelation, and when they taught, they taught with power and authority of God." (Alma 17:2-3).

We let the Spirit teach us.

We read in the Doctrine & Covenants how the Lord was moved to observe of the Saints in Zion that they were "truly humble and (were) seeking diligently to learn wisdom and to find truth." (D&C 97:1). We have been repeatedly counseled to trust in the Lord with all our hearts and lean not unto our own understanding. (See Proverbs 3:5). This is why B.H. Roberts "said after a coherent and vigorous presentation that he loved books; indeed, that in some degree books had made him. But then, in a most vehement way, he said 'But I am not dependent on books. I am dependent for what I really know and really trust, on the direct experience of God.'" ("Defender of The Faith" p. 374). We testify that repentance brings us into the realm of that direct experience with Deity.

We know of a surety and truth that the words of our leaders concerning repentance will guide us to eternal life, "because of the Spirit of the Lord Omnipotent, which has wrought a mighty change in us, or in our hearts, that we have no more disposition to do evil, but to do good continually. And we, ourselves, also, through the infinite

goodness of God, and the manifestations of His Spirit, have great views of that which is to come, and were it expedient, we could prophesy of all things. And it is the faith we have had on the things which (our prophets) have spoken unto us that has brought us to this great knowledge, whereby we do rejoice with such exceedingly great joy." (Mosiah 5:2-4).

We make a behavioral commitment.

In the best of circumstances, repentance is encouraging, motivating, and catalyzes our capacity to change our behavior. It widens our perspective, creating the desire to renew binding commitments, and especially strengthens our testimony of Jesus Christ, our witness of the power of His Atonement, and our dedication to observe the principles of The Plan of Salvation. We think of the example of "King Benjamin," who "thought it was expedient, after having finished speaking to his people, that he should take the names of all those who had entered into a covenant with God to keep his commandments." (Mosiah 6:1). Everyone in the audience beyond the age of accountability was given the opportunity to pledge their allegiance to the Lord. "And it came to pass that there was not one soul, except it were little children, but who had entered into the covenant and had taken upon them the name of Christ." (Mosiah 6:2).

Joshua had drawn a similar line in the sand a thousand years earlier, in the Promised Land of Israel. "Fear the Lord," he said, "and serve him in sincerity and in truth; and put away the gods which your fathers served on the other side of the flood, and in Egypt; and serve ye the Lord. And if it seem evil unto you to serve the Lord, choose ye this day whom ye will serve ... but as for me and my house, we will serve the Lord." (Joshua 24:14-15).

Choice is at the heart of the Gospel of Jesus Christ, and repentance nudges us off our comfortable cushions of complacency directly onto the hot-seat of personal accountability. "There are many called, but few are chosen," wrote Joseph Smith

from Liberty Jail. "And why are they not chosen? Because their hearts are set ... upon the things of this world." (D&C 121:34-36). Repentance strengthens spirituality by promising the peace that accompanies the righteous exercise of our agency as we follow The Plan of Salvation. The prophet Joel saw in vision the path that lies before us, exclaiming: "Multitudes, multitudes, in the valley of decision, for the day of the Lord is near in the valley of decision." (Joel 3:14).

<u>In our repentance, we are encouraged by the Spirit.</u>

Repentance figuratively paints the portrait of a turtle on a fence post. When we repent, we know one thing for certain. That turtle had help getting up there. When we repent, we draw upon the power of our covenants that point us in the direction of the Savior and His Atonement. On the other hand, when we try to skip some of the necessary steps of repentance, it is like putting roller skates on an octopus; we will have no control over the direction we will go.

We cannot skip any of the uncomfortable steps of repentance. These require that we Recognize our transgression, experience Remorse, Renounce the self-defeating behavior, Resolve to do refrain from it, and to do better, make Restitution to injured parties whenever possible, and thereby establish a Reconciliation with the Spirit, in order to Receive a Remission of sin through the grace of God Who is our Redeemer. Repentance thereby strengthens our testimony of The Plan of Salvation. Its lynchpin is the Atonement, which makes a powerful statement that through the grace of God, we may experience self-improvement by practicing what the Savior has preached.

Repentance invites us to reach out to firmly grasp the rod of iron, and then to press forward through the darkness, until we come forth out of its mists to behold the light and to partake of the fruit of the Tree of Life. (See 1 Nephi 8:24, & Alma 5:34).

We are reassured by repentance, and are energized to know that although "the stars

fade away, and the sun himself grow dim with age and nature sink in years ... we shall flourish in immortal youth, unhurt amidst the war of elements, the wreck of matter, and the crash of worlds." (Joseph Addison, "Cato" Act 5, Scene 1).

The principle of repentance is the embodiment of the standard to which we must strive. It is nothing less than perfection, for the Savior said: "I would that ye should be perfect even as I, or your Father who is in heaven is perfect." (3 Nephi 12:48).

Repentance is founded on principles rather than on values, and so it bridges the cultural, economic, political, and social boundaries that might otherwise artificially limit its implementation. The principle of repentance speaks to our spirit without bias or reservation, because each of us is entitled to guidance from the Light of Christ. Everyone on earth is intuitively led to repentance. Because it is universally understood, it is immune to conventional wisdom or cultural bias, it resists dogmatic interpretation, and it withstands the twisted influence of private interpretation.

Under the best of circumstances, both in and out of the Church, "we talk of Christ, we rejoice in Christ, we preach of Christ, we prophesy of Christ, and we write according to our prophecies, that our children may know to what source they may look for a remission of their sins." (2 Nephi 25:26).

We never forget, however, that a restoration of truth was necessary to realign religious practice with the eternal principle of repentance. The Restoration of the Gospel gave the servants of the Lord "the power to lay the foundations of this Church, and to bring it forth out of obscurity and out of darkness, the only true and living Church upon the face of the whole earth, with which ... (He is) well pleased." (D&C 1:30). The Church was restored, "lest any man spoil (us) through philosophy and vain deceit, after the tradition of men, after the rudiments of the world, and not after Christ." (Colossians 2:8).

With the Restoration of the Gospel, the principle of repentance was reignited as a

torch of truth, and it became a homing beacon. Once again, as in the apostolic age, we quietly listen to the whisperings of the Spirit, and we feel that angels will attend us. (See Acts 2:37). We feel that "whoever speaks to us in the right voice, him or her

I shall follow as the waters follow the moon, silently, with fluid steps, anywhere around the globe." (Walt Whitman).

John Greenleaf Whittier wrote of his own introduction to truth, as he sat at the feet of the Prophet of the Restoration. "There was a straight-forward vehemence and intense earnestness in his manner, which at once disarmed my criticism. And what was the secret of this power! His faith in God! In listening to these modern prophets, I discovered, as I think, the great secret of their success in making converts. They speak to a common feeling; they minister to a universal want. They contrast strongly the miraculous power of the Gospel in the apostolic time with the present state of our nominal Christianity. They ask for the signs of divine power; the faith, overcoming all things, which opened the prison doors of the apostles, gave them power over the elements, which rebuked disease and death itself, and made visible to all the presence of the living God. They ask for any declaration in the scriptures that this miraculous power of faith was to be confined to the first confessors of Christianity. They speak a language of hope and promise to weak, weary hearts, tossed and troubled, who have wandered from sect to sect, seeking in vain for the primal manifestations of the divine power." ("A Mormon Conventicle," p. 461).

The power of which he spoke is manifest as all three members of the Godhead participate with us in the process of repentance. The Holy Ghost brings out the best in each of us, by helping us to avoid being "caught in the bind of building a church and killing the articles of its faith, or permitting form to triumph over spirit. The Church and Kingdom of God is built by the ardor and conviction of its members." (Alvin R. Dyer, "A Foundation for Education").

Repentance is alive with interactive communication with God. "These currents and

many more are part of the flowing fountain of the Church. If we do not drink, if we die of thirst while only inches from the fountain, the fault comes down to us. For the free, full, flowing, living water is there." (Truman Madsen, "Christ and The Inner Life" p. 31).

Quickened by the Spirit, we recognize the source of the life-giving water that is offered, and we gratefully accept in our hearts the sacrifice of the Savior manifest in His Atonement. When we transgress, we speedily repent and return unto God, and find favor in His sight, and are restored to the blessings which He has ordained to be poured out upon us. (See D&C 109:21).

"If the inhabitants of the earth shall repent of their wickedness and abominations, they shall not be destroyed, saith the Lord of Hosts." (2 Nephi 28:17).

Quid Magis Possum Dicere?

About The Author

Phil Hudson and his wife Jan have 7 children and over 25 grandchildren. They enjoy spending time with their family at their cabin nestled in the Selkirk Mountains, on the shore of Priest Lake, the crown jewel of North Idaho. Phil had a successful family dental practice in Spokane, Washington for 43 years, before retiring in 2015. He has an eclectic mix of hobbies, and enjoys the out of doors. He always finds time, however, to record his thoughts on his laptop, and understands Isaac Asimov's response when he was asked: If you knew that you had only 10 minutes left to live, what would you do?" He answered: "I'd type faster."

Phil received the inspiration to write this book while he and Jan were serving as missionaries for The Church of Jesus Christ of Latter-day Saints, in the Kingdom of Tonga. While there, they celebrated their 50th wedding anniversary.

"Your brethren in Zion begin to
repent, and the angels
rejoice over them."
(D&C 90:34).

3

By The Author

Essays

>   Volume One: Spray From The Ocean Of Thought
>   Volume Two: Ripples On A Pond
>   Volume Three: Serendipitous Meanderings
>   Volume Four: Presents Of Mind
>   Volume Five: Mental Floss
>   Volume Six: Fitness Training For The Mind And Spirit

First Principles and Ordinances Series

>   Faith - Our Hearts Are Changed Through Faith On His Name
>   Repentance - A Broken Heart and a Contrite Spirit
>   Baptism - One Hundred And One Reasons Why We Are Baptized
>   The Holy Ghost - That We Might Have His Spirit To Be With Us
>   The Sacrament - This Do In Remembrance Of Me

Book of Mormon Commentary

>   Volume One: Born In The Wilderness
>   Volume Two: Voices From The Dust
>   Volume Three: Journey To Cumorah

Doctrine & Covenants Commentary

Volume One - Sections 1 - 34
Volume Two - Sections 35 - 57

Minute Musings: Spontaneous Combustions of Thought

Volume One
Volume Two
Volume Three

Calendars:

In His Own Words: Discovering William Tyndale
As I Think About The Savior
Scriptural Symbols

Children's Books

Muddy, Muddy
The Thirteen Articles of Faith
Happy Birthday

Professional Publications

Diode Laser Soft Tissue Surgery Volume One
Diode Laser Soft Tissue Surgery Volume Two
Diode Laser Soft Tissue Surgery Volume Three

These, and other titles, are available from online retailers.

CPSIA information can be obtained
at www.ICGtesting.com
Printed in the USA
LVHW060000100719
623636LV00010B/119/P